BACK TO THE POSTINDUSTRIAL FUTURE

EASA Series

Published in Association with the European Association of Social
Anthropologists (EASA)

Series Editor: Aleksandar Bošković, University of Belgrade

Social anthropology in Europe is growing, and the variety of work being done
is expanding. This series is intended to present the best of the work produced
by members of the EASA, both in monographs and in edited collections. The
studies in this series describe societies, processes, and institutions around the
world and are intended for both scholarly and student readership.

For a full volume listing, please see back matter.

BACK TO THE POSTINDUSTRIAL FUTURE

An Ethnography of Germany's Fastest-Shrinking City

Felix Ringel

berghahn
NEW YORK • OXFORD
www.berghahnbooks.com

First published in 2018 by
Berghahn Books
www.berghahnbooks.com

© 2018, 2020 Felix Ringel
First paperback edition published in 2020

Library of Congress Cataloging-in-Publication Data
A C.I.P. cataloging record is available from the Library of Congress

British Library Cataloguing in Publication Data
A catalogue record for this book is available from the British Library

ISBN 978-1-78533-798-7 hardback
ISBN 978-1-78920-805-4 paperback
ISBN 978-1-78533-799-4 ebook

For my mother, Martina Ringel,
who I take with me into the future

Contents

Illustrations

All photographs are the author's unless otherwise stated

Preface

Ethnography in Hindsight

Writing ethnography is akin to time-travelling: we are bound to a present that has already gone. Anthropological data is hence always out of date; its 'best before' date is reached at the end of fieldwork. But thought needs time, and time does not stop to elevate the representational concerns of a social scientist. Consequently, we keep on travelling back in time, trying to capture what was there. However, studying the relations to the future of my informants and their hometown might tempt author or readers to evaluate which past predictions prove true. This book argues we should avoid such temptations. We have to take the present we explored as what it was: a short stretch of time, during which we have shared life with the people we study. This book aims to take the reader back to Hoyerswerda in 2008 and 2009 and to account for the conditions and problems that were prevalent then. These problems might resemble the ones 'currently' important in Hoyerswerda, but to establish whether they are the *same*, is impossible.

To capture the present I encountered in sixteen months of fieldwork is hard. There is simply not enough space to represent the ethnographic material that I assembled during this time in one singular argument. In hindsight, I have not captured this particular present or period in its entirety, and my argument restricts itself to matters of time, particularly of the future. Since the future was on everybody's mind then, I am assured that my informants will appreciate why it takes centre-stage now. Sadly, this means I had to leave many things out. Therefore, the readers will not read about Waltraut Skoddow's delicious asparagus salad or the resounding laughter of elderly women from the Cultural Factory's knitting club. They will not be taken at night to the spooky emptiness of an abandoned eleven-storey apartment block awaiting demolition. They will not stand on its roof, seeing the lights and straightforward lines of the

New City's impressive modernist architecture. They will not see the numerous pieces of art that decorate the interiors of so many apartments in the city or sit around a dinner table with one of my host families, discussing matters of the day, tidings from the local newspaper or plans for the weekend. There is also not enough space to see the many sculptures from the socialist past displayed throughout the city, or the local zoo, another true accomplishment from the same historical period. We will not enjoy ourselves in absurd costumes at the local anarchists' 'Coke, Puke, Communism II' (*Koksen, Kotzen, Kommunismus II*) party or dance the conga line with the seniors' club Spätlese e.V. after its annual fashion show, where the models were recruited from among their own active crowd. We will not go on a wolf tour with Stephan, join a few of the remaining miners on their way to work much too early in the morning, or carefully cycle home after a splendid *Weinclub*-dinner at the best restaurant in town on a bike exhibiting a sticker advocating the renovation of a house in the city centre with the slogan (in English) 'Born to Survive'. We will not stop for a beer in front of the *Schlucki* drinks market, listen to a private Gundermann concert by young singer-songwriter Florian in district 5 or visit Moni on her lovingly cared for garden plot that is part of what is still called the 'Bright Future' (*Frohe Zukunft*) allotments. We will not stand on stage with the grandmother who, in lieu of her grandchild, awaits the introductions for the ceremony of the former socialist confirmation equivalent: her grandchild will arrive the next morning from her family's new West German home, where the East German *Jugendweihe* is not celebrated.

As I focus on drastic postindustrial decline and the presumed loss of the future, the readers will not be introduced to the 'normal' small city lives that people, too, live in Hoyerswerda. They will be taken to moments of conflict and argument, of critical commentary, creative work and existential negotiations. These moments do not allow much time for silence and introspection. But for the sake of the argument of this book, they are important to attend to because they help to underline that the everyday life of a shrinking city is in many ways not normal. The future looms over it and demands thought, care and reflection. This book documents this postindustrial urban community's response to a presumed loss of the future and the new kinds of social relations this loss creates.

Acknowledgements

I owe thanks to the citizens of Hoyerswerda, foremost for teaching me so much about life, but also for their hospitality, openness and kindness. When I arrived in Hoyerswerda in January 2008, it was the height of the international financial crisis. My informants could only shrug at this crisis. 'A new crisis? We had a crisis for years already.' With the same stubborn attitude, they first eyed a young anthropologist embarking on his first fieldwork. What then happened was as unexpected for them as it was for me. Cycling through the city, from an appointment in the New City to a meeting in the Old City and then back to a party in some abandoned apartment house at the outskirts, I met a lot of very different people. They always treated me kindly, answered my numerous questions, and guided me through the city and its surroundings. Young and old shared a lot of thought, wit, tea and cake with me. Many schools, clubs and other institutions opened their doors to me, and endured the odd onlooker into their professional and private lives. I think it is fair to say that we have mutually learned a lot from one another on a very transparent journey back to a city that kept on shrinking in the meantime.

Throughout my sixteen months of fieldwork, my host families and newly found friends were simply wonderful and sustained me in many ways. I want to express heartfelt gratitude to my overall seven host families for providing me with much-appreciated new homes during my fieldwork: Regina, Andreas and Franzi Schütze with Markus, Oma Helga as well as Jule and Axel Kiermeyer; Heike, Micha, Franzi and Basti Kalkbrenner; Kersten Flohe; Angela and Hajo Donath; Katrin, Rocco and Sebastian Schäfer as well as Oma Brigitte; Moni, Ralph and Genia Büchner; and Dorit, Carsten and Ria Baumeister with Dirk Lienig. Just a few of my friends include Benni, Willy, Ria, Ise, Rick, Proksch, Ollum, Fidschie, Hanni, Dennis, Alex, Florian, Uwe, Sabine, Röhli, Angela, Elke, Claudia,

Marita, Jo, Ute, Gerhard (Schlegel and Walter), Waltraut, Helfried, Rosemarie, Renate and Peter. Special thanks go to Steffi Schneider for sharing the joys and burdens of the 'AnthroCamp' project, and to her, Mandy Decker and Inge Williams for making the 'PaintBlock' project happen. Mirko Kolodziej has been the best 'office manager' I could wish for when writing journalistically, and thinking generally, about Hoyerswerda.

I would also like to acknowledge the many members of the following social clubs and institutions, whose continuous patience and hospitality contributed enormously to my research: Seniorenakademie Hoyerswerda e.V., Kunstverein Hoyerswerda e.V., Kulturfabrik Hoyerswerda e.V., Spätlese Hoyerswerda e.V., Kulturbund Hoyerswerda e.V., Braugasse 1 e.V., AntifaAG Hoyerswerda, Initiative Zivilcourage Hoyerswerda, StadtZukunft e.V., the *Hoyerswerdaer Tageblatt*, the Stadt Hoyerswerda, particularly Lord Mayor Stefan Skora, and the Lessing-Gymnasium Hoyerswerda, especially the musical class and the theatre group of the year 2008/09.

I applaud the courage, enthusiasm and hard work of Hoyerswerda's inhabitants. To paraphrase Leo Tolstoy, happy cities might as well be alike, and every unhappy city might be unhappy in its own way. However, cities are also unique with regard to the manner in which they reclaim their future (and) happiness, and respond to their problems. Hoyerswerda's problems are similar to those in Flint, Michigan (United States), Yūbari (Japan), Nowa Huta (Poland) or, indeed, Durham (United Kingdom), where I am writing these lines. In particular smaller postindustrial cities have to find their very own way out of the structural crises that affect their existence. The people living in Hoyerswerda, I hope, have found their response and are – as some of my friends had it – 'deeply relaxed' (*tiefenentspannt*) about, and still 'fervently' (*mit Inbrunst*) working on, their prospects. I wish them and their city all the best for the future.

Many institutions have funded this project: the German Study Foundation, the University of Cambridge, Sidney Sussex College, Cambridge, and the Economic and Social Research Council of the UK (PTA-031-2006-00210). I thank them for making this work possible. Parts of Chapter 2 have been published in *FOCAAL* 66 (2013) and an earlier version of Chapter 5 has appeared in the *Journal of the Royal Anthropological Institute* 20(S1) (2014).

I have presented aspects of this work at several research seminars. I owe debts to colleagues at the Anthropology Departments at Brunel (United Kingdom), Cambridge (United Kingdom), Maynooth (Ireland), Copenhagen (Denmark) and Vienna (Austria). I also owe

Laura Bear and the colleagues of her 'Conflicts in Time' research network for inspiring conversations, Maya Shapiro for co-organizing the 2013 AAA panel on Urban Affect, and Tatjana Thelen and the Postsocialism reading group in Vienna for continuing debates. Nina Gribat and Wolfgang Kil have been co-explorers of Hoyerswerda many a time, and I hope we can at some point put these conversations in writing. I am also grateful for the advice of three anonymous reviewers, the old and new series editors Eeva Berglund and Aleksander Bošković, and the rest of the team at Berghahn Books. Over the years, many scholars have influenced my thought and facilitated my intellectual wellbeing. Special thanks goes to Paul Rabinow, Alexei Yurchak, Marilyn Strathern, Susan Bayly, Chris Kaplonski, Stef Jansen and, most importantly, Nikolai Ssorin-Chaikov.

Finally, I am endlessly grateful to my family and friends from my original home, especially to my father Thomas, my sister Nadja with Norbert, Clara and Hannes, and my grandmother Ilse Purfürst. Alice von Bieberstein and Eirini Avramopoulou have shared the burden the whole way. Even more so has Emily Thomas, who continues to impress me with her own metaphysics everyday anew. She has endured much in relation to this book. To spend as many presents with her as I can is my best reward.

Notes on Translations

All translations are mine. I provide as much of the original German as possible, either in brackets or in footnotes. Some German terms such as *Neustadt* (New City), *Herr* (Mr) or *Frau* (Mrs) are used throughout the book.

Abbreviations

e.V.	*eingetragener Verein*/registered association
FRG	Federal Republic of Germany
GDR	German Democratic Republic
IM	*Inoffizieller Mitarbeiter*/Informal Collaborator
KuFa	*KulturFabrik*/Cultural Factory, referring both to the social club and their domicile, Hoyerswerda's sociocultural centre
MfS/Stasi	*Ministerium für Staatssicherheit*/Ministry for State Security
SED	*Sozialistische Einheitspartei Deutschlands*/German Socialist Unity Party
SuB HY	*Stadtumbau und Bürgerbeteiligung Hoyerswerda*/Urban Redevelopment and Citizens' Participation Hoyerswerda
WK	*Wohnkomplex*/residential complex

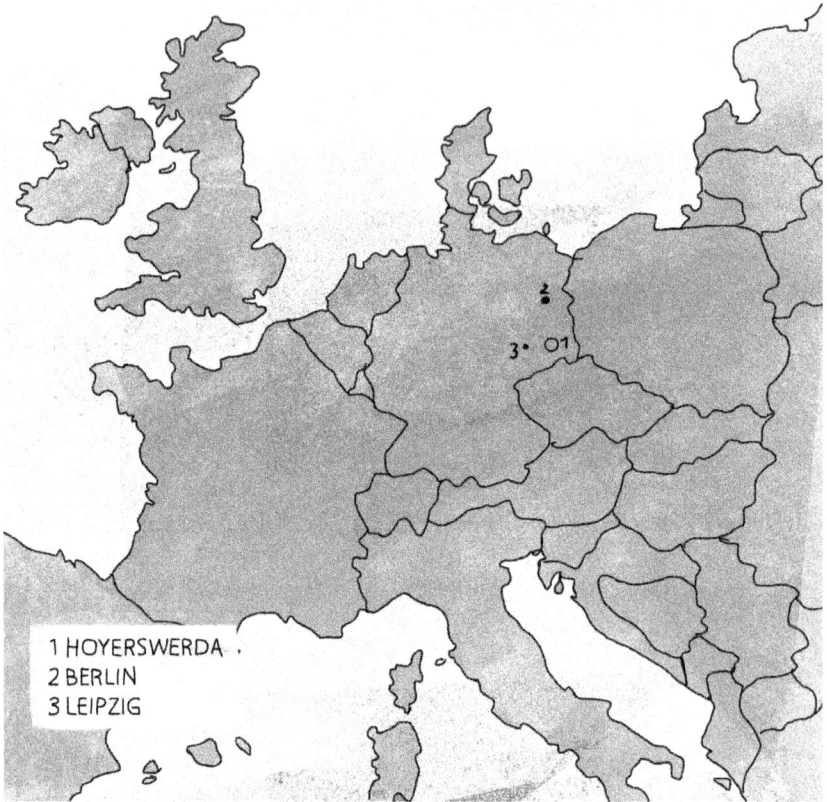

Hoyerswerda, Germany, in Europe. Map designed by artourette

Introduction

Anthropology and the Future
Notes from a Shrinking Fieldsite

The future is a flying bullet.
It carries my name and it's going to hit me no matter what. /
My question is, How shall I catch it? –
With my head, my arse, my hand or with my cheek? /
Does it hit me like a torpedo, or brush me like a kiss?
—Gerhard Gundermann, 'The Future'[1]

I started fieldwork in the East German city of Hoyerswerda in 2008. On my arrival, huge excavators were busily tearing down several of the socialist apartment blocks in Hoyerswerda's New City (subsequently *Neustadt*). Some used the usual wrecking ball; others deployed enormous forceps, breaking up these formerly five-, six- or eleven-floor buildings piece-by-piece. The piercing sounds of the heavy machines contrasted with the dull noise made by the falling concrete units. When mounting the heaps of rubble left over from what just months before had still been people's homes, the excavators wobbled like a ship on a sea of concrete, adding a crunching sound to the somewhat eerie situation. Only the water pumps, fighting the dust formation, ran constantly. Once in a while, a former resident would pass by, take pictures and start a chat with the usually smoking operator of the excavator. The latter might have already heard some stories from the lifeworlds he was deconstructing here. He was, however, more eager to answer the not uncommon question of where all the debris would be going when his work is done.

Figure 0.1 *Excavator on remains of the 'PaintBlock' building, WK 10, winter 2009*

The process of the city's large-scale physical demolition had started exactly ten years earlier in 1998. That same year, the local singer-songwriter Gerhard Gundermannn performed a song, 'The Future', for the last time. In this song, whose first lines open this Introduction, Gundermann describes the future as a 'flying bullet', which carries his name and is going to hit him 'no matter what'. In Hoyerswerda, which would later in 2009 be officially labelled Germany's fastest-shrinking city, the future indeed appeared to relentlessly bring its demise. However, Gundermann adds a twist to his deterministic, hopeless characterization of the future as a flying bullet: 'My question is, How shall I catch it?' Instead of giving in to the inevitable flow of time, he claims that we have the power to relate to the future in our own ways: we can – arguably – determine whether this future is to hit us 'like a torpedo' or brush us 'like a kiss'.

For the urban community of a shrinking city, the future poses an ongoing problem. This monograph explores the ways in which inhabitants of Hoyerswerda relate to their oncoming futures and shows how their experiences of shrinkage can help anthropology as a discipline to properly constitute the future as an integral part of its analysis. In the following sections, I will first introduce my fieldsite and then sketch my vision of the anthropology of the future, continuing an old tradition in the anthropology of time by taking inspiration from recent philosophical work on metaphysics. Having linked 'ethnographic' to 'metaphysical' presentism, I show how in Hoyerswerda the future has been rendered problematic and how it has become an epistemic object in its own right – for both my informants and myself – in the third section. In the last two sections, I proceed by conceptualizing knowledge and time in relation to one another I close by reviewing my overall argument. This book's general aim is to provide the reader with an ethnography of hope and the future in a city that, for many, was doomed to have neither of those. However, I read this city's present not through the lens of its (failed) past(s) – socialist or post-socialist – but from the perspective of what my informants considered a much more pressing concern: their personal and collective futures.

Introducing Hoyerswerda

Gundermann's song poses the question for the whole book: how is the urban community of a shrinking city to relate to the future; and how is the discipline of anthropology to account for this effort? Gundermann's life is intimately linked to Hoyerswerda's past, and I will briefly reconstruct it here by way of introducing the troubled history of my fieldsite. Importantly, Hoyerswerda is much more than an old town in the *Lausitz* region (Lusatia)[2] near to the Polish and Czech borders, which rose to national and international fame as a model industrial city during state-socialism. As will become apparent, Hoyerswerda's current problems might be intimately linked with the recent political and economic past of Germany. However, these problems are similarly, if not more, drawn to the dystopian futures they seem to prefigure.

Gundermann grew up in Hoyerswerda during *Neustadt*'s construction. The construction started in the mid 1950s and was part of the socialist government's response to a widespread existential housing crisis. The socialist part of Germany, the German Democratic Republic (GDR), like all of Germany – indeed, most of Europe and many other places in the world – lay bare and devastated at the end of World War II. After the official division of Germany in 1949, early Cold War conflicts were fought out between capitalist Western Germany and the GDR by competing in terms of state provisioning and economic success (Borneman 1992), and Hoyerswerda, part of the GDR, was quickly caught up in this conflict: which political system could overcome the war legacies quicker and provide its population with the much-needed material goods, housing and sociocultural infrastructure? Which system could better live up to its promises of a better future?

Gundermann was part of the second generation of *Neustadt*'s inhabitants, the children of those workers who had come to build Hoyerswerda's *Neustadt* as the GDR's second socialist model city and the major settlement for the nearby emerging brown coal industrial complex exploiting the region's vast lignite deposits. He was raised in an avant-garde city that was constructed from scratch on top of the endless Lusation sands and the heaps of brown coal, which, as a local Sorbic myth has it, the devil himself had placed beneath it. And the different political economies surrounding the exploitation of lignite proved to be a blessing and a curse for Hoyerswerda's existence – although at first a blessing. Hoyerswerda *Neustadt* was the first city in the world solely erected using industrially prefabricated concrete units; a vanguard socialist-modern project – meticulously planned, quickly expanded and fervently drawn towards a socialist future. Hoyerswerda was a GDR state experiment, full of personal promises and splendid future prospects for those privileged to live and work there.

During the 1960s and 1970s, Gundermann witnessed the construction of most of *Neustadt*'s ten living complexes (*Wohnkomplexe* – subsequently WK), including their many schools, kindergartens, 'WK-shops' (*Nahversorger*), playgrounds, parks, sculptures, streets and pavements – everything that belongs to a new city. He attended local schools, did his A-levels in the Old City's prestigious Lessing Gymnasium and then found a job in the mines, as did so many Hoyerswerdians of the first *Neustadt* generation. On his arrival, the city's population had already dramatically increased in size, from previously 7,000 to over 70,000 inhabitants by the early 1980s. Besides being a professional operator of one of the huge coal excavators (the length of which is twice the height of the Eiffel Tower, I was told proudly by many informants), he also played in Hoyerswerda's most famous band of that time: the 'Brigade Firestone' (*Brigade Feuerstein*). This band was not part of the socialist plan for the city. Neither were the many social, cultural and musical clubs and associations founded by those inhabitants who were 'hungry for life' – as a local idiom has it – in an environment dominated by planned efficiency and functionality.

With German reunification in 1990, the Cold War ended in Germany. The former GDR's sudden incorporation into the capitalist world system had severe social and economic consequences all over East Germany: unemployment roared and outmigration skyrocketed. With the modernization of the industrial complex, for which Hoyerswerda was originally built, Gundermann lost his job too. Of the original 30,000 'miners and energy workers', only a tenth were still needed. The city's population shrank drastically in a very short period of time, eventually causing the widespread demolition of *Neustadt*'s cityscape. In the mid 1990s, Gundermann tried to retrain as a carpenter. Meanwhile, he was touring around the former GDR, celebrated as 'the voice of East Germany'. For many, he was one of the few public figures expressing the feelings and problems of a whole society in rapid transformation. Change, justice, solidarity and the future were topics of his songs. He found words for what – from one day to the next – had hit the whole region, but Hoyerswerda most dramatically: deindustrialization, decline and the loss not only of the socialist future it once had, but also the future of the 'imaginary West' (Yurchak 2006: 158ff). It was the latter capitalist future that earlier came to dominate the nascent East German peaceful revolution and later, after the 1989 'turn' or *Wende*, failed to deliver on its promises of post-reunification prosperity. Another recurrent theme in Gundermann's work is the inevitable finitude of life. His own premature death in 1998, at the age of forty-three, tragically underlined the melancholy of his songs.

As an ethnography of the failures and aftermath of German reunification, this book could be an elaborate account of dying, vanishing or demise. Hoyerswerda is a city of 'historically unprecedented decline and deconstruction in peacetimes', as German journalists were recurrently eager to point out. Between 1989 and 2009, Hoyerswerda's population halved from approximately 70,000 to less than 35,000 residents. The average age of the remaining inhabitants had doubled over the course of four decades. Demographically speaking, Hoyerswerda had turned from Germany's youngest city in the 1950s into one of its oldest by 2009. The future prospects were, to put it mildly, bleak, and especially the young and well-educated continued to leave the city; already at the beginning of my fieldwork in 2008, the population was predicted to halve yet again by 2020.

Furthermore, Hoyerswerda not only had the reputation of having 'no future', it was also widely known to be of the past in at least two different ways. First, as a socialist model city, it seemed stuck in the socialist past, unable to enter the capitalist present and future. The local election successes of the leftist successor party to the former state-ruling Socialist Unity Party seemed to confirm this in the early

1990s. The same goes for the city's apartment houses built in prefab style architecture (*Plattenbau*; see Hannemann 1996), which – as in West Germany – soon became defamed as soulless social housing for the poor and a representative of the failed project of state-socialism. Second, in September 1991, Hoyerswerda was also the first city in Germany to showcase xenophobic attacks on foreigners – newly arriving asylum seekers and former contract workers from other social states. The images of a drunken mob harassing innocent refugees went around the world and linked the city to the even more distant past of Nazi Germany.

However, rather than providing an ethnography of dramatic demise or heroic survival, this monograph seeks to advance something different: an ethnography of the future.[3] From a presentist perspective (and despite the initial historical contextualization), this study takes as its ethnographic objects the many explicit, tacit and always concrete temporal notions that are sparked by – as much as they relate to – the temporal dimension of the future. These temporal relations to the future include all kinds of representational and non-representational forms of knowledge that pertain to this dimension. In Hoyerswerda, they obviously first of all deal with the negative developments the city faces. However, relations to the future have been rendered problematic in many parts of the world. The postindustrial era, which arguably started with the 1970s oil crises, has had severe effects. As Jane Guyer argued in her seminal 2007 article on contemporary forms of temporal reasoning, people worldwide have lost their hold particularly on the near future. In place of five-year plans and widespread construction, they experience what Guyer labels 'enforced presentism': they are coerced to live only in the immediate present, having lost the ability to plan ahead. The post-Cold War era and its numerous new crises have, indeed, forced many people to face a reality in which the (better) future seems to be lost to the realm of fantasy (Guyer refers to this as fantasy futurism). However, the idea of the modernist future, of ongoing economic growth as well as urban and other development has been overthrown in Hoyerswerda and in many other parts of the former socialist bloc much more suddenly than elsewhere in the postindustrial world. In less than a decade, the city had changed from a booming and lively mining settlement to a drastically shrinking city without a future. In 2008, this loss of the future constituted the city's most important problem.

In what follows, I ethnographically explore Hoyerswerda's future. My central thesis is that the future as an ethnographic object should be an integral part of anthropological analysis – regardless of whether it seems lost or not in a specific fieldsite. Anthropologists as much as other social scientists tend to think that our present lives are the results of complex historical processes of causation. Accordingly, when analysing peoples' presents, their pasts are frequently discussed to the exclusion of their futures (see Persoon and van Est 2000). Against this, I argue that the different ways in which people relate to the future is as, if not more, crucial for understanding their presents. This book explores the postindustrial condition and its social, cultural and epistemic repercussions in one social setting by mapping the loss, and reappropriation, of the future by a particular urban community. Hoyerswerda is an ideal place to study this. No longer a vanguard socialist industrial city, it can be understood as a vanguard city of a different kind: a herald of the postindustrial future in Europe and beyond, to which, as I claim in the book's title, we should return more consciously. Although it is a most drastic example, Hoyerswerda is only one of the many shrinking cities produced in the postindustrial era of finance capitalism. Outside of the former Eastern Bloc, particularly cities in the United States (for Chicago, see Walley 2013; for Flint, Michigan, see Young 2013) and broader cultural changes in countries such as Japan (for example, Allison 2013) caught scientific attention. However, it is no coincidence that the comparative literature on shrinking cities first emerged in East Germany (Hannemann 2003; Oswalt 2005, 2006; Oswalt and Rieniets 2006, see also Bude et al. 2011; Willisch 2012; Cliver and Smith-Prei 2014), and cities such as Hoyerswerda might as well provide a unique perspective on the postindustrial future.

To explore how Hoyerswerda's inhabitants have overcome their postindustrial representational paralysis with regard to the future and how social scientists can follow suit analytically, I argue for a particular way of studying the future. I claim that anthropology, with its inherently presentist methodology of ethnographic fieldwork, allows us to come to a better understanding of the role the future plays in human life than other social science disciplines. Once this new conceptualization of the future is established, it will also change our understanding of the past. To assist in the elucidation of these two related arguments, I will briefly discuss the philosophical theory of presentism. Like Alfred Gell (1992), I take inspiration from the metaphysics of time in order to draw from this renewed transdisciplinary conversation a link to our own concerns (compare Bear 2014; Hodges 2008).

Anthropology and Presentism:
Past, Present and Future Reconsidered

In the metaphysics of time, presentism is the account of time that holds that only the present exists, while the past and future are in some way unreal; it is contrasted with eternalism, which holds that the past, present and future are equally real. Metaphysical presentism resembles the approach of those anthropologists who hold that both the past and the future do not exist other than in their not necessarily accurate representations in the present (for example, Gell 1992; Munn 1992). Kirsten Hastrup's 1990 definition of ethnographic presentism argues that in the discipline of anthropology this form of presentism is not just a literary device; it is the essentially presentist methodological approach to ethnographic material, which shapes anthropology's 'necessary construction of time' (Hastrup 1990: 45). Pushed to the extreme, as Alfred Gell so convincingly showed in his discussion of the temporal quality of the Magna Carta, it does not matter from an anthropological point of view whether a document held in a British library or cathedral dates from 1215 or not. What matters is how people attach meaning to it, that is, whatever 'temporality' or 'historicity' they construct in their respective presents (see Ringel 2016b). To focus on the ethnographic present therefore does not detemporalize anthropological analysis (de Pina-Cabral 2000), but helps us to put invocations of pasts that potentially never were and of futures that potentially never will be on their proper metaphysical footing.

However, historically minded scholars can easily counter the idea of ethnographic presentism. In their view, although any future might be open, the present came to be the way it is through a long and complex process of historical causation. Hence, for them, it would be important to read Hoyerswerda's postsocialist present through the lens of the socialist or an even earlier past. This seriously downplays the influence the representations of the future might have in and on the present, and it severely restricts human agency or, more specifically, human temporal agency (Ringel 2016a). In their conceptual framework, the present is reduced to a momentary pause in an ever-continuous process of causation. Only the past gains a proper ontological quality. To undermine the view that the present is determined by the past, I turn to a recent discussion of presentism in the metaphysics of time.

In 2006, the philosopher Craig Bourne published a defence of metaphysical presentism – entitled *The Future of Presentism* – and the work contains a piece of reasoning that is relevant to my concerns. Bourne seeks to identify and invalidate deterministic fallacies, using an argument that I simplify here.

The first premise is that, given a certain degree of contingency and indeterminacy, at any moment in time, we face the probable emergence of a variety of possible futures. In other words, Bourne claims that our future is not predetermined, as at any point in time many possible futures may come to pass. I suspect that most anthropologists would accept this premise (although many philosophers would not). Otherwise, meaningful action is hard to envision: most people at least seem to presume that their decisions have an impact on the future. The second premise is that if our future is not predetermined, then our actual pasts – events, which were once one of these possible futures, but have actually become a present and then a past – were at no point predetermined to become an actual present either. Given both premises, the conclusion follows that neither our future *nor* our past is or was predetermined.

Bourne's understanding of metaphysical presentism does not entail that there is no causal relationship between past and present. Rather, it puts the past and the future on an equal ontological footing: neither past nor future exists in the present, and neither is predetermined. For a presentist, only the present exists. This framework suggests a new way of understanding anthropological presentism, both theoretically and methodologically: we should treat the past and future symmetrically in anthropological analysis, paying in-depth attention to *all* the temporal relations and experiences – pertaining to the past, present and future – found in our fieldsites' many successive presents. Building on this, I attempt to reconceptualize the anthropology of time with an increased and explicit attention to the future.

This approach helps me to avoid two traps: first, explaining postsocialist change solely through the perspective of the socialist past (Ringel 2013a); and second, projecting my own hopes and wishes for a better future, as much as my fears and worries, onto my informants' lives and struggles (Ringel 2012). As the experiences of my informants prove, any future might hold various surprises, as past futures have already done. For instance, had my informants been told twenty years ago that their city's population would decrease by half in 2008, the dystopian imaginaries to capture such an allegation would have had their own self-fulfilling prophetic effects. However, now that people live in the deindustrialized future, the new present suddenly allows otherwise unforeseen spaces for hope and different, if still tentative, ideas of other futures. What counts for the future also has to count for the past: from a presentist point of view, neither of these temporal dimensions exists ontologically outside the present, in which they are presented and negotiated (see Adam 1990: 38). These temporal representations stem from a temporal agency all human beings have (see Ringel and Moroşanu 2016) and are usually subjected to all kinds of temporal politics (for example, Antze and Lambek 1996; Kaneff 2003).

For their analysis, this book follows Jane Guyer's aim 'to develop an ethnography of the near future of the 21st century' (Guyer 2007: 410) and thus empirically explores the (epistemic) repercussions of a much broader collapse of formerly powerful modern and postmodern narratives of the future. Therefore, it is not about memory, nostalgia or other representations of the past (see Gilbert 2006); rather, it approaches change through the perspective of alterations in temporal knowledge in relations to the future. Following its presentist inclinations, it proposes that these temporal relations are primarily of an epistemic kind, which in turn entails our own practices of knowledge production (compare Fabian 1983; Wolf 1982).

This analytical decision has major repercussions for the study of change and transformation. Primarily, I have to reconsider the role of knowledge in times of change, exploring its adaptability and flexibility, without repeating the anthropology of postsocialism's initial tendency of depicting the former socialist 'other' (in Fabian's terms) as surprisingly adaptable to new socioeconomic environments (see Buyandelgeriyn 2008). By that I distance myself from the implicit idea of a postsocialist ontology, fully predetermined by – and mostly directed to – the past, which took hold in many academic and non-academic circles, particularly in the field of transitology. As other accounts from the vast and diverse body of literature in the field of postsocialist anthropology (for example, Pelkmans 2003; Boyer 2006; Gilbert 2006; Pedersen 2012; Jansen 2014; Knudsen and Frederikson 2015), my case study depicts one example in which this paradigm ultimately fails. Instead of memories of – and concerns with – the past, I encountered an abundant variety of local knowledges, imaginaries and affects pertaining to the future, which, for a presentist, remain not (fully) predetermined by the past.[4]

Under the heading of postindustrial shrinkage, I foreground the future in all its openness, indeterminacy and malleability, rather than depict the past as powerfully predetermining the present and the future. This is particularly important because, as Nancy Munn observed, in the discipline of anthropology, 'futurity is poorly tended as a temporal problem … in contrast to the close attention given to "the past in the present"' (Munn 1992: 116). It also challenges academic hopes that postsocialist persons because of their socialist past can articulate a fundamental critique of Western capitalism and actively partake in some form of 'co-determination' (Dunn 2004). Such new solutions, ideas, concepts and practices were also locally awaited, but never really occurred; rather, a new present demanded altogether new solutions for novel, problematic futures. By inspecting the diverse modes of temporal agency of Hoyerswerda's inhabitants in relation to the future, my ethnographic material contributes to the overall discipline what the subdiscipline of postsocialist anthropology has always been concerned with: the issue of time.

Gilbert et al. (2008: 11) already put it rather felicitously regarding the potential theoretical contributions of postsocialism: 'If anthropology is the social science of the present, it ought to offer insight into the future *in* the present.' They aspire to assemble a 'social historiography of the future – a futuricity to complement historicity' (ibid.). However, my approach also substantially differs from such culturally exclusive prescriptions. For instance, in contrast to Hirsch and Stewart's 2005 take on historicity, I doubt that we can convincingly account for the historical predetermination of relations to the past (and by extension to the future), that is, what Hirsch and Stewart refer to as the *historically specific* and thereby determined 'relevant ways in which (social) pasts and futures are implicated in current circumstances' (see Ringel 2016b). Futuricity, as a coherent, homogeneous and collectively shared way of relating to the future, does not account for how my informants relate to the future (see again Ringel 2016b). Instead, as the overall postsocialist experience (Yurchak 2006) captures: things seem rather less determined and homogenous; they might radically change from one day to the other, and we should not be surprised by how (comparatively) easily humans adapt to this. As I claim throughout this book, for a presentist, both change and continuity are in some way subject to people's temporal agency: in each present, different relations to different pasts and futures are possible.

Faced with the contemporary epistemic changes, the inhabitants of Hoyerswerda deploy their knowledge and experience to problems that are 'conceptual' and 'new'. They refer to them as problems of 'shrinkage' (*Schrumpfung*), thus establishing a *post*postsocialist epistemic arena. Superficially, the term 'shrinkage' might be understood to describe the merging of three different processes of transformation: postsocialist transition, (neoliberally orchestrated) globalization and (post-Fordist) deindustrialization. I propose to study the concurrence of these processes not through a political economy perspective, but by regarding their epistemic impact on the life of the inhabitants of this shrinking city. My ethnographic material maps the final establishment and acceptance of the trope of shrinkage, and then tracks how this temporal regime too has been challenged. The emergence of the possibility of asking a new, rather simple question regarding the future depicts this challenge. 'What happens after shrinkage?', however, incorporates a local revolution in epistemic terms; it gives Hoyerswerda a new future by epistemically reclaiming it. The fact that futures can be lost and exchanged for other futures is an essential part of Hoyerswerda's story, and I show how its citizens overcame their particular forms of enforced presentism and dystopian fantasy futurism, and established a new present from which to relate to yet other futures.

As Dominic Boyer (2006, 2010) suggested, this strategy has further political implications: such local concerns about the future might provide a position that finally allows East Germans – or anybody else, for that matter – to take their future in their own hands. Since the postindustrial decline hit East Germany faster and harder than their West German countrymen, the latter are less interested in what is officially seen as a specifically East German problem. In turn, knowledge in and about this shrinking city is locally specific, practical, malleable and adaptable – not just postsocialist or East German in kind. This reconsideration of presumably postsocialist knowledge practices entails the reconceptualization of the notion of 'East Germanness'. Accordingly, this ethnography is not a study of East German culture. Beyond the construction of alterity between East and West Germany, which was the core object of study in the anthropology of East Germany (compare Borneman 1992; Glaeser 2000, 2001; Boyer 2001a), I leave the comparative reference to 'the West' out of my analysis. Hoyerswerdians, like many other East Germans, face problems of their own, and it is their responses to these concrete epistemic problems that I analyse here.

Still, I also refrain from celebrating the many attempts of Hoyerswerda's inhabitants involved in the endless endeavour to regain or uphold a sense of a personal and the city's future. By that, I do not follow the future solely via uncovering the epistemic logic of the 'method of hope', as Hirokazu Miyazaki (2004) so admirably did for his Fijian fieldsite. Rather, I attempt to approach the future as an ethnographic object that is – in many different ways – not only an epistemic problem for my informants in their presents, whose solution needs the constant 'redirection of knowledge', but is also a social, ethical and political concern. Importantly, the local production of knowledge is linked to the future not by myself as the analyst, but explicitly by my friends and informants in the field. My informants establish these links foremost because they face a situation in which their hometown's future is rendered fundamentally problematic. The next section answers Jane Guyer's question, which follows from this observation: 'What kind of "stories" does imagination create when the reference points lie in the future?' (Guyer 2007: 417).

The Future in the Present

In Hoyerswerda, the overwhelming omnipresence of the future in daily life entails mundane long-term and short-term decisions; official planning practices; business development plans; strategy papers of local social clubs, organizations and associations; private and public investment plans; and the conceptualization and organization of potential future projects. It also comprises more intimate aspects: personal future prospects; expectations of the local youth's outmigration; individual feelings and collective affects of fear, hope and despair; issues of trust and the lack of self-confidence; and the constricted capacity to envision one's own life in the future.

In recent years, topics such as hope (Appadurai 2002, 2013; Miyazaki 2004, 2006, 2010; Zigon 2006, 2009; Pedersen 2012; Jansen 2014; Kleist and Jansen 2016) and planning (Alexander 2007; Guyer 2007; Weszkalnys 2010; Nielsen 2011, 2014; Baxstrom 2012; Abram and Weszkalnys 2013; Bear 2015) have received special attention as modes of relating to the future. In this book, I follow the more thoroughly collective, socially embedded, and continuously negotiated and contested future-relations (see Bear 2014, 2015). I thus focus on a specific set of collective epistemic practices and conflicts: public negotiations of temporal problems, specifically with the future, in which the citizens of Hoyerswerda collectively scrutinize their own and their hometown's existence in time. This, in the first half of the book, combines different local arenas, such as educational and sociocultural projects, and controversial discourses, in which, for example, urban development strategies and the city's future are passionately debated in moral, social, political or technological terms. Later in the book, I focus on two further aspects: the systematic imposition of affects of the future – spurred by dystopian predictions – and teleological practices of permanence and endurance. I use such sets of practices in order to reconsider issues of, and relations between, hope, knowledge and temporal agency. The analysis of these heterogeneous practices

Figure 0.2 *View from the Lausitz Tower in* Neustadt's *city centre towards WK 10 (beige buildings, centre left), with the coal-fired power plant* Schwarze Pumpe *in the background (centre right)*

draws together very different local groups, events, institutions, perspectives and opinions. The links between these different persons, places and situations were upheld by the widespread problematization of postindustrial shrinkage, the then characteristic feature of what I refer to as the local economy of knowledge: the collective exchange and contestation of ideas and opinions about the city and its future.

All of these practices conceptually, practically and affectively targeted the temporal dimension of the future (in the present). Nonetheless, they still did not add up to a local temporal culture. Rather, my informants' production of knowledge and affects about themselves, their city and respective futures remained concrete and situated. Their epistemic practices answered specific questions and concerns, and indicated in their variety a complex, diverse and even contradictory reservoir of temporal thoughts and relations, and a certain flexibility in people's capacity to negotiate this multiplicity. If anything, it was the then current omnipresence of potential and widely feared repercussions of the drastic local economic, social and demographic decline that characterizes this local economy of knowledge.

Despite the fact that actual shrinkage has very different effects on different people, depending on their socioeconomic standing, age, education and personal conviction, all Hoyerswerdians were forced to ask themselves what kind of future their hometown has. In concrete terms, this meant that they had to define what for them, in their particular circumstances, the locally ubiquitous phrase 'quality of life' entailed and how much of that they were ready to sacrifice when facing a bleak future. Is life worth living in a shrinking city? The sometimes prosaic, performative claim that Hoyerswerda was, after all, a 'loveable and liveable city' (*liebens- und lebenswerte Stadt*) – a phrase continuously brought forward by the Lord Mayor, local journalists and other public voices – has a somewhat empty and sober, but at the same time passionate and desperate appeal to it.

However, actual shrinkage as well as its imagined future consequences impeded on the most intimate, relational aspects of social life – and even there sparked the production of knowledge about the future. The severe holes in the city's social fabric affected every citizen. For example, all of the seven host families I stayed with during my sixteen months of fieldwork faced important changes stemming from their children's outmigration. Out of my seventeen host siblings (all in their late teens to early thirties), thirteen had already left the city when I was doing fieldwork; by 2011, only four remained with three more to leave soon. Most host families usually housed me in the bedrooms of their offspring, who had already left the city. Even if the parents' own futures in the city seemed secure (and three of the seven families seriously considered leaving during my time in Hoyerswerda), there were still potentially dramatic changes ahead. My first host parents, both teachers, worried about the future of the respective schools they worked at. If one of them closed down due to a lack of new pupils, where would they be allocated to – another school in Hoyerswerda or another city altogether? My second host mother's main concern was the impending move out of her WK 10 apartment. Already in 2008 WK 10 was widely predicted to be completely demolished by 2013 (which, indeed, it was) despite being Hoyerswerda's youngest living district. Should she move to Dresden where her two sons live? Should she stay in Hoyerswerda where she is only precariously employed? Until that decision was made, she had to endure all the concerns of living in a WK that is doomed to be demolished: the ongoing deconstruction of nearby apartment houses, the decay of green spaces and playgrounds, the accelerating departure of neighbours and friends. My third host parents faced leaving after their two children finished their A-levels and started university degrees elsewhere. They seriously considered moving to Dresden, Berlin or some alternative living project in the countryside. My host mother was constantly on the brink of being made redundant from her job as a headmistress of a local nursing school due to the school's potential closure. My host father commuted daily to Berlin – why not move there for good?

Such personal concerns, problems and impediments are themselves not unusual and can be found in most parts of the world. Everywhere, institutions, shops and surgeries shut down; people face migration, insecurity and temporary hopelessness. Worldwide, children are leaving their parents' homes, and communities are forced to deal with fundamental alterations stemming from such outmigration. In particular, what is known as the former First World suffers from ageing populations and demographic implosions. The division into winners and losers of contemporary changes has set into motion new flows of people, goods and investments, which severely affect – as this account's focus on outmigration suggests – not only those going away, but also those staying behind (compare Ferguson 1999; Walley 2013; Young 2013; Gaibazzi 2015; Vacarro et al. 2016). In Hoyerswerda, it is not the kind of social, economic and cultural change – postindustrial, after all – that is significant, but rather its magnitude and rapid intensity. For many inhabitants, the actual survival of their city is under threat, since there seems to be no end to this accelerated process of change. At its core, then, 'shrinkage' precisely entails this problematization of the future because it pre-emptively prescribes to current changes a bad outcome, directing them to a future that seems already lost. It is for this reason that inhabitants of Hoyerswerda continuously renegotiated their personal and collective futures with one another.

The Future as an Epistemic Problem

> Once a city decreases in size, do its citizens subsequently increase in relevance?
> —Uwe Proksch, CEO KulturFabrik e.V., September 2008

At the end of my fieldwork in the spring of 2009, the Federal Office for Building and Regional Planning pronounced Hoyerswerda to be Germany's fastest-shrinking and soon (demographically speaking) oldest city. More than before, the term 'shrinkage' came to signify the myriad intricate and large-scale changes experienced by

Hoyerswerda's citizens, and put their city in the national media spotlight. The future dimension, as shown in the previous section, had a special role to play in locally perceiving and making sense of these alterations. But how did shrinkage – or what it refers to – come to be a problem, and with which epistemic and social repercussions? In particular, the search for a proper context, out of, in and with which to create new meaning for the present and the future in it, was essential in Hoyerswerda, since the daily encounters with the deconstruction of major parts of the cityscape and continuous threats of further deconstruction, closure and new impediments kept on influencing my informants' lives. Although many Hoyerswerdians claimed that they got used to the sight of the huge excavators tearing down apartment blocks, the noises of the concrete panels crashing down on huge heaps of rubble or the smell of the irrigated cement residue, they, like I, often still experienced a sense of confusion when stumbling yet again over the absence of a particular apartment house, school or kindergarten – not to mention the absence of friends, children and neighbours.

In my first chapter, I scrutinize the following possibility: anthropologists could convincingly approach life in Germany's fastest-shrinking city from the perspective of postsocialism – composing a narrative about postsocialist failure and the burdens of the socialist past, tracking in detail what Caroline Humphrey aptly referred to as the 'unmaking of socialist life' (Humphrey 2002a). In a bleak version of this – common in German media – the Hoyerswerdians could then be seen not as facing problems with their future, but as postsocialist subjects who have never been fit for the new (Western) future in the first place. Accounts of nostalgic attachments to the past (which I hardly ever encountered during my sixteen months of fieldwork) would neatly illustrate this situation, and the failure of German reunification could remain as depoliticized as it is in most public discourses in Germany. As I argue, however, the fundamental upheaval in Hoyerswerda cannot be reduced to being merely a postsocialist phenomenon. Rather, much broader processes simultaneously come to bear in Hoyerswerda, producing an unprecedented dimension of change, which my informants tackled daily in their personal and professional lives.

From Hoyerswerda alone, approximately 50,000 people have left, with far fewer people moving to the city. What happens when more than half of a city's population leave in a comparatively short period of time, and when urban life and sociality suddenly lose their endurance, permanence and predictability? In Hoyerswerda, the answer to these questions required the production of new knowledge in my informants' continuously problematic presents. The shift from the refusal of the term 'shrinkage' to accepting it as a valid description of the process gave a new structure to this knowledge. One of the crucial understandings it entails is an ethical one, namely that a 'good' life is not only possible in times of growth. Rather, in the eyes of my informants, life in times of shrinkage and decline is to be lived in as good a way as possible, despite (or even because of) their hometown's current decline. Established practices and institutions are to be maintained, and new forms of practices have to be tried out. At the core of this ethical response are the profound temporal operations in the form of temporal reasoning. This particular form of temporal agency allows for the reappropriation of the temporal dimension of the near future in concrete terms, and beyond the local politicians' dubious invigorations of the 'chances of shrinkage' (*Chancen der Schrumpfung*).

That the city and its future are rendered problematic therefore invites an analysis with reference to the anthropologies of time and of knowledge. The key term 'temporal reasoning' combines these two aspects most effectively. In Jane Guyer's definition, it refers to the different ways of 'implicating oneself in the ongoing life of the social and material world' (Guyer 2007: 409). In its original sense, it comprised 'the reach of thought and imagination, of planning and hoping, of tracing out mutual influences, of engaging in struggles for specific goals' (ibid.) – all regarding relations to the near future, particularly in modern times (see Bear 2014; compare Pels 2015). I explore with it knowledge practices also aimed at other temporal dimensions, in particular the past and the present, thus expanding its meaning to all epistemic investments in issues of time and particular temporal periods. Additionally, an analysis of human knowledge practices, temporal politics and the local production of meaning for the future also entails affective and ethical issues and questions about the efficacy of future knowledge more generally. The problematization of the city's existence in time creates the city of Hoyerswerda as an object of knowledge and stimulates the personal and public production, exchange and dissemination of knowledge about it. Virtually all citizens are drawn into these discursive or representational practices. They are genuinely concerned about their hometown's future and a potential loss of their quality of life in it. Since Guyer specifically attends the potential privatization of the near future, I focus on the *public* explication, dissemination and negotiation of the (near) future.

In the following chapters, I refrain from extensively describing disappearance, absence, change and hopelessness or the ongoing process of spatial and material deterioration, decay and deconstruction of lifeworlds and former socialist *and* postsocialist living spaces. Studying the epistemic or conceptual repercussions of the process of shrinkage, I instead focus on specific local clashes in – and through – which particular knowledge about the city and its future is made explicit. In an urban context, public arenas of knowledge explication are multiple, but in my case remain linked by the widely acknowledged problematization of Hoyerswerda's future.

Problematizing urban life and the city's future also entails a problematization of local citizenship and these citizens' contemporary role and agency. What does it mean to be a citizen in and of a shrinking city? Uwe,[5] the CEO of Hoyerswerda's sociocultural centre, posed the ingenious question: 'Once a city decreases in size, do its citizens subsequently increase in relevance?'[6] He drew attention to the fact that those staying in Hoyerswerda are much needed for essential social responsibilities and functions. With every person leaving, the city's quality of life was seen to further deteriorate – so the worth of each citizen should be at the centre of all political decisions in these troubled times. Such considerations were not new in Hoyerswerda. During the time of Neustadt's erection, a time of constant growth, the famous East German author Brigitte Reimann publicly intervened on behalf of the young population and approached the problem of the quality of urban life by asking a simple question: 'Is it possible to kiss in Hoyerswerda?' In critique of the increasingly more economically restricted and functionally inclined official plans under state-socialism, she insisted that the city's architects should include the new Hoyerswerdians' social, cultural and emotional needs in their planning. She demanded more social meeting places, a central alley with shops and cafes, a theatre, a cinema, bars and a literature café. A socialist model city, she underlined, should consider the human beings in all their complexity. So should a shrinking postindustrial city, I hasten to add, because it is not only that socialist life, or modern industrial life, is being unmade, but a new form of life is emerging, and we – as my informants – should aim at finding words to capture this emergence.

In 2008, such questions were asked again in relation to the repercussions of the process of shrinkage. As Dorit Baumeister, a local architect, put it: 'In this process of shrinkage, which we have come to accept as such, it is our aim to intervene positively, to remain capable of exercising agency. We want to create an optimistic atmosphere, which in turn produces a different, a new quality and culture of life.'[7] Her club's response was and is sociocultural: more 'togetherness'

(*Miteinander*) of those who remain in Hoyerswerda. However, it is precisely these sociocultural arenas that faced the lack of public funds most severely. Since state money is allocated to local communities in relation to their population numbers, Hoyerswerda procured increasingly lower levels of funds, but still had to maintain the same urban infrastructure at increasing costs. The conservative Lord Mayor Stefan Skora was acutely aware of the fact that if he followed regional and state financial demands, he would have to close down most cultural institutions, all of which are sponsored – in legal terms – voluntarily by the city. He refused to do so in order not to 'expel' even more of his inhabitants. As he underlined, Hoyerswerda was, is and will be 'a loveable and liveable city'. The quality of life the city was seen to provide is not only in this way an essential political, technical and personal tool to handle shrinkage; its invocation might also be a crucial, if nascent attempt to recolonize the city's presumably lost near future.

For the same reason, Skora introduced another group intervening in the public definition of the city's qualities: marketing and advertisement experts. In search of unique selling points, they approached Hoyerswerda's quality of life as a major tool in the increasingly fierce competition between small- and medium-sized cities. For their survival, these cities compete not only for investors and state funding, but also for the similarly scarce resource of citizens. Imagine there is a city and nobody wants to live in it. In particular, the competition for increasingly scarce skilled personnel defines cities, towns and communities as quality providers for the lives of those much-desired citizens who promise tax income and the potential attraction of more people. However, the marketing experts' job was also to convince those living in Hoyerswerda of their own city's advantages, thereby creating a sense of togetherness like the architect's sociocultural club had in mind.

For a social anthropologist to intervene in such discourses on a city's quality of life, already captured as a neoliberal unique selling point, entails several problems. For one thing, the emphasis on the social and cultural dimensions of human life often similarly reflects the anthropologist's hopes and concerns. As Sara Ahmed (2008) warned, there is a danger in our interventions in such discourses, onto which we impose our own conceptualizations of social harmony, for example, by wanting to put the 'social glue' back into moments of crisis and divergence. I accept her critique. However, the problematization of the core social relations that make up personal, public, urban, professional and everyday life in Hoyerswerda (i.e.

the local urge for more togetherness and social cohesion) is in itself an ethnographic fact. As an outcome of various knowledge practices that centre around the city's fate and future, it should not be easily debunked out of concerns about our own ethical and political convictions. In order to explain what is theoretically at stake when local forms of reasoning about the city's worth in the present and the future are approached via their temporal characteristics, I present a few thoughts on the anthropologies of time and knowledge in relation to one another.

Knowledge and Time/Knowledge in Time

> There is no need to be in awe of time, which is no more mysterious than any other facet of our experience of the world.
> —A. Gell, *The Anthropology of Time*

In the eyes of many Germans, Hoyerswerda is just another East German city with 'no future'. A former avant-garde settlement where the socialist future was daily facilitated, Hoyerswerda faces social decline more strongly than other postsocialist cities, a continuously decreasing and ageing population, and unrestrained physical deconstruction. It has lost its economic foundation and with it its modernist raison d'être. By all accounts, Hoyerswerda is perceived as a hopeless case. Still, as shown in the previous sections, the city remains infused with an urge towards the future. However, the new temporal framework of shrinkage fundamentally questions any future prospects for Hoyerswerda. It outruns in bleakness the disillusioning loss of the hopes of the postsocialist transition. As shown above, in the process of shrinkage, uncertainty prevails not only in the domains of urban planning, the housing market, the education system and other public domains, but also in personal lives. People have lost the security they needed to plan the future. They cannot be sure that their jobs, schools, dentists, favourite restaurants or football clubs will continue to exist in the years to come.

The commonly expected responses to problems with the future – nostalgic attachment to the (in this case socialist) past[8] or Guyer's otherwise accurate enforced presentism/fantasy futurism-dyad – set strong limits to the capacity of Hoyerswerda's inhabitants to discern not only change and a different future, but to the ability to envision a future altogether. They also do not provide convincing reasons for the fact that people nonetheless continue in myriad ways to direct their practices and lives to the future (see Crapanzano 2007). What kind of ethnographic object and analytical tool are hope and knowledge of the future? And how should we approach temporal agency in this context of shrinkage?

My ethnographic material consists of the local mediation of Hoyerswerda's present and future by its citizens. As Donna Haraway (1988) pointed out, knowledge is always situated; this means it is part of a specific social context and manifests there as the interface of sociopolitical processes of negotiation (Boyer 2005) and personal interpretations of the world (Barth 2002). In a presentist framework, I account for both the 'radical historical contingency for all knowledge claims and knowledge subjects' and the 'radical multiplicity of local knowledges' (Haraway 1988: 579). Accordingly, I approach knowledge less as an access point to local cultures (something ontologically given) and more as radically contingent, collectively negotiated outcomes of a multiplicity of local knowledge practices. In Hoyerswerda, as elsewhere, these negotiations happen in discourses among friends and family members, at all sorts of social gatherings, professional city planning procedures, in expert circles, around conference and coffee tables, at public speeches and sociocultural projects targeting the city's future. This book maps a variety of public engagements with the city, presenting a citizenry that passionately produces and discusses knowledge about its own life, city and future.

Such a practice-based approach to time and knowledge (see Rabinow 1986) throws light on local politics and the way in which the future is made to play a role in Hoyerswerda's citizens' lives and experiences. It has a longstanding tradition in the discipline of anthropology. As Gell in *The Anthropology of Time* pointed out, Durkheim in his *The Elementary Forms of Religious Life* already made clear 'that collective representations of time do not passively reflect time, but actually create time as a phenomenon apprehended by sentient human beings' (Gell 1992: 4). However, I concur with Gell's critique of Durkheim, whose 'thesis of the social origination of human temporal experience offers the prospect of a limitless variety of vicarious experiences of unfamiliar, exotic, temporal worlds' and 'their distinctive temporalities' (both ibid.). In contrast to such an ontologizing idea of temporality as a homogeneous, closed cultural system (compare Ringel 2016b), and in accordance with Gell, I define time as an issue of (knowledge) practices, politics and changing social conventions, but not as an aspect of culture, a term that, for example, one of the most influential theorist of knowledge, Michel Foucault, in his early works uses only very unreflectively (for example, Foucault 2004 [1961], 2005 [1966]).

As Gell emphasizes, instead of searching for distinct temporal cultures, we should instead account for a more specific 'contextual sensitivity of knowledge' – including temporal knowledge: 'how much a person "knows" about the world depends not only on what he has internalized and what … is in his permanent possession, but also on the context within which this knowledge is to be elicited, and by what means' (1992: 109), that is, the present context of its production. For example, as he observed in Bourdieu's early work, the Kabyle 'operate with a multitude of different kinds of temporal schemes, appropriate to specific contexts of discourse or action' (Gell 1992: 296). In Hoyerswerda, I am going to discern different forms of reasoning in similar ways. In both cases, political claims to time are part of the 'continuous production of socially useful knowledge' (ibid.: 304). Gell very successfully poses this idea of 'contingent beliefs' against 'the doctrine of temporal "mentalities" or "worldviews"' (ibid.: 55).⁹

Carol Greenhouse also emphasizes the politics of time, and reminds us that we have to think about time and temporal representations always in relation to, in her case, changing or contested conceptions of social order and agency (1996: 4). As in Gell's analysis, this goes beyond wondering about the 'geometry of time' (ibid.: 5), that is, its presumed cyclicity or linearity. Whereas she still focuses on temporality as an aspect of culture, I concentrate on the particular knowledge practices that reference different temporal dimensions. As she observes, however, any dominant formulation of temporality is, in fact, hard to be maintained (see ibid.: 82). Following Greenhouse, we could define shrinkage as the dominant formulation of time in Hoyerswerda, and it comes with the dominance of a particular version of temporal reasoning, what I call 'enforced futurism' – a constant attention to and problematization of the temporal dimension of the future. This form of temporal reasoning might have its histories (compare Rosenberg and Harding 2005; Pels 2016) or buy into particularly long-lasting problematizations (Rabinow 2003: 56), but I claim that there is no historical force that determines these practices. From a presentist point of view, the agency expressed in them might yield surprising results against all odds. Indeed, relations to the future in postindustrial modernity require the production of specific kinds of knowledges. As Ferguson has pointed out, these different kinds follow 'the need to come to terms with a social world that can no longer be grasped in terms of the old script' (Ferguson 1999: 252), in which dominant temporal frames fail to convincingly deliver epistemic clarification.

Ferguson claims that we should focus on the epistemic consequences of such changes. In *Expectations of Modernity*, he advances an ethnography of decline in which he strongly argues against modernist linear narratives, whilst emphasizing our discipline's own investments in these temporal knowledge regimes. He contrasts their counterparts (deindustrialization, deurbanization and de-Zambianization) to his informants' various expressions of agency. His aim is to trace the decline's 'effects on people's modes of conduct and ways of understanding their lives' (ibid.: 11–12). Whereas he sees most hope for overcoming the decline in the past as a resource for countering the false future promises of the modernization narrative, I want to establish the future as a resource for countering narratives of decline and shrinkage.

Facing widespread problems of and with knowledge itself, how do we specifically approach knowledge about the future? As I have pointed out above, I investigate particular forms of temporal thought, practice, affect, ethics and agency in a context where the future is rendered problematic. In short, the future is not just a matter of professional planning practices in local, regional and national state institutions or their citizen's responses. Rather, the future is created, related to and represented in a variety of different arenas, such as art, social, cultural and other communal milieus, and many more places. Accordingly, through their practices, many inhabitants of this shrinking city have become new experts of the (postindustrial) future.

However, if we follow the German philosopher Ernst Bloch's central predicament of *The Principle of Hope* (1986 [1959]), namely, that men are essentially determined by the future, we have to acknowledge that most social sciences still lack a comprehensive methodological and analytic toolkit for accounting for the future and the role it plays in human life. Liisa Malkki describes this as the 'theoretical invisibility of the future'[10] (2000: 326). Akin to my approach, she concludes that 'futures as well as traditions and histories are constituted in and constitutive of present struggles, identities … communities, and social formations' (ibid.: 28–29). The acknowledged abundance of relations to the future – 'Once we start looking, it becomes clear that much of our political energy and cultural imagination is expended in personal and collective efforts to direct and shape (and, sometimes, to see) the future' (ibid.) – provides enough ethnographic material to the future as an important matter of knowledge, particular in contexts of crisis such as Hoyerswerda.

Surprisingly, for Malkki's informants (Hutu refugees in Canada), it is not the past that is problematic, but the future. However, as Bamby Schieffelin pointed out, since the 'future is the most unknown of the temporal dimensions', it 'has to be marked in the present' (Schieffelin 2002: 12). As a result, we can access the future's 'existence' in the present through the knowledge, which is produced and reproduced about it in the present.

In modernity proper, as Rabinow claims in his discussion of the German sociologist Niklas Luhmann, the future has been configured as a problem: it 'appears as a contingent set of possibilities about which decisions are demanded; decisions are demanded because the future appears as something about which we must do something' (Rabinow et al. 2008: 57). In times of postindustrial shrinkage, this seems as impossible as the undisturbed production of other narrative trajectories. Rather, the change of the content and form of particular (temporal) knowledge practices also accounts for the ways in which human beings position themselves and their agency vis-à-vis the changes they are experiencing. The trope of shrinkage, like other epistemic tools, provides a very distinct imagination of the future and yields specific epistemic repercussions. This book tries to locate, map and conceptualize agency in this context of shrinkage (see Ringel 2016a, 2016b). The methodological question – less about how to study time and more about how to study knowledge (about time) and the temporal dimensions of knowledge – translates into a focus on what Morten Nielsen (2011) calls 'anticipatory actions', which for him are guided by both unknown and known futures, and that help to reorient individual life trajectories by exploiting the former's imaginative potentials.

However, 'unknown futures' are not 'no future'. As a city with 'no future', Hoyerswerda could, indeed, be seen as one of the places where the unequal distribution of hope (Miyazaki 2010) drew away the prospects of a better future. Deploying Miyazaki's own work (2004), this entails the loss of hope's epistemic function: with no hope, people lose the ability to (radically) redirect their knowledge. However, as Zigon (2009) argues, this urge for a radical redirection of thought is not necessarily hope's main point. Rather, hope entails particular incitements to *maintaining* practices – conceptually, ethically, and relationally (Ringel 2014). Apart from the need to diversify analytical approaches to the future, there is still an issue with the logic, practicality and efficacy of representations of the future in the present, which also needs to be taken into consideration. However, as I claim, this will only ever allow new insights into the present in which this knowledge is produced. As Miyazaki, for example, underlines in a different context, once the future is feared or otherwise made concrete, the present is itself imagined 'from the perspective of the end' (Miyazaki 2006: 157; compare Miyazaki and Riles 2005). However, 'the end' in my informants' temporal knowledge practices is much more indeterminate than Miyazaki suggests. In the context of shrinkage, the challenge is to have an accurate idea of the future in the first place. As I will show in the following chapters, under this paradigm, Hoyerswerda's citizenry continuously establishes arenas for the common imagination of the future whilst struggling daily with the imposition of official dystopian demographic, economic and social visions of the city's future. This hopeful reappropriation of the future has been described by Appadurai (2002, 2013) as a political right, a right to aspire and to participate in the social practice of the imagination.

Finally, any consideration of our informants' hope and future knowledge should also involve what is at stake with regards to the hopes and futures of the ethnographer and analyst. Most of the aforementioned scholars attach a particular form of hope to including the temporal dimension of the future in their analysis. As Ernst Bloch has it, only 'philosophy that is open to the future entails a commitment to changing the world' (quoted in Miyazaki 2004: 14). Miyazaki remains cautious with regard to the 'ongoing effort in social theory to reclaim the category of hope' in a broader 'search for alternatives' in times of the 'apparent decline of progressive politics' (ibid.: 1–2). The hopeful moments sustained in his fieldsite's many knowledge practices show one efficacy of hope to be a *method* for the production of future knowledge: the continuation of thought (and) practice against all odds. Methodologically, Miyazaki answers his own questions of 'how to approach the infinitely elusive quality of any present moment' (ibid.: 11) by looking at concrete knowledge practices over time whilst being aware of their indeterminacy. In a presentist vein, he thus resolves the mundane paradox 'to cherish indeterminacy and at the same time expect it to be resolved' by showing how that 'requires constant deferral of … closure for the better' (ibid.: 69). For him, the maintenance of hope, despite its constant failure, affects not only our informants' lives, but also our own academic practices. In Hoyerswerda, a city with supposedly no hope and no future, the analysis of questions of knowledge and the future require a similar continuous reflection upon my own hopes and relations to the future. This also allows for a different methodology.

Once we conceptualize issues of time to be matters of representation and understand that the production of knowledge about the future in a dramatically changing fieldsite keeps on changing too, anthropological representations of these practices remain necessarily inapt. All they can do is become part of this process by joining the search for more sustainable or convincing takes on the future. This methodological move is based upon an understanding that my informants are recursively adjusting their social metaphysics in order to find contexts and narratives for describing their current and past experiences. They do so collectively, passionately as much as pragmatically and in conflict with one another. As I claim in more detail elsewhere (Ringel 2013b), this continuous epistemic work allowed for several different forms of intervention during fieldwork. I therefore published weekly newspaper columns in the local newspaper over the course of a whole year, conducted a week-long anthropological research camp for sixteen local youths and initiated a two-week community art project.[11] However, the instability of local representations, particular with regard to the future, also prevents me now in the process of writing from authoritatively imposing my own conclusive representation upon this local processual heterogeneity.

To sum up this section, the analysis of time has long focused on particular and situated social practices. The undoubtedly interesting theoretical concerns regarding the distinction between linear and cyclical time have been dissolved in a general trend to de-ontologize human understandings of time. In contrast, with attention being paid to the local construction of temporal knowledge – that is, knowledge about time and knowledge that reaches out in time – recent anthropology acknowledges that the flexibility and multiplicity of forms of temporal reasoning challenges notions of temporal knowledge as culture or given temporalities (Ringel 2016b). With a strictly ethnographic approach, anthropologists could subsequently show how this particular kind of knowledge is infused with political and ethical relevance, since it is deployed for fundamental claims on both the past and the future in the present, and on life and what it means to be human. The future in particular thereby gains a newly prominent standing in anthropological analyses. Representational and non-representational dimensions of human relations to the future allow insights into the efficacy of knowledge about the future as much as the wide-ranging registers that are deployed in many different forms of practices to relate to the future. In this book I map a variety of local temporal knowledge practices and their relation to the future in order to continue this theoretical quest. To rephrase Gell slightly, there is, indeed, no need to be in awe of the future.

Figure 0.3 *Anarchist graffito, KuFa building, Hoyerswerda, men's toilet, 2009, 'Utopias to Reality; Shit to Gold!!!'*

Conclusion: Knowledge in Motion

As the song mentioned above by Gundermann indicated, the question at the heart of this study is how people relate to the future. Gundermann rightly draws attention to the human agency involved in one's positioning towards the future. This requires an understanding of knowledge itself being in motion. The ways in which people relate to the future are not fixed and stable. They evolve in (and are reproduced by) everyday practice, in which all things social, political and ethical are at stake. With this in mind, I explore diverse aspects of a more general shift in local reasoning that occurred during my fieldwork in 2008 and 2009, a shift that can loosely be described as one from a postsocialist to a postindustrial temporal framework. I also encountered many moments when both frameworks were overcome. In specific social, cultural, political and educational projects, such moments bear witness to the indeterminateness of human thought, agency and practice, which East Germans and other people affected by decline are so often seen to have lost. This then is a 'presentist ethnography', and I see my analysis as an invitation to ponder on the issue of (temporal) knowledge, particularly on its efficacy and its relationship to present hopes and futures.

In the following chapters, I understand 'knowledge in time' in three different ways. First, I chart the ways in which knowledge (in terms of content, form and practice) changes over time: new concepts emerge, are negotiated and have particular effects (compare Rabinow 2003, 2007). Second, I consider the temporal dimension of knowledge as the many different ways in which people in their knowledge practices reach out in time to the past or the future, both near and far (compare Guyer 2007). Third, I approach the affective aspects of knowledge practices and according temporal implications, scrutinizing the phenomena of hope and fear and their relations to knowledge about particular temporal dimensions, especially the future (Anderson 2006a, 2006b; Berlant 2011; Povinelli 2011). This does not deploy the concept of temporality as usually attributed to particular objects, forms, relations and situations. Instead of discovering some inherent quality that allows such analytical objects to exist in time, I approach issues of time via the politics that are done with them, the effects they have and their own existence in time (Ringel 2016b).

In this book's overall structure, one form emerges. First, I analytically zoom in on the theoretical issue of the future in Chapters 1 and 2, laying the groundwork for a more complex understanding of local practices of contextualization and narrativization, and local forms of temporal reasoning, which initially include the past. In Chapters 3 and 4, I investigate two aspects of local futurity more thoroughly. Whereas Chapter 3 enquires into the temporal dimension of the near future regarding conflictive local politics and forms of reasoning, Chapter 4 focuses on affect and affective politics, and their relations to the future. Chapter 5 accompanies the preceding two chapters by zooming out again, that is, proliferating the approach to the future. It presents the issue of maintenance and endurance in consideration of local beliefs in (and hopes for) the efficacy of future knowledge.

Through this explorative strategy, my overall account provides answers to the question posed in Gundermann's song – by depicting a surprising variety of human relations to the future and bearing witness to a community's hard work to regain its own sense of the yet-to-come in the conceptual space of the process of shrinkage. This impressive, continuous and multifaceted work stems from the choice that Gundermann had in mind, which motivated my own intellectual engagement with the lives of the inhabitants of Germany's fastest-shrinking city. Its efficacy is hard to judge, but it keeps my informants going in their diversity towards a future that remains in many ways indeterminate by the past that once was their present. It keeps time, and knowledge about it, in motion.

Notes

1. The lyrics in German read rather beautifully: 'Die Zukunft ist ´ne abgeschoss´ne Kugel, / auf der mein Name steht und die mich treffen muss. / Und meine Sache ist, wie ich sie fange, / mit'm Kopf, mit'm Arsch, mit der Hand oder mit der Wange. / Trifft sie mich wie ein Torpedo oder trifft sie wie ein Kuss?' For the rest of the song, Gundermann uses further sets of metaphors, describing the future as an 'unexplored country' (*ein unentdecktes Land*), in which one has to choose sides with prey or predator; a 'handed-in package' (*abgegebenes Päckchen*), which could contain either a time bomb or precious issued stocks; and 'a pale small woman' (*kleine blasse Frau*), who is leaving and who one at this very moment could let go, force out or hold back. Despite their bleakness, these metaphors focus on the agency involved in how one might potentially define one's relationship to the future.
2. Lusatia (*Lausitz*) is the name of the region surrounding Hoyerswerda. For centuries, it has been inhabited by the Slavic minority of the Sorbs (*Sorben*).
3. For another, although very different example of an ethnography looking at the future, see Lorenzo Cañás Bottos' monograph on *Old Colony Mennonites in Argentina and Bolovia* (2008). He looks at the future relations of a community that for different and self-professed reasons was considered to be of the past. See also Holbraad and Pedersen 2013; Krøijer 2015.

4. I contrast this to theories that account for the influence of the past through a history of knowledge (practices). For example, Pels (2016) recently argued that we have to understand contemporary modes of representing and relating to the future in the West by accounting for the dominance of these modes over a time span of more than 500 years.

5. All names used in this monograph are real names. However, in reference to contentious issues, I altogether refrain from mentioning names and instead circumscribe the people involved via social status, age, gender, etc.

6. 'Wenn eine Stadt kleiner wird, werden die Menschen in ihr dann größer?'

7. 'Unser Ziel ist es in diesem Schrumpfungsprozess, den wir als solches akezeptiert haben, hier positiv einzugreifen, handlungsfähig zu bleiben, und darüber eine positive Stimmung zu erzeugen, die dann für eine andere, neue Lebensqualität und Lebenskultur sorgt.'

8. For critiques of East German *Ostalgie*, cf. Berdahl (1999, 2009) and Boyer (2001a, 2001b, 2006, 2010). Both authors show that temporal references to the GDR past should not be analysed as expressions of some form of past-fixation, but instead as critical contemporary statements with an inherent claim on the future.

9. He later strengthens this point by reference to the work of phenomenologists such as Husserl, who proposes that 'our daily lives are lived within the set of temporal "horizons" which shift continually' (Gell 1992: 221), 'horizons of a temporally extended present' (ibid.: 223), which still retain some continuity. Gell positions his own concept of temporal maps with regard to the key concepts of Husserl's temporal phenomenology of perception, 'retention' and 'protention'.

10. Guyer et al. draw attention to a particular disciplinary 'prioritization of different temporal frames' (2007: 7). In the field of anthropology, the future did indeed not play any prominent role for a long time (see Munn 1992).

11. For more detail on the newspaper columns, see the archive of the local newspaper, the *Hoyerswerdaer Tageblatt*. For visual material on the *AnthroCamp08*, the youth camp on anthropology, see www.kufa-hoyers werda.de/anthro-camp-2008-2.html and https://www.youtube.com/ watch?v=iwmuMOZVe18. For visual material on the community art project *Malplatte*, see http://www.kufa-hoyerswerda.de/2009-malplatte. html.

1

'There Can Only Be One Narrative'

Postsocialism, Shrinkage and the Politics of Context in Hoyerswerda

I, as a political person, can change my politics
by … shifting my spatiotemporal horizon.
—David Harvey, *Spaces of Hope*

Demographic knowledge is powerful, particularly when it refers to the future in something that the title of this book describes as postindustrial times. During my fieldwork in 2008 and 2009, the demographic future of Hoyerswerda looked devastating: although the city had already lost more than half of its population over the previous twenty years, many of its citizens where expecting yet another wave of shrinkage in the years to come. Hoyerswerda's population had reached one of the highest age-averages of all German cities, so what would happen, as a friend put it, once 'all of these old people started to die' (*wenn die auch alle anfangen zu sterben*)? Indeed, in the long run, there was no end in sight to the city's demise, and dystopian narratives of decline were widely communicated in local, regional and national media. They had an impact on local thought about life and future prospects, but they did not take away people's agency. As I claimed in the Introduction, the response to this kind of knowledge about the future and my informants' everyday experiences of decline was not simply despair or lethargy. Rather, it sparked the production of new kinds of knowledge, deployed to make sense of the city's problematic present and its unpromising future. Given the undeniably dramatic challenges ahead, such knowledge was in constant need for the right kind of midrange social metaphysics; in order to make (renewed) sense, it needed a context or narrative to fit in.

This chapter tracks the vast variety of contexts and narratives, in and through which my informants made sense of the problems and changes they faced. In its first half, I assemble a collage of short ethnographic examples in order to account for the local diversity and heterogeneity of such contexts. Instead of providing more ethnographic detail about the city's demise, I focus, still ethnographically, on its inhabitants' epistemic and conceptual responses to this demise. In its second half, I follow more closely what came to fruition during my time in Hoyerswerda – the emergence, establishment and final acceptance of one particular context: that of shrinkage. This chapter therefore pays tribute to the local diversity of expressions of epistemic or conceptual agency, and follows the contested social production of a context in an economy of knowledge one could rightly describe as 'inchoate' (Carrithers 2007), 'unstable' (Greenhouse et al. 2002), and characterized by a 'loss of coherence' (Lakoff and Collier 2004: 422) and a 'crisis in meaning' (Ferguson 1999: 14). It also constantly reflects upon potential academic contexts, which might and might not correspond with local ones. In lieu of a 'normal' first chapter, which would introduce the field through accounts of local history and geography, I offer an initial analysis of Hoyerswerda's local economy of knowledge and ask which context is the best for this book to account for Hoyerswerda's present.

However, as an epistemic tool, any context is simultaneously restricting and enabling, both for my informants and for me. A particular spatiotemporal context allows for a specific vision of the future, and has its specific repercussions on understanding one's and others' (temporal) agency. It affects what local inhabitants as well as external analysts can subject to thought and how they do it. This explains the clashes and conflicts that arise when different ideas about the city's present collide. However, despite local contextual diversity and my own methodological interventions in search of a better or more promising context, the factual results of shrinkage and outmigration seem all too inevitable. Indeed, in times of postindustrial decline, one has to ask whether, after all, there can only be one narrative. The first ethnographic example of an art project in, and slightly out of, context will help me to expand on this question. It offers, for a start, a somewhat external perspective on the city's past, present and future.

Figure 1.1 *'ONE NARRATIVE': 'ArtBlock' building, WK 10, Hoyerswerda* Neustadt, *August 2008*

ONE NARRATIVE

In August 2008, Bjarke, a young Danish artist, attached the slogan THERE CAN ONLY BE ONE NARRATIVE in white capital letters onto the upper front of a soon-to-be-demolished five-storey apartment block in Hoyerswerda's New City (*Neustadt*). His intervention was produced during an international student art residency, which took place in *Neustadt*'s youngest residential district WK 10. The district's main landlord Lebensräume e.V., the LivingSpaces cooperation, temporarily offered thirty-six young international artists two abandoned apartment blocks, which gave the project its title: 'ArtBlock' (see http://www.art-block.blogspot.com). Initially, the project's initiators had searched for other kinds of abandoned places. Such places, they told me, were increasingly common all over Western Europe and North America: places of no further use, redundant cities, factories and train stations, abject spaces of the postindustrial era. They had initially sought a dilapidated West German detached housing area, which in their understanding offered itself neatly for critical remarks on *capitalist* mainstream culture. Then they stumbled across the former socialist model city of Hoyerswerda and its *other* houses of *other* times and in *other* spaces. The officials and inhabitants of Hoyerswerda nonetheless happily provided the artists from Chile, Peru, Brazil, the United States, Israel, Botswana and several different European countries with 'free space' (*Freiraum*) in the German two senses of the word: physical *and* 'conceptual space' (Buyandelgeriyn 2008: 237).

The choice for Hoyerswerda changed the artists' agenda as they suddenly confronted buildings arguably of – and in – a very different context from what they initially expected. Based at the outskirts, these blocks overlooked the fields towards an adjacent Sorbic village, only disturbed by a forest of young pine trees, which must have been planted here around the time of WK 10's erection in the late 1980s. The two blocks – one housing the artists, the other supplying individual studios – were surrounded by either other abandoned apartment houses or the uncanny absences of those blocks that had already been torn down. The parking lot in the courtyard in front of the two blocks was empty and slightly overgrown with weeds; only Frau Meyer's little silver car parked there regularly during the time of the project. Frau Meyer still lived in the third, neighbouring block (third entrance, fifth floor on the right). Of all the inhabitants of this courtyard, she was the last to move out with her young son, being relocated to a refurbished flat in WK IV a few days after the end of the two-week art project. The artists had suddenly parked their small, used student cars next to hers (not that there was a shortage of parking space) and the courtyard was revived one last time. But how were they to account for Hoyerswerda's fate in general or Frau Meyer's life and her current experiences in particular in the language of art?

When walking through the city, these artists saw more of the same, since they first had to cross the three districts most affected by deconstruction and decline before reaching the huge, shiny shopping centre in the New City's central district or the Old City's picturesque centre with castle, church and market square. In a city currently torn apart by demolition dredgers, they were as much in need of context in order to make their practices and interventions meaningful as were my informants in their everyday work and life. However, I think Bjarke had a very important point to make: both as a former socialist model city and as Germany's fastest-shrinking city, Hoyerswerda did not fit the common paradigms easily – the changes were too dramatic and a superficial postmodern critique might not capture that.

WK 10 incorporates these changes. It can probably be described as the epicentre of Hoyerswerda's shrinkage and deconstruction. Although it was only completed after the fall of the Berlin Wall in 1989, it was, according to plans in 2008, the first district to be completely dismantled by 2013 or, as German bureaucratic jargon has it, 'area-wide back-built' (*flächendeckend zurückgebaut*). During the 'ArtBlock' project most of the flats in WK 10 were already empty, because Hoyerswerda's extreme loss in population specifically affected *Neustadt*'s outskirts, which housed the youngest and hence most mobile inhabitants. The buildings' abandonment makes this loss blatantly visible. Bjarke's initial idea, he confessed, stemmed from this apparent tragedy, capitalizing on the blocks' totally unexpected life history: finished in the late 1980s and early 1990s, they were torn down less than twenty years after their erection. But the buildings did not embody the local context alone.

The artistic production of meaning was strongly influenced by the many reminders of the previous lives these blocks had housed – random household items, old posters, leftover furniture, wooden slides and personal memorabilia.[1] In addition, many former and remaining inhabitants of WK 10 – as well as a wider Hoyerswerdian public – revisited this marginal part of Hoyerswerda during the time of the project and shared their memories with the new, though temporary residents. References to Hoyerswerda's contemporary problems and the former inhabitants who embody them (again, many literally revisiting their old homes) thus abounded in the pieces of art: Christián from Chile painted Hoyerswerda's official 'Three Oaks' crest with massively pruned branches; a German artist wrote excerpts from the GDR constitution's sections on housing – then a constitutional right – over the walls of her studio to highlight the political and legal changes of the present; two other artists spanned a thread out of their fifth-floor workshop all the way across the courtyard to the adjoining forest, referencing the common local narrative that *Neustadt* is given back to – or reclaimed by – nature; in another exterior project and with the help of local firemen, an artist attached giant reproductions of photographs of trophies and socialist medals (all found in local homes he had visited) to adjacent blocks in order to, as he claimed, 'honour their achievements'; an American art student built little miniature blocks out of sand (the main postmining residue) and her German friend used finely cut pieces of the blocks' concrete walls to assemble a kit for building one's own miniature castles – a project entitled 'Make Your Self at Home' – for those who were forced to leave. By relating meaningfully to the material and social spaces in which they intervened, the artists tried to ensure a dialogue with their local audience, particularly on the work-in-progress open days and the final weekend's exhibition.

Meanwhile, the last inhabitants were moving out of next-door staircases, underlining that Bjarke had it right from the beginning:

there is, after all, only one narrative that contains the many stories the Hoyerswerdians and the artists were telling one another, with only one directionality towards the future – that of decline and demolition. But how does the new surprise – the 'ArtBlock' building itself – fit into this narrative? And what other narratives could handle the heterogeneous complexity of the city's present changes and the multiplicity of stories and perspectives produced in response?

When the Hoyerswerdians came to visit the 'ArtBlock' building, their reactions were shaped by their own experiences. People talked about how desirable these flats once were, how they already back then had come to take pictures of their allocated flat's construction and how, with the changing times, they were now taking pictures of their demolition. But despite the apartments' dilapidated state and the concrete's much-discussed poor quality, most visitors remarked on the fact that they were 'still OK' (*noch in Ordnung*) and what a shame it was to tear them down. The context of art, which the artists had drawn them into, made them think about their city's fate, its past, present and future. Just by coming to this site of demolition, it seemed, they halted the accepted changes for a moment and were invited to reflect on them.

This unexpected encounter thus provided different means for the production or reactivation of knowledge about their city. But, after all, there were no new narratives emerging – no ideas for alternative futures that could allow for the blocks' survival (although one person suggested that the studios should remain opened indefinitely as a museum). Nonetheless, the Hoyerswerdians were impressed by the artists' intervention: that the blocks could so unconventionally be used yet again seemed, if only for a moment, to challenge the idea of the *one* narrative of decline, even without factually overcoming it. Bjarke's assertion might be contradicted by the unexpected premortem blossoming of those houses – and only the narrative of its final deconstruction held true. Still, I claim, even these blocks' decline can be narrated, contextualized and directed towards the future in many different ways. Even in Hoyerswerda's all too bleak present, one can find a whole variety of different contexts and narratives, a few of which I present in the next sections.

The differences between local forms of contextual reasoning partially resemble local political and spatial divisions: conservative Old City inhabitants and winners of the postsocialist changes contextualize their presents differently from left-wing *Neustadt* inhabitants, who have suffered from unemployment after the 1989 fall of the Berlin Wall. The following examples help to circumscribe the local economy of knowledge and some of its surprisingly far-reaching metaphysics. In them, specific local tropes such as 'healthy shrinking' (*Gesundschrumpfen*), 'economic expulsion' (*Wirtschaftsvertreibung*) and 'the chances of shrinkage' (*Schrumpfungschancen*) are used as epistemic tools and discursive armoury. Their analysis explicates differences in spatiotemporal reasoning. I focus on their explanatory and political value in their respective local sociopolitical contexts (see Strathern 1995b: 132) in order to assess whether Bjarke's claim was right.

The Local Construction of Context

The contexts constructed for and in Hoyerswerda's present situation are manifold; they involve both meaningful spatial and temporal relations. For example, spatial concerns in Hoyerswerda often involve the city's actual distance from the Saxon and the federal capitals Dresden and Berlin respectively. This distance is bemoaned as a hindrance in Hoyerswerda's development towards a better future. Another spatial imaginary stems from its citizens' unparalleled outmigration, and the many better 'imagined elsewheres', where friends, relatives and colleagues had settled. The more than 50,000 inhabitants who have left Hoyerswerda over the last two decades link spatial distance and mobility to social relations and feelings of belonging. In contrast, temporal concerns, the overall focus of this book, include the considerations of different pasts, presents and futures. Giving a city a particular past or future, we often presume, helps to determine its existence in the present. Such positioning, however, is for many reasons far more complicated – and remains all the more contested. Although finding the 'right' context or narrative promises to stabilize the city's existence in this crisis of meaning, the construction of context is highly contested and recurrently reproduces internal political fissures. In order to clarify this point, let me sketch out a few potentially more extreme and polemic examples. With them, I also show what is politically at stake for my informants.

Just before Christmas 2008, a group of young men dressed as Father Christmas stood on *Neustadt*'s central Lusatian Square (*Lausitzer Platz*), at the entrance to the city's main shopping centre. They were handing out oranges and chocolate Santas, to which they had attached little propaganda leaflets. The narrative the leaflets told were about how democracy has led to the 'fatal' process of shrinkage, increasing poverty and inequality, and how it is to be blamed for harming the German *Volks*-body. The same group of local neo-Nazis propagated similar narratives at the 1 May Labour Day demonstrations. Hoyerswerda's high unemployment, outmigration and subsequent physical deconstruction were presented as the results of the rule of 'self-proclaimed democrats' (*selbsternannte Demokraten*). For the future, the neo-Nazis' historical implications evoked a swift return to National Socialism in order 'to save the German people'. Otherwise, they predicted, 'this system will bring us *Volks*-death' (*Das System bringt uns den Volkstod*). As yet another flyer proclaimed, the Federal Republic of Germany is itself 'planned *Volks*-death' (*geplanter Volkstod*).

In the autumn of 2008 in the Seniors' Academy (*Seniorenakademie*), an institution for lifelong education and concerted economic activity founded by a group of former engineers and miners after the changes of the early 1990s, a former hydrologist gave a talk entitled 'Hoyerswerda – City on the Waterfront'. He informed his audience about current issues of climate change and their relation to the long-standing history of the extraction of coal and other resources in the area. In his contemplations, the retired expert reached much further into the past than the city's right-wing youth in their nationalist ideas. In order to find a way out of the current crisis, he covered the period from the end of the last Ice Age, which left the region of Lusatia as a huge 'swampland' (the original meaning of the word 'Lusatia'), the Stone Age, when coal extraction started, and the comparatively recent era of industrialization. Out of this long-term scope, the speaker developed an idea about how Hoyerswerda could tackle its present economic problems by being transformed into a city based on green energy and with new future perspectives. His strategy was hydrological; it implied that the many old waterways, in fact a geological result of the last Ice Age, can help restore Hoyerswerda to what it once was: the 'Lusatian Venice' (*Venedig der Lausitz*). They were to be revitalized by channelling water to Hoyerswerda from the distant river Elbe. Subsequently, tourism, the fishing industry, green energy production and large-scale CO_2 reduction (the latter two points remained rather unclear) could create a renewed symbiosis between natural resources and the regional economy, determined, as history explained, by the region's long-term natural conditions. By putting the current changes into an extensive geohistorical context, the hydrologist saw chances for the city's future, but only 'if one can understand the past and learn from it' – as the academy's head underlined in his introduction to the talk.

The third example follows this logic too. Seventy-year-old Helfried, a former mining engineer, embedded Hoyerswerda's present more thoroughly in the region's nineteenth- and twentieth-century history of industrialization. On our many tours through Hoyerswerda's surroundings in his flashy black Mercedes Benz, he showed me two of the mines still working; several landmarks of the coal industry such as the huge F60 cool excavator; old villages recently abandoned by their inhabitants because of the progressing mines as well as new ones built from scratch for resettled communities in the 1990s; and former model towns and villages from the 1920s and 1930s whose construction then accompanied the industrialization of open pit mining and energy production in the region. He even pointed out the hardly discernible reforestation areas from the same historical period, where an early specialist in forestry successfully implemented measurements to 'renaturalize' the postmining landscapes. On our way to the lakes of the emerging touristic Lusation Lake District (*Lausitzer Seenland*), we stopped along the many new cycle and rollerblade tracks for future tourists, looking at the channels connecting already half of the sixteen lakes. All of this supposedly 'natural' landscape, he underlined, was purposefully manufactured over the course of more than a century. And postindustrial planning continued in this longstanding effort despite the several regime changes of the last century: each tree, hill and stream was accurately positioned in the planners' minds; each lake was prescribed one function or 'unique selling point': motor racing; canoe touring, water skiing, sailing, etc. In this context, spanning a history of industrial (and postindustrial) modernity intervening in the region, Hoyerswerda was just another manmade, planned, functional project, and its changes were subject to the same, enduring modernist logic. In the 1950s and 1960s, *Neustadt* was indeed the worldwide first city completely erected by industrially prefabricated concrete units. Such engineered projects can either succeed or fail.[2] However, the time of industrialization and planned progress was over – even the Swedish company owning the mines and power plants was predicted to retreat from the region (a plan it realized in 2016). In 2009, however, new hopes in the narratives of modernity and industrialization arose with the rediscovery of copper north of Hoyerswerda and a foreign investor promising the establishment of thousands of new jobs (which thus far remains unrealized). As much as the Lusation Lake District project, this plan provided new hopeful imaginaries for local life and future economic prospects by potentially slowing down or even reversing the process of shrinkage. Such hidden hopes, I often felt, also shaped Helfried's take on Hoyerswerda's present.

For many of my young informants, in contrast, such hopes did not hold much currency in 2008/2009. Rather, for those who grew up in the time of postsocialist changes and increasing shrinkage, Hoyerswerda had no future perspectives at all. For most of them, it was a city of no hope, and having no future was, for them, somehow related to having no past. The commonly denied socialist-modernist past, which their parents and grandparents had advanced, seemed as far away as other historical epochs. For the city's youth, present concerns were important and a historically informed context was therefore hardly of quintessential use. 'Nothing is happening here either way' was the most common description of their lives in Hoyerswerda.

Like other peripheral small cities, Hoyerswerda had not only lost its economic foundations with reunification, but it also quickly lost its attraction. People's expectations of a city's quality of life aspired to metropolitan centres elsewhere. Although for a town of its size Hoyerswerda exhibited astonishingly many local sociocultural activities, the majority of local youth still aspired to go to Berlin, Dresden, Leipzig or even further away. There was no realistic narrative with which to describe their future in the city either in the near or in a more distant future of a potential return. Their older family members repeatedly supported such a view by expressing the fears and concerns in relation to their children's seemingly inevitable outmigration. In contrast, many city officials and sociocultural clubs argued against such dystopian predictions and invested much of their professional and personal activities in providing local youth with an imaginary for staying *in* Hoyerswerda – invoking feelings of belonging and homeliness[3] as well as pointing out potential job prospects in the region (see Chapter 3).

These attempts at convincing Hoyerswerda's youth to stay indicate the conflicts that can occur when different contexts, like those presented in this section, oppose one another. Having discussed three examples to show the diversity of local contexts deployed in the city's economy of knowledge in contrast with one which showed the absence of a coherent narrative (the youth's no future narrative), let me now discuss three further examples in more depth in order to underline the varying epistemic and political repercussions such contexts can have, as well as the conflicts they spur.

The Politics of Context

One interview partner, a self-describing *Altstädter* (inhabitant of the Old City), gave me a rather peculiar account of the process of shrinkage. He asked me to imagine a graph of Hoyerswerda's population – stretching not just over the last fifty or sixty years, but incorporating data from almost two hundred years altogether. With such a broad scope, he explained, the current demographic changes do not look too bad. Rather, on such a graph we see Hoyerswerda slowly gaining a population of 7,000 inhabitants throughout the nineteenth century and until World War II, due to the region's industrialization. With World War II, the city loses half of its inhabitants, until refugees from Silesia and other formerly German parts of Eastern Europe settle in Hoyerswerda. Then, suddenly in the 1950s and 1960s, we encounter what he called an 'unnatural' development: the unforeseen socialist explosion in Hoyerswerda's population, enlarging the old city ten times with the incoming miners, engineers and energy workers of *Neustadt*. The rise to more than 72,000 inhabitants, he underlined, has already peaked in the early 1980s, that is, before German reunification. My interview partner suggested that rather than the economic changes following reunification, it was wealth and prosperity that slowed down Hoyerswerda's population growth, not to mention the impact of female emancipation and the contraceptive pill. The following implosion in numbers of inhabitants will, he predicted, stop soon and Hoyerswerda will stabilize its population in the near future at around 20,000 or 25,000 people. From his point of view, Hoyerswerda *proper* (which for him most importantly referred to the Old City) will not have lost half its population, but rather will have gained triple its initial number – depending on the temporal context in which you understand the recent changes. For him, shrinkage is thus nothing abnormal. If anything, this graph's – in his words – 'socialist pimple' (*der sozialistische Pickel*) is abnormal. As people were migrating to Hoyerswerda in the socialist past, coming to the then attractive expanding model city, this direction was now reversed. The 'market' determines these developments, he proclaimed, which allowed him to legitimize and naturalize them. Hence, he saw hardly any actual problems or a need to counteract them: Hoyerswerda is simply 'shrinking to a healthy state' (*sich gesundschrumpfen*). For him, the process of shrinkage remained unquestioned, uncritical and incontestable, rendering the many stories of those affected by these changes inevitably out of sight.

In contrast, another interview partner thoroughly repoliticized Hoyerswerda's present situation. A committed socialist and *Neustädter* (inhabitant of *Neustadt*), this person's account did not accept the loss of more than half of the population as a 'natural process'; rather, he embedded shrinkage in the current political economy of (globalized) capitalism. In his eyes, this extreme form of outmigration should be called 'economic expulsion' (*Wirtschaftsvertreibung*). Similar to political expulsion (in a German context, the expulsion of Germans after the end of World War II immediately comes to mind), this form of migration was enforced and happened involuntarily. Indeed, facing the imminent demolition of his apartment house as well as his district's decay, one WK 10 inhabitant expressed the same logic by saying: 'One is downright expelled here!' (*Man wird ja regelrecht vertrieben hier!*). My leftist interview partner denounced the fact that the market dictates the movement of people; rather, it prevented them from freely deciding where to stay whilst political leaders refrained from intervening in this enforced process.[4] Such supposedly enforced mobility, he underlined, could have been prevented. The repercussions the city contemporarily incurred are the outcome of many different and politically initiated failures: German reunification and the politicians who designed it; the privatization of the brown coal complex by imported new West German political elites[5]; and the way in which the market economy is more broadly (not) regulated. His reasoning provides a critical analytical framework. Shrinkage and massive outmigration should not be accepted; in order to understand and stop it, one should embed it into a critical understanding of contemporary global capitalism. In an open letter to the local newspaper and as a response to one of my weekly newspaper columns, he even publicly encouraged me to write this book solely about economic expulsion as the cornerstone of contemporary forms of capitalism.

A last approach was neither really depoliticizing nor repoliticizing the process of shrinkage. It was the common practical approach of most city officials, especially Hoyerswerda's Lord Mayor. It attempted to focus on what is widely propagated in bureaucratic jargon as the otherwise unspecified chances of shrinkage. As the Lord Mayor repetitively proclaimed, Hoyerswerda was, is and will remain a 'loveable and liveable city' (*liebens- und lebenswerte Stadt*). Like many others, he accepted the process of shrinkage as a given and suggested that the people of Hoyerswerda should focus on their own strengths. It was the responsibility of all inhabitants as much as of the city officials to preserve and use these advantages against looming negative developments. This approach took change itself as the context for practice. It did not develop the idea of a context that could account for this change. As I will argue in Chapter 3, it finally failed to provide new stabilities, also because there is then obviously no need of further politicization. This arguably pre-empts both analytical rigour and the production of new, alternative or different

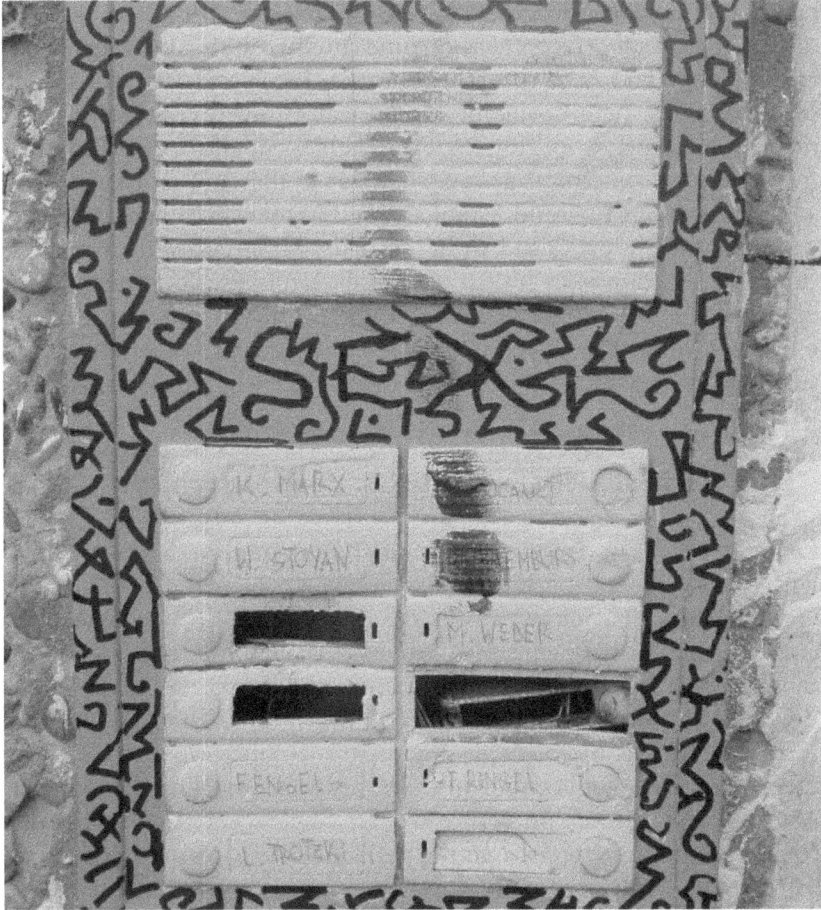

Figure 1.2 *Fake bell button panel, 'PaintBlock' building, summer 2008*

narratives. It also shows the limiting impact that a context can have on human agency in times of crisis.

To sum up the argument thus far, local accounts of shrinkage followed two main contextual logics. One was to accept and naturalize the outmigration of people; the other perspective focused on the potential political regulation of this process by depicting these changes as being unnatural and not given. Both convictions stimulated particular practices: on the one hand, educational practices targeting local youth and their knowledge about Hoyerswerda and its future prospects, as I will discuss in subsequent chapters; on the other hand, a more general critique of contemporary capitalism. To account for such narratives or contexts is all the more important since each contextual construction entailed, as Greenhouse (1996) showed for different cultural conceptions of time, further understandings about one's agency and how the world works. Do we as analysts simply combine these heterogeneous local metaphysics by constructing a metacontext or by choosing between them – and, if so, on which analytic, political or ethical grounds? What is the context or narrative an anthropologist should establish for Hoyerswerda and the many diverse contexts produced in it? In order to circumvent this question, one solution is to transform these narratives into ethnographic objects (as I have done in this section); another is to scrutinize our own involvement in the contexts we deploy in our academic knowledge practices, which I will pursue in the following three sections.

Social Science Contexts: Postmodernism

From an academic point of view, several perspectives come to mind with which to approach Hoyerswerda's problematic present. The German social science literature on East Germany, for instance, often embeds what is happening in Hoyerswerda in a narrative of failed reunification, presenting Hoyerswerda as a prime example of this 'failure'.[6] In a broader postsocialist approach too, a narrative of failed transformation could be deployed, especially since Hoyerswerda as a former socialist model city lends itself neatly to explaining why it was not prepared to catch up with the West. Such account could be used for different aims: to critique the elites in charge of the transformation or to celebrate the many local responses. With a wider temporal perspective, one could also claim that Hoyerswerda is yet another city affected by the post-Fordist changes in the dominant modes of capitalist production and distribution. Hoyerswerda could then be presented as a prime example of deindustrialization or postindustrialization and the inequality resulting from a neoliberally orchestrated form of globalized capitalism. This approach could concentrate on new flows of people and other demographic repercussions of contemporary socioeconomic changes.

On the one hand, all overarching contexts create useful insights via their potential for broader comparison and subsequent abstractions and generalizations; on the other hand, they might also prevent rather than enable a detailed analysis of local specificity. For example, postmodernism as the cultural clothing of flexible accumulation (Harvey 2000) is indeed somewhat traceable in Hoyerswerda, especially in the architectural reshaping of the city after 1990. A whole postmodern architectural axis was spread right across the former socialist city centre, which despite all plans for a better socialist future remained unfinished until the fall of state-socialism. The axis evoked a very specific historical and spatial context, that of the region of Lusatia, in order to add symbolic value to its new, and typically postmodern, entertainment-based and consumption-orientated socioeconomic foundations. Hence, the *Lausitz Square* was grouped with the *Lausitz Center* (a big shopping centre) and the renamed concert venue *Lausitzhalle* (the former Mine- and Energy-Workers' Cultural House – *Haus der Berg- und Energiearbeiter*) lined up with the *Lausitz Tower* (*sic*; a newly renovated eleven-storey apartment house turned architectural landmark with iconic red illumination of its roof terrace) towards the *Lausitz Bad* (the city's new leisure and aquatic centre). These shopping, leisure and architectural spectacles were built or renamed after 1990, and may indeed be seen as indicative of the actual postmodern forces at work and the respective changes they brought by. In their stereotypical postmodern character, they were only outdone by the never-realized plans for a Karl-May-Leisure Park, which would have used the sandy postmining areas for a Wild West amusement park in reference to Karl May's still very popular cowboy and Native American stories around the characters of Winnetou and Old Shatterhand from the late nineteenth century.

However, the apparent impact of the global phenomenon of postmodernism would only rarely be the context of reference used in my fieldsite. Rather, my informants very specifically talked about the West German head of the post-1989 urban planning department, who left most of these postmodern traces in Hoyerswerda's cityscape, as a 'postmodernist'. He was repeatedly remembered as not understanding 'Hoyerswerda's modernist architectural spirit'. My informants also bitterly remarked that his West German architect friends realized many of his projects rather than one of the many local architects. Indeed, such invocations of the context of postmodernity are situated political attempts, embedded in the local economy of knowledge, in which different issues are at stake. If I were to impose any of the common academic contexts (such as neoliberalism, postmodernism or globalization), I might miss out on exactly these diverse local meanings and situational uses of (contextual) knowledge and specific narratives and stories. The same applies to two further predictable contexts: that of Marxism and postsocialism, which I respectively discuss in the following sections. After that, I suggest that the local context of shrinkage combines some of the advantages of other contexts and still entails new imaginaries because its main focus is not on the past, but on the future.

Marxism as/in Context

Marxism could be one of the overarching perspectives as well as a good strategy to repoliticize Hoyerswerda's current changes. Interestingly, Marxism rather than, for instance, 'postsocialism' was actually often invoked in my fieldsite, despite being generally devalued in German political discourses. In Hoyerswerda, Marx himself was often accused of having made an anthropological mistake, namely, misunderstanding that the human being, as it were, 'is not made for socialism' (*nicht für den Sozialismus gemacht*). However, even his own otherwise convincing narrative of history as class struggle seems hard to deploy. Once we dissolve the metacontext of historical materialism and class exploitation, again, into the actual social context at place, it gains, if anything, unexpected explanatory value.

On a class trip in July 2008, eighteen-year-old Willy and some of his classmates had a passionate discussion about the *Communist Manifesto*. Willy had bought a cheap paperback version of the *Manifesto* because of his interest in leftist theory. In a long debate, the application of its insights to their hometown's current problems proved more difficult than expected. No classes to be easily identified; only the ever-looming confrontation with the big historical disproval of actually existing socialism: its own failure. Instead of problematizing their hometown's present, Marx's text made this group of young anarchists reconsider the GDR, a country most of them were just about born into, as yet another ideological project in world history. This project of socialist modernity was as 'unfree' and 'oppressive' as any other ideological project, such as contemporary global capitalism. The context, in which their hometown gained so much prominence, was thus put in another temporal frame (anarchist if you wish), which in turn devalued Marxism as a context to think with.

Furthermore, their direct exposure to Marxist thought forced the friends' analyses to remain in the past, stopping before the process of shrinkage was in reach. To counter this, I tried to problematize the effects that Marx's theory had on their hometown during state-socialism, linking the *Manifesto*'s infamous vision of lavish palaces for farmers and workers to Hoyerswerda's *Neustadt* and the blocks in which most of them grew up. However, other concerns, proliferated in German media discourses or their school history lessons, were more important for the overall discussion. The conversation therefore focused on 'the Stasi' (the GDR's much-dreaded Ministry of State Security) and ideas of 'freedom', and made them defend the post-1989 changes as a form of liberation, whilst still critiquing contemporary capitalism. Thus, the application of a Marxist context, for this group of local youth, did not cast new light on Hoyerswerda's present. Despite reading Marx, they refrained from depicting shrinkage as an expression of a systematic crisis of capitalism.

In contrast, this is exactly what another informant passionately did. Against his own liberal political convictions, the WK 10's former District Mayor convincingly claimed that his Marxist political education in GDR schools ('citizen's education' – *Staatsbürgerkunde*) had foreseen this all: 'In fact, Marx had it all right!' For him, what was rather surprising was that his fellow East Germans, having received the same education, were at all surprised about what contemporarily (during the 2008 global economic crisis) happened. The loss of jobs and the rise of poverty are what occur in a capitalist context time and again. Still, he was certainly not nostalgic about the decline of state-socialism, nor was he revolutionary in any specific sense. On the contrary, after 1989 he became politically involved in the German Liberal Party. His postreunification dissatisfaction still sparked critical thought with Marx's help, but with no further consequences. He and his wife were to leave WK 10 soon, either in order to move to Dresden or to Munich, where their daughters had already moved to pursue their carriers.

As these two examples underline, the local deployments of Marxist ideas might contradict academic hopes for their emancipatory, critical potential. The anarchist youth did not use this context for further critique, whereas a liberal politician did for his own analysis, but to no wider actual avail. Although Marxism would have to offer much for any academic analysis, I will present another ethnographic example in relation to Marx before scrutinizing the academic context of postsocialism. This example again underlines how local social practices and relations themselves create a context that, I argue, some academic contexts might fail to address in the first place.

The 'ArtBlock' artists' temporary neighbour, Frau Meyer, was rather intimately touched by Marx's spectre. On her last day, she took me up the stairs to floor five and showed me her empty flat, sadly pointing out the beautiful view from her balcony. On this balcony, she told me about her time in this apartment, her many wonderful experiences and what might await her and her son in WK 4, where they were allocated a new flat. 'It isn't too bad', she remarked, but she would have preferred to stay here. The last days and especially nights alone in the house were frightening, though, she said, particularly because of 'this strange guy' who had been looking at them through the window. She felt a bit weird about it, she said, and pointed to what I already knew to be the portrait of young Marx, which Christián, a Chilean artist, had painted in his atelier just across the courtyard. However, the rather unusual depiction of young Marx, at an age not older than the walls he had been drawn onto, was not frightening at all. He resembled a young revolutionary romantic poet, full of hope, full of revolutionary desire.

On my way down I heard Frau Meyer do the last *Hausordnung* (the cleaning of the stairs, which during socialism was the weekly task of the people living in one staircase). She said she wanted to leave the house with dignity. And she knew that her house would soon be deconstructed – at an age, I am reminded, in which Marx himself had not even written about socialism's upcoming palaces. In this peculiar moment on her balcony, a young single mother was at eye level with a portrait of the man who, some 150 years ago, had inspired most of the experiment which she grew up in – indeed, who had provided the epistemic context for her upbringing. Whilst the real Marx (and, even more so, Engels) witnessed the creation of the urban proletariat, Frau Meyer's home was demolished because there was no longer enough work for *Neustadt*'s workers. Analytically, there might be a rather different and surprising presence and influence of Marx's ideas in the context of Hoyerswerda. Before choosing the context that should frame the remainder of this book, let me turn to the context of postsocialism, which in contrast to Marxism had, surprisingly, little currency in Hoyerswerda.

Postsocialism as Context

The realm of postsocialism has often been described as either an area with a clear-cut temporal context – the narrative of transformation directed towards catching up with the West – or, alternatively and with an informed and ethnographic critique of the former, as a region of the world in which life is shaped by the absence of context due to living in an era of 'epochal' change (Burawoy and Verdery 1999: 1). Analytically this latter approach includes both the 'macro-institutional' (ibid.) changes and the 'small transformations' (Róna-Tas, quoted in ibid.) of everyday life. Particularly the anthropology of postsocialism (Verdery 1996; Bridger and Pine 1998; Burawoy and Verdery 1999; De Soto and Dudwick 2000; Hann 2002; Dunn 2004; compare also Buyandelgeriyn 2008), similar to the anthropological literature on development and modernity (e.g. Escobar 1995; Ferguson 1999), have successfully criticized the transitional and teleological (meta)narratives of other disciplines. Such critique had theoretical as well as empirical reasons. Empirically, the actual course of history often turned out to differ from previous predictions.

The notion of context is of importance for the studies of postsocialism because the shift in context was defined as dramatic. Postsocialist subjects seem to have been thrown out of their old (socialist) contexts into a new one. Hence, both postsocialist subjects and anthropologists take the uncertainty of social change as a starting point for reflection and analysis (see Nafus 2006). Interestingly, in anthropological analyses the initial loss of orientation in postsocialism was often made to last forever, or at least for the last two decades: people were described as *constantly* being in change (Buyandelgeriyn 2008), as if other regions in contrast were not undergoing any changes at all. However, postsocialist studies nonetheless helped the wider discipline to reconsider how 'deeply' people are contextually invested, if you will, in particular ideologies, relations of power and institutional structures. Human beings appeared suddenly to be much more adaptable to change than expected – even by themselves (Yurchak 2006).

However, for a long time anthropologists approached their informants in the area of postsocialism with Katherine Verdery's famous question 'What was socialism, and what comes next?' (Verdery 1996). Especially stemming from the literature on former Yugoslavia and East Germany, this concern has been overcome by other questions and considerations. Gilbert et al. (2008) thus rightfully detected the anthropology of postsocialism's problems with its own periodizations. One of the subdiscipline's earlier responses to the question whether postsocialism will ever lose its legitimacy as a major organizing epistemic category was a widening of scope: from postsocialist studies towards the studies of the post-Cold War era (see Hann 2002; and specifically Humphrey 2002b; Kalb 2002; Verdery 2002: 17ff). One could, indeed, claim that the local processes of extreme economic, social and demographic decline – and the subsequent physical deconstruction of the city – resulted from a combination of three translocal or supralocal developments: postsocialist transformation in its detrimental particularities of German reunification; East Germany's integration into a neoliberal global political economy; and the currently dominant and increasingly palpable process of deindustrialization.[7] This approach emphasizes that the whole world had entered a new era, with new and globally shared problems. It deploys a spatially widened, increasingly inclusive metanarrative of change.

Whereas Nafus claims that the point about the postsocialist realm is that it has 'endured without becoming conventionalized' and thus 'resists overarching description' (Nafus 2006: 622), in Hoyerswerda, on the contrary, we encounter the emergence of a new context, narrative or description from within. However, this context does not extend the postsocialist perspective spatially, but temporally: since the postsocialist analytical framework (i.e. the reference to before and after the 1989 turn or *Wende*) locally stopped to provide convincing meaning for what was perceived as new and unprecedented forms of decline, people more forcefully invested in the temporal dimension of the future. This temporal logic is inherent in the context of shrinkage, which is directed towards a future that is rendered problematic. By being focused on this bleak future, it rarely has to reference the socialist past, or any past for that matter. Instead of approaching it as a variant of a narrative of transition, I treat it as a 'description' in its own rights, but a description of the future. The proclaimed loss of the future is not the loss of the future of the postsocialist transformation, which Hoyerswerda cannot live up to, but a more fundamental loss.

By taking this local context seriously, I follow Caroline Humphrey's helpful strategy to attend 'whatever other frameworks of analysis arise from within' what we perceive as postsocialism (Humphrey 2002b: 13–14). At the same time, I also take Mertz's critique into account that in 'unstable places' such as Hoyerswerda, we should not only 'notice, respect, and take account of the systematicities' (Mertz 2002: 370) our informants produce, but should also see them as a potential 'lure of a mythical, fixed, safe reality … a drive for stability, a will to make a coherent story even where none exists' (ibid.: 371). As she claims, we risk supporting the invocations of security that contradict actual lived realities and fail at providing a critical analysis.

In Hoyerswerda, the context of shrinkage due to its novelty and openness – and despite its dystopian logical repercussions – is often productive and challenging instead of disempowering in its actual application. As James Ferguson (1999: 257) had it in his account of postindustrial Zambia, in some sense, decline is 'good to think' with, and many Hoyerwerdians participate in the production, dissemination and critical evaluation of their city's present and future. The local production of context is, however, not occupied with issues of former 'Eastern' and 'Western' Cold War politics and the past (see Boyer 2001a). It is rather very concrete and, especially as the future is at stake, it opens up a new perspective on the arguably 'postsocialist' present, in which the socialist past only remains a strategically exploited (Kaneff 2003) and continuously scarce resource (Appadurai 1981) amongst other concerns. In contrast to shrinkage's future logic, the inherent past-fixation of the term 'postsocialism' is one of the reasons why postsocialism faces problems of contextualization (see Gilbert 2006; Gilbert et al. 2008; Ringel 2016b). With Hoyerswerda's dominant context of shrinkage in mind, we might ask the now more immanent question – what is *post*socialism and what comes next? – but only to keep raising the same question to the context of shrinkage in an attempt to determine when it stops making sense. It is in this future-orientated sense that the context of shrinkage offers a new take on the postindustrial future, as I will explore in the next section. Apart from James Ferguson's ground-breaking work on Zambia (1999), the postindustrial condition, with its specific take on the future, has been most productively approached in the social science literature by scholars of affect (Stewart 2007; Berlant 2011; Povinelli 2011), in autobiographically inspired writing projects (Walley 2013; Young 2013) and only recently with an anthropological perspective in its own right (Vacarro et al. 2016).

Shrinkage as Context

During my fieldwork in 2008 and 2009, the term 'shrinkage' gained great local prominence and dominated the local economy of knowledge. As an often-used trope, it structured most local discourses and imaginaries, including expert debates and intimate considerations amongst families and friends. Originally, it had emerged in the late 1990s, being incorporated from academic discourses into local attempts at making sense of the city's problematic present. In the early years of harsh denial, aversion, taboo and accusations, the first people to use it publicly were denounced as traitors or 'nest-soilers' (*Nestbeschmutzer*). Retrospectively, some of my informants believe that the 2003 sociocultural project SuperReconstruction (*SuperUmbau*) facilitated the first major propagation of the term. In contrast, some city officials retrospectively claimed that they had been working with the term all along from the mid 1990s onwards. Either way, its public dissemination and increasing accreditations bore essential consequences. Apart from formulating existential anxieties, the self-attribution of being a 'shrinking city' was long seen to have detrimental effects for Hoyerswerda's future. Who will live – not to mention invest – in a city of decline and with no future? The context of shrinkage was therefore seen critically for acting like a self-fulfilling prophecy. At the end of my fieldwork in the spring of 2009, Hoyerswerda was finally officially declared to be Germany's fastest-shrinking city by the Federal Planning Office. By then, city officials and inhabitants had already been familiarized with the idea that their city was shrinking. Many sociocultural projects had been conducted to reflect on this process; many public debates had been most passionately argued. Thus, the population was prepared for this official declaration. A staff member of the Lord Mayor's office even quickly proposed to market Hoyerswerda as the 'City of Demographic Change' (*Stadt des demographischen Wandels*), finding in shrinkage its current unique selling point (USP). Indeed, in recent years, dozens of experts, researchers and journalists have come to visit Hoyerswerda and glimpse into the postindustrial future. In this official's reasoning, the city should reclaim its vanguard position and become a showcase example for the ways in which people deal with shrinkage.

Nonetheless, there are many problems with the concept of shrinkage. Like any context, it subsumes details and differences under its unifying epistemic umbrella. For instance, it does not distinguish between the various ways in which different people are affected differently by shrinkage – there are indeed winners and losers of this change. Because of its holistic character, it is also not helpful in pointing out particular problems and finding concrete solutions. Rather, as in the example of the 'socialist pimple' from above, it portrays the thus-captured changes as a process that is to be passively accepted and endured. Shrinkage was thereby depoliticized, inasmuch as it was often used to shut down the discourses aiming at new solutions. It quickly prestructured local discourses rather than opening them up and using its own novelty as an incentive for critical self-reflection. Being dystopian in character, it also imposed a negative relationship to the future in form of the prediction of an increasingly 'worse' local future. It foretold an expansion of the problems of the present into the future, with all sorts of actual and epistemic repercussions.

The main question then is whether it is better to have no context at all rather than a wrong or restrictive one. For the case of the academic context of postsocialism, I would argue for a better and more differentiated use of such categories (Thelen 2011). One aim should be to retain a certain openness to other contexts and narratives, and to reflect upon their ethical and political implications. The partial openness of the term 'shrinkage' has become apparent by its own changes in connotation and meaning. As one of my host uncles, forty-year-old filmmaker Dirk, who had recently returned to Hoyerswerda from Australia, described: 'If people hear that I moved back to Hoy[erswerda], they usually ask how on earth one could live in a shrinking city?' In response, he turns the temporal implications around. He sees this process as a challenge, which will soon confront most parts of the world. It is in places like Hoyerswerda, he claims, 'where we already have to practice these new forms of living and working'. However, his idea of the chances of shrinkage differs from the political claims inherent in describing Hoyerswerda as a loveable and liveable city. Contrary to an old joke in Hoyerswerda (namely, that only demolition companies, elderly care homes and undertakers have a future in Hoyerswerda), he sees Hoyerswerda as a city of the future *because* of its shrinkage – a future that is already affecting and will soon increasingly affect most parts of the world. On top of this, he also simply wants to spend time with his family, which brings me back to the social context in which the above-mentioned contexts have been uttered and used (both in the academy and in my fieldsite). What counts in these social contexts are the specific social relations, conflicts, solutions, ethics, etc. They are not just what we as anthropologists try to capture ethnographically, they are also part and parcel of the nature of contexts in the first place: namely that even the most powerful contexts and narratives are hard to maintain. In turn, such maintenance work, to which I will return in Chapter 5, is best captured from a presentist perspective, because it underlines the indeterminacy of changes in the local economy of knowledge as well as people's capacity to determine, adjust and reflect upon their own present contexts. The work that goes into maintaining or adjusting one's or others' stances to the present is an expression of agency.

As Dirk's sister, a local architect, demanded, 'we, the Hoyerswerdians, have to find our own path' through these changes. I follow this strategy and turn again to ethnography, collaboratively assessing where the locally dominant context of shrinkage might take us. After providing one more ethnographic vignette about shrinkage and outmigration, I conclude this chapter with a last example, in which shrinkage as a narrative allowed the emergence of a new perspective. This will suffice to legitimize my own use of the term and will provide further initial insight into Hoyerswerda's economy of knowledge. In the vein of studies of postsocialism, my approach includes the many breaks, fissures, multiplicities and new connections of and in a continuously changing context. It shows how Hoyerswerda itself has become a very specific problem, constituted as a shared and disputed object of knowledge – about the past and the future – and of conflicting passions, hopes and anxieties. Virtually everybody in Hoyerswerda partakes in this problematization, or is forced to partake in it. At stake are political and economic issues as much as more intimate, personal, social and conceptual ones, and I want to understand them in the same way as my informants do: not with an eye on the past, but with a focus on the future.

Leaving the City

It was on a Friday, late afternoon, in the summer of 2009. I was looking at the small stage of Hoyerswerda's sociocultural centre, the *KulturFabrik* (Cultural Factory). I had rushed in from Berlin a month after the end of fieldwork. One of my host sisters was giving her farewell party. She is going to New Zealand – 'as far away as possible', one of her teachers jokingly remarked. Eighteen-year-old Franzi, since July a proud A-level graduate, is not the only girl from her year to go away. Candy, Maria and Theresa are flying off to Chile for half a year soon; Marie-Luise and Susi have already left for Latvia, as has Sarah for the Dominican Republic; and Kristin is going to Canada in exactly three weeks. Since so many are leaving, Franzi wanted to have a big farewell party. Not just the normal 'sit-in, drinking beer, talking' kind of gathering, as she emphasized, but a splendid evening with a self-made cultural programme: live entertainment, self-composed music, some theatre sketches. The final departure from their hometown should be celebrated. Especially for her best friend Linda, the only girl of this group of friends who will remain in Hoyerswerda, this was a hard task. Later that evening, Linda gave a speech, during which she (and many others) started to cry whilst thinking of the future when Franzi and all the others will no longer be around – and because of the general changes that had lately become so apparent: finishing school, searching for a place at a university, moving out from their parents' flat. The memories of the last school days, the prom, the many good-byes to their teachers and classmates had already started to fade away.

The men within that same group of friends laughed loudly when yet another sketch reminded them of all the funny things they had put on stage during their eight years at their grammar school, the Lessing Gymnasium. We all concluded that this might be one of the last times for such a shared re-enactment of past memories. The future, which was awaiting the boys, did not help to exchange the feelings of loss with some anticipatory hope. Most of them would stay for their year of civil service, during that time still the only alternative to the obligatory German military service. A lot of thought had already been invested in the years thereafter. Most of the boys only wanted to get this interim year over and done with as quickly as possible. Surely, the city was no longer the same for them without half of their friends. With these kinds of expectations in mind, nobody enjoys a gap year and even the smallest chance of considering staying in Hoyerswerda and finding a job in the region disappeared quickly. 'Without my friends, why would I stay in Hoy? Nothing happens here in any case.' Hence they will also go and only return to visit their parents and grandparents for major family holidays – as so many young persons from Hoyerswerda have done before and will continue to do after them. No wonder the city is packed with temporarily returning expatriates during Easter and Christmas, the only times when there is an actual shortage of parking lots in the city. Cars from all over Germany then suddenly block the streets. Enjoying this elaborate celebration, I begin to calculate: if all of the people who have left Hoyerswerda after 1990 had celebrated a party like Franzi, there would have been at least six parties each day until the summer of 2009. I wish Hoyerswerda's citizens had cultivated this format more forcefully, like the artist who attached the medals and trophies to the soon-to-be-demolished apartment blocks.

Frau Groba, Franzi's former English teacher, who attended the party, seemed to have read my thoughts. She dragged me out since she had to leave earlier, and on our way to her car, she said: 'Isn't that a pity! You see how wonderful these youngsters are – their talents, their creativity, their warmth and character. It hurts so much: you invest in them for eight years, help them where necessary, then they turn out so well – and still you only have to let them go. Shit that is. This city could be such a different place if they could somehow stay.' She was right. It was and is a pity for the city and its inhabitants: most members of the younger generations will live lives elsewhere. Indeed, Benni, one of the boys staying for another year and a talented singer-songwriter who happened to contribute the cover image and the map to this book, once called Hoyerswerda a 'school for life' (*Lebensschule*), but only 'a temporary one'. Like many of his friends committed to his hometown, Benni could not see a future for himself in Hoyerswerda. In one of his songs he put it poetically: 'Once hope will die, here will be its grave' (*Wenn die Hoffnung einmal stirbt, hier liegt dann ihr Grab*), bemoaning the lack of local future prospects – their own personal tragedies of shrinkage.

In very different times, Heike, Franzi's mother, had started her job in the local hospital. Having gained a higher degree in the early 1990s, she still leads the local nursing school. She is needed, she told me in order to explain why she was not seriously considering moving to Berlin or West Germany, where she would be paid much more for the same job. Lots of changes awaited my second host family. Franzi's year off in New Zealand was accompanied by her older brother's start at a university near Halle/Saale. In contrast to parents in prospering regions, Heike and her husband Micha could be sure that their children will most probably never return home 'for good'. The jobs they will be educated for will not be on offer in a continuously shrinking Hoyerswerda.

I had asked Heike about their future plans because Micha still commuted daily to Berlin. Less than two hours might not sound too bad, but starting your way to work daily at 5am consumes a lot of time and energy. Still, though, they are needed, she emphasized. For the Braugasse-building in the centre of the old city, for whose desperately needed reconstruction they had been fighting for in a social club founded for this purpose; for the *KuFa*, the club running the city's sociocultural centre; for her children's former school, which was also in need of reconstruction and for which she fought in yet another association; and last but not least for her own nursing school – all of these institutions being in danger of being closed down in the not too distant future. Nobody would do the job, she remarked, especially regarding her real job, which would become even more difficult with the local clinic's planned partial privatization. Who in her stead should win the annual fight for the still decreasing subscriptions of new students?

In times of shrinkage, she underlined, one is needed and one can find a way to shape local life, not only one's own – and to make one's own narrative against all dystopian predictions. She is probably one of the people Uwe had in mind in his quote from the Introduction about the increasing relevance of people in a shrinking city. Despite her commitment, Heike clearly saw the negative impact of broader economic and political forces, but as she underlined in a couple of follow-up emails: 'I am alright; I can see and name problems and despite seeming futility do my job (or at least stay busy) and stay in good humour. However, I am annoyed when people pretend that everything is fine, when they with slogans like "it's all in our hands" and "yes, we can" belie the fact that this neoliberal system with its gigantic redistribution from below to above diminishes our ability to deal with each other human(e)ly.' She concluded by saying: 'I just try to retain, to preserve, to hold the position, at which I am placed – if I go, nobody will fill my void. And I suffer from that.'[8] And she carries on despite this suffering and despite her contextual knowledge.

Conclusion: In and out of Context

Heike's use of contextual knowledge underlines a heightened awareness of the issues at stake. Such knowledge catered to her critical faculties, but it did not help much in her daily practices. Since this book aims to understand such concrete practices, it can also only link them to broader considerations rather than using such broader narratives for their analysis. The novel trope of shrinkage includes many different contexts by evoking an emerging reversal of modernity and the postindustrial era. It focuses less on the socialist past or its post-Cold War successor, and subsumes either of them in the context of deindustrialization. More importantly, however, it establishes a clear-cut link to the future as an analytical dimension. This temporal aspect is crucial in local practices and hence I concentrate on it throughout the subsequent chapters. Such a concrete approach mirrors my informants' agenda in their manifold attempts to do what they refer to as the 'shaping of shrinkage' (*Schrumpfungsgestaltung*).

Once the context of shrinkage is conceptualized with regard to the concreteness of the lifeworlds of people living through these processes, I can use it to throw new light on other potential contexts, but specifically on that of postsocialism. Substituting 'postsocialism' with the term 'shrinkage' acknowledges that the changes that Hoyerswerda is currently undergoing stem from a multiplicity of different external forces and thus are comparable to many broader ongoing processes. It also acknowledges that ethnographically, we encounter a multiplicity of contexts and narratives deployed in daily practices and attempts at making sense of these changes. However, shrinkage does not constitute a new master-trope or metanarrative in its own right. Due to its then current dominant position in local discourses, it shall function here as a heuristic device, which opens up new perspectives on the issues at stake. After the 'un-making' (Humphrey 2002a) of postsocialist life, the final question regarding shrinkage will consequentially and against its own logic only ever be: what comes after shrinkage? Such fluid approach frees Hoyerswerda from partially restrictive narratives and thereby follows its own (epistemic) politics. It also opens up new directions along which people can in many different ways orientate their practices in response to contemporary concerns and problems regarding the future.

However, the city's existence remains influenced by forces also at work elsewhere. These similar developments might gain more global prominence – at least this is what experts on East Germany and increasingly the Hoyerswerdians themselves claim, to their pride. Hence, the world can once again learn from this little East German city; as in earlier decades, Hoyerswerda can again be a city of a future. This is a future that will confront most people with new problems. One of the analyst's tasks, following Greenhouse et al. (2002), will be to scrutinize particular broader forces by drawing attention to their negative consequences in places such as Hoyerswerda. Ethnographically, my aim, like that of my informants', is rather to detect moments when yet a different idea of and for the future emerges – one that is different from decline and nonsurvival.

Lastly, there is surely a tragedy in the demolition of 'ArtBlock' building and of the many other parts of the city of Hoyerswerda. The building's late revival found its logical yet radical destination in its own destruction. Its windows were taken to some Eastern European country; the rubble remaining from its walls was sold for high prices to be reused in new building projects. The block had yet again sheltered many different people only to be itself prematurely demolished. Its material existence resembles the little socialities it had accommodated and that were similarly cut off and dispersed following the fall of the Berlin Wall. The grumpy (de)construction worker, who had problems tearing down the 'ArtBlock' building's ruin coincidentally underneath the slogan's 'CAN', is not the last person connected to this block. I started this chapter from exactly the block that heroically held Bjarke's big white letters in order to question his claim. As Bjarke had it, the tragedy is that despite all past hopes and expectations of a better future with which this city and its blocks in particular came to be invested, history has proved them to be untrue. After all, there can only be one narrative. My choice to write about Hoyerswerda from the perspective of shrinkage as one point of access into its contemporary complexity is not aiming at some nostalgic account of a better socialist past, but to account for the complexity of the presents in which my informants lived. For them, at any point, history might yet again have taken other paths in(to) the future, beyond other narratives, including that of shrinkage. Hoyerswerda can be the right space to think about such possible alternatives and to overcome an analytical overemphasis on the past and neglect for the future.

As one unintended aftermath of the 'ArtBlock' project, another big art residency took place in another block in WK 10 in June 2009, at the very end of my fieldwork. This time, it was Hoyerswerda's citizens who were invited to produce their own artistic interventions (see Ringel 2013b). Many of them were inspired to reflect upon their hometown's current problems. In their contributions, they came to ask basic questions about life, urbanity, sociality, labour, security and happiness. One particular idea grabbed my attention. For me, it provided a different perspective, a different narrative for the problem of outmigration, which was usually discussed as outlined above: either as something naturally happening or as something that has to be stopped with drastic measures. The CEO of the Cultural Factory, Uwe, had

Figure 1.3 *Side façade of the 'PaintBlock' building, artwork by local artists Richard Leue and Steven Proksch, summer 2009 (photo by Mirko Kolodziej)*

a different story to tell. For this, he cut out of a former living room's remaining carpet the silhouettes of a family of refugees, a true-to-life copy of the famous 'Refugees Are Welcome' icon, and glued them up against the wall opposite the room's door. Outside that door, he attached a quote by the already mentioned singer-songwriter Gerhard Gundermann. Uwe used one of Gundermann's ideas about the finitude of live, but in a radically different context (that of Hoyerswerda's shrinkage), thereby invoking a new take on the much-proclaimed freedom of mobility, which GDR citizens had fought for in their peaceful revolution, but that had had its rather unexpected consequences in places like Hoyerswerda. Gundermann wrote: 'Whoever wants to leave, shall be free to leave. Whoever wants to come, shall be free to come. Whoever wants to stay, shall be free to stay.'[9] From his own use of the context of shrinkage, Uwe claimed something I had not considered beforehand: the right to stay, that is, the right not to have to be mobile – an actual *freedom* of mobility. He thus mirrored Harvey's initial statement about politics and underlined that there does not have to be *only one* narrative (of migration, this time) after all.

Notes

1. For a discussion of the affective qualities of abandoned spaces and their influence on knowledge production, see Navaro-Yashin (2009).
2. Another friend pointed out to me the peculiarity that after the changes in 1989/1990, the 'dug-away' (*abgebaggert*) villages replaced WK 8's street names. Previously, these streets had been named after GDR soldiers who were killed at the inner German border. This renaming served as a symbol of political change and tried to finally include the many stories of those severely afflicted by socialist modernity's expansion. However, due to large-scale deconstruction, some of these streets together with the buildings that stood along them have – like the villages they were named after – already been demolished. 'What does that say about the present?', my friend asked.
3. On the notion of homeliness (*Heimat*) and belonging in an East German city, see James (2012).
4. His reasoning applies globally, but even in Germany the migration from former East to West Germany is significant as it leaves many towns, cities, villages and whole regions in the East in severe crisis. Approximately two million East Germans have gone to the more prosperous West in the two decades following reunification. With a previous total population of sixteen million, this exodus was made all the more severe since East Germany was also affected by the infamous postreunification implosion of birth rates. The combination of both processes creates serious long-term demographic repercussions.
5. I once clashed with a postreunification West German 'construction helper' (*Aufbau-Helfer*). He accused me of having misrepresented the immediate application of capitalist market rules to the formerly planned economy, which proved so tragic for Hoyerswerda. I had written in a newspaper column that the consequences of economic adjustments on Hoyerswerda as the settlement (*Wohnstadt* – city for living) of the

nearby brown coal industrial complex *Schwarze Pumpe*, once deprived of its economic base, were predictable. One could thus have claimed that West German political and economic elites had willingly decided on Hoyerswerda's future. Having talked to Hoyerswerda's last socialist major and the industrial complex's last director, I also proclaimed that the industrial complex had been willingly destroyed (*wurde kaputt gemacht*). The West German former politician in charge of the complex's modernization then confronted me over coffee with endless figures and numbers proving that the re-adjustments were necessary and inevitable. Obviously, he did and could not apply the GDR's context to evaluate the worth of the plant, people and technologies. The numbers he repeated only made sense in his West German context. The full automation of the power plant, which is now among the most modern brown coal power plants in Europe, the closing down of most mines and the total neglect of the fairly advanced carbon-chemical unit remained unchallenged in his eyes. He did not see the incommensurability of the two systems, the two different contexts, which were neglected in the reunification treaty – to the loss of many East German industries. Interestingly, the brown coal industry in West Germany increased its capacities in the early 1990s and many Hoyerswerdians vividly remember that there was only West German coal sold in regional stores during these years.

6. As was done by media outlets too, for instance, in an article in *The Independent* in October 2009, entitled 'A Monument to the Failure of Reunification'.

7. In their critique of the term 'postsocialism', Gilbert et al. (2008: 11) follow this strategy more specifically by claiming that the 'postsocialist experience resonates with and exemplifies critical social, economic and political transformations globally: postindustrial political and economic restructuring; the reconfiguration of personhood around flexible labour and niche-market consumption; the displacement of alternate forms of political practice in favor of liberal models or representation and participation; and the wedding of military intervention, US foreign policy and democratization'.

8. 'Mir geht's nicht schlecht, ich kann Probleme sehen und benennen und bei scheinbarer Vergeblichkeit trotzdem meine Arbeit tun (wenigstens noch tätig sein) und sogar bei Laune bleiben. Aber mich nervt es total, wenn so getan wird als wäre alles tutti paletti und mit Sprüchen wie "es liegt nur an uns selbst" oder "yes we can" darüber hinweggetäuscht wird, dass uns dieses neoliberale System mit der gigantischen Umverteilung von unten nach oben zunehmend der Möglichkeiten beraubt, menschlich miteinander umzugehen. Ich versuche nur fest zu halten, zu bewahren, den Platz zu halten, an den ich gestellt bin' – 'wenn ich gehe, füllt niemand die Lücke aus. Und ich leide daran'.

9. 'Alle, die gehen wollen, sollen gehen können. Alle, die kommen wollen, sollen kommen können. Alle, die bleiben wollen, sollen bleiben können.'

2

Reasoning about the Past

Temporal Complexity in a City with No Future

> The present is charged with the past and pregnant with the future.
> —B. Adam (*pace* Leibniz), *Time and Social Theory*

There is obviously more to a postsocialist city than its socialist past. On entering Hoyerswerda, one encounters a variety of references to many different temporal periods, including the future. Already in 2008/2009, many apartment blocks of its socialist New City, for instance, rested wearily in the postsocialist present. They stood empty, but mostly intact, or half-demolished, when bad weather prevented the demolition's completion. Others still housed some inhabitants, but had not seen any maintenance work for years. They still exhibited GDR windows (not the Western models introduced widely after 1990) or remained uninsulated. Only blocks with a future were actually taken care of and invested in. And so the deconstruction continued as the town kept on shrinking.

Many others, however, had been renovated. On their surfaces, too, different layers of paint nonchronologically referred to different pasts and futures: on top of the colourful postsocialist restorations, themselves signs of the recent promises of a new future, there were prominent references to a more distant past – 'National Socialism Now!' was sprayed in black, abrasive letters. Elsewhere, stickers commemorated the 'Heroes of both World Wars'. Swastikas, SS-runes and numerical Hitler-encodings were found throughout the city as common currencies amongst the local youth's right-wing faction, who I briefly introduced in the previous chapter. Apart from the Nazi past, they pointed to Hoyerswerda's more recent history: the infamous 1991 attacks on foreign contract workers and asylum seekers, the first xenophobic pogrom in reunified Germany. At the time, several neo-Nazi gangs chased anyone they perceived to be 'foreign-looking' through the streets of Hoyerswerda while the utterly overwhelmed police forces looked on; eventually the asylum seekers were evacuated from the city – an appalling defeat of state forces. Scenes of cheering crowds of so-called normal citizens were repeatedly shown in the national and international media, like ghosts re-arisen from the Nazi past in a former socialist (i.e. anti-Fascist) model city and predicting a similarly horrible nationalist future. How, then, to characterize Hoyerswerda's existence in time – as postsocialist, post-1991 or post-1945? How do problems with the future alter the importance given to such historical turning points in academic and local analyses – when the city, for instance, is only ever seen as being *pre*demolition?

Reasoning about the Past

Jane Guyer (2007) has argued that anthropologists should pay more attention to issues relating to the future. She urges us to redirect our analytical focus on the past and proposes a more complex understanding of the issue of time as it plays a role in local thought and practice. Before exploring how the future becomes problematized and acted upon in everyday life in subsequent chapters, in this chapter I want to discuss the issue of the past through the perspective of what I call 'temporal complexity'. By the term 'temporal complexity', I refer to the variety of locally coexisting temporal references, which involve references to very different temporal periods, but at the same time occur in concrete practices of social negotiation. I use this term to challenge the idea that particular social groups – foremost 'postsocialist' people – can be ascribed one specific temporal orientation due to their respective and unique position in history. In contrast, I present a variety of simultaneously activated and strategically deployed temporal – and not only historical – references.

Whilst including the past in my analysis of Hoyerswerda's economy of knowledge, I also indicate the many links made between different temporal dimensions. This strategy will underline how thoroughly embedded in present dynamics and concerns such temporal references are. A presentist approach either way quickly adds the temporal dimension of the future to the analysis. In the following sections, I investigate a particular set of temporal practices, namely two projects of moral education of local youth regarding Germany's socialist and Nazi past vis-à-vis the local youth's own politics of the past. I thereby scrutinize the many and diverse temporal concerns voiced and debated with regard to Hoyerswerda's problematic present. For the analysis of the role the past and the future play in local practices, I introduce Guyer's helpful notion of temporal reasoning, which approaches the issue of time and temporality as a matter of knowledge (practices). Guyer defines temporal reasoning as 'the process of implicating oneself in the ongoing life of the social and material world' (Guyer 2007: 409). Originally, she uses the term to explore human relations to the near future. In contrast, I extend this notion of epistemic investment to all kinds of temporal dimensions: near and distant past and future as much as the present itself. Such investment does not have to be methodological or rational in kind. Rather, temporal reasoning invests particular temporal relations with meaning, value or affect in particular ways. Guyer also points out that in different spatiotemporal or cultural contexts, different temporal dimensions can be differently emphasized or, in contrast – as she puts it – 'evacuated'. Since Guyer is herself worried about a culturalist understanding of temporal reasoning, I follow Crapanzano's (2007) engaging critique and explore these practices' diversity and multiplicity further, which open up spaces for agency vis-à-vis these presumed epistemic trends. The ethnographic material presented in this chapter indicates that differences in temporal reasoning occur within particular social groups, and may result in particular political and moral conflicts in as well as between different groups.

By conceptualizing the past and the future as a matter of knowledge practices and social negotiation, Leibniz's quote from above can be drastically reformulated as a question about how the present is *made* to be charged with the past and *made* to be pregnant with the future. To answer this question, I extrapolate the always-contemporary temporal politics at place in the clashes discussed below. The focus on clashes between those educating and those interpellated into a particular form of temporal reasoning will be accompanied by further remarks on the issue of the past in Hoyerswerda. I take one of my tasks to be showing how – in the connections between these different, artificially disconnected temporal domains – concerns with the future facilitate practices related to the past and vice versa. Another aim is to first of all point out such different forms of temporal reasoning. Although enabled and constrained by their own historical conditions of possibility, these forms are neither predetermined by some homogeneous, bounded, postsocialist (i.e. past-fixated) culture, nor by personal, historical or generational[1] experiences. Rather, they remain thoroughly embedded in contemporary sociopolitical dynamics and at the same time respond to very specific concerns about the future. Their analysis should thus include both past *and* future as matters of current local knowledge practices, social relations and temporal politics.

This epistemic approach to 'time' via the analytical focus on particular knowledge practices and their respective sociopolitical characteristics and repercussion is not new in the social sciences. Barbara Adam (*pace* Mead) has already pointed out that the issue especially with the future, but also importantly with the past, is that: 'Any reality that transcends the present must itself be exhibited in it' (1990: 38). As Marilyn Strathern has it, in 'one sense, everything is in place: sociality, the values, relationships. But what must be constantly made and remade, invented afresh, are the forms in which such things are to appear' (Strathern 1991: 98). I include in this ongoing process of explication the many temporal considerations that bear relevance in local practices. In this vein, we can analytically transcend the simple 'recognition that people make history in conditions outside their control' (Adam 1990: 98) and reconsider with the help of Michel de Certeau the embeddedness of the present in the past anew as a matter of practice, imbued with politics, moral and, indeed, other temporal concerns. I will thus treat the role of the past in present temporal practices as 'a concern with representation, with how people make things known to themselves' (Strathern 2005: 42). This is a first step towards a more thoroughly presentist approach to time.

Arjun Appadurai (1995) already pointed out that time (as part of a broader understanding of locality) is produced in such practices: people in their daily practices familiarize themselves with – and thus appropriate – their surroundings, and locality (including temporal embeddedness) is therefore never 'a non-negotiable here-and-now' (ibid.: 206). Munn (1992) also asks us to attend practices of strategic temporalization as indicative of 'ways in which time is not merely "lived," but "constructed" in the living' (ibid.: 109). For her, time is temporalization: 'a symbolic process continually being produced in everyday practices' (ibid.: 116). However, specifically in the temporal regimes of postsocialism and shrinkage, these practices can be seen to be restricted by dominant forms of temporal reasoning. As Burawoy and Verdery (1999: 2) put it for the case of postsocialism: 'Because the postsocialist moment means constant change in the parameters of action, actors tend to strategize within time horizons that are short.'

Figure 2.1 *Repository, City Museum Hoyerswerda, 2008*

Above, I argued against such analytic prescriptions of particular forms of temporal reasoning. I claim that if we see people as being constantly overwhelmed with change, we restrict our understanding of their agency. To counter such limiting understanding, I introduce the concept of temporal flexibility at the end of this chapter, which I develop further in Chapter 3.

With this in mind, I claim that the city's problematic present does not restrict, but rather incite a broad variety of temporal references. Because the process of shrinkage has profoundly challenged its inhabitants' self-understanding, manifold ideas, interpretations and imaginations drawn from different pasts and directed towards competing future visions have become essential tools for dealing with the current changes. Importantly, not the socialist past, but the present of shrinkage and particularly its problematization of the future thus shape current practices.

Still, the socialist past does have local currency, but also in relation to the future. Interestingly, it is foremost local youth's relations to the past, which are rendered problematic due to their presumed lack of historical experience and the potential of being exposed to nostalgic, benevolent perspectives on GDR times. Consequentially, the younger generation is transformed into a special target for a strategic (temporal) interpellation into their position vis-à-vis the GDR and other pasts. Specific historical projects try to constitute them as specific moral subjects. In the tradition of German attempts of 'mastering the past' (*Vergangenheitsbewältigung*), newly configured in the East with German reunification, the pupils are encouraged to learn from the past in certain, prescribed ways. Before discussing two youth projects in more depth, I introduce the issue of the past and temporal politics with a few ethnographic vignettes from one specific day at the beginning of my fieldwork. Although it only covers material collected in the course of a few hours, it already depicts a whole variety of temporal references and aspects, and indicates the vibrancy of Hoyerswerda's economy of knowledge.

Temporal Complexity

My first interview on 18 January 2008 took place in the Johanneum, Hoyerswerda's recently founded Christian grammar school. I met up with the history teacher Herr Oswald, who briefly introduced me to his school's history. I was surprised to hear that according to its own understanding, the school was founded as a Christian response to the above-mentioned 1991 right-wing attacks. As such, I was told, its mission was the reintroduction of supposedly lost Christian moral values into the 'Red City of Hoyerswerda' (*das rote Hoyerswerda*) and against its post-1989 neo-Nazi problems. Herr Oswald underlined that many of its founders see a lack of democracy and postsocialist residues of a – in Hannah Arendt's term – 'totalitarian dictatorship' as a convincing explanation of the dreadful 1991 pogroms, and it was the church's moral duty to intervene. As Oswald put it: 'The Church has to go where it really hurts!' In such argumentation, references to a particular historically predetermined mentality and not contemporary economic and political factors explain the post-reunification violent outbursts. The city's socialist history, not its postsocialist present, creates an epistemic framework for local analysis. Despite its moral-educational vocation, the school, like any other in Hoyerswerda, nonetheless faced problems with an unsecure future. In a shrinking city, fewer and fewer children are born and thus fewer schools are needed. Like other parts of the local infrastructure, schools found themselves in danger of losing their means of existence – or they were threatened that they will lose them in the near future. Shrinkage, I thought, does not stop before the Johanneum school's vigorous post-1991 moral calling.

One of the ways to secure one's survival was local publicity. Media coverage abounded with articles on a particular school's sporting, artistic and educational achievements. In particular, the big extracurricular projects promised good reviews and thus higher future subscription. Herr Oswald and I started discussing a project that happened two days earlier. It was the twelfth annual convention of the project 'Against Forgetting' (*Wider das Vergessen*), a project commemorating Germany's Nazi past, which is funded by the city but organized by local representatives of a leftist organization. The project mainly capitalizes on organizing discussions in all Hoyerswerdian schools with survivors of the Holocaust and Nazi terror. In his opening speech and beyond all political fissures, the conservative Lord Mayor described the project as an exemplary project for all of Germany, thereby portraying Hoyerswerda as a vanguard city of German *Vergangenheitsbewältigung*, praising its institutionalized ways of dealing with the past. However, even for him, this historical project had some future currency. He did not mention the 1991 attacks in his speech, but alluded to this project's relevance for a city like Hoyerswerda, whose two main reputations – as a Nazi town and as a city of deconstruction – posed a threat to the city's present and future.

As Herr Oswald explained, for more than a decade already a dozen survivors of Nazi concentration camps come to the city each year in early January and conduct two days of intense discussions with local youth, in their official role as contemporary witnesses (*Zeitzeugen*; literal translation: time-witnesses). The first day is usually dedicated to a book presentation and a placid dinner reception, at which the survivors mingle with the participating history teachers. It was at this year's reception that I first met Herr Oswald. At this event, the Lord Mayor had welcomed the witnesses more informally. His address of welcome was followed by a speech by the local head of the organizing Association of the Prosecuted of the Nazi-Regime/German Anti-Fascist Federation (VVN/BdA: *Verbund der Verfolgten des Nazi-Regimes/Bund deutscher Antifaschisten*). The concern about the commemoration of the Nazi past had temporarily united the Christian-conservative Lord Mayor and this leftist organization.

In her speech, the head of the VVN/BdA had emphasized the value of the project and her joy that most of the witnesses 'had made it yet again to Hoyerswerda', but also her concerns about the future. Soon, she feared, there would be nobody left to give accounts of the Nazi past through first-hand experiences. She also detailed the other parts of the project which are conducted throughout the year: excursions to nearby sites of Nazi terror, lectures and a formal wreath ceremony, at which every year a different participating school is in charge of organizing and conducting the official procedure. These activities and experiences will not only produce knowledge about the Nazi past, they will also shape the intended relationship to it, and thus a desired commitment to a better future. At the wreath ceremony, the pupils are asked to proclaim their will to prevent such atrocities in the future in front of the assembled Hoyerswerdian public. The 'right' historical knowledge gained throughout the project is the foundation for this moral stance.

After her speech, the mingling started and the whole group had become very lively and agitated. Nothing was left of the solemn seriousness with which they were previously introduced to the classes at the official reception. In particular, one Auschwitz survivor from Poland kept cracking one good joke after the other. However, the evening's main topic was the disturbing interference at the presentation of a recently published book about the Buchenwald concentration camp, which took place earlier that day. The presenter had been one of the witnesses, a survivor of this concentration camp near Weimar. In his book, he had commented on his life after their liberation. In front of the assembled pupils, he said that for him the GDR as an actual anti-Fascist socialist state was the only serious response to fascism, which is why he passionately and in high party position partook in its construction. Then, socialism was the only future option he had, and he still believed that despite its failure, it continues to be an important idea. At that point, a white-haired man in his late forties raised his arm and yelled: 'Isn't this not a bit too much AgitProp [*Agitation and Propaganda*]?' He assertively pointed out that there was a lot of anti-Semitism in the GDR too. He had even heard that it was the GDR's State Security Agency that faked neo-Nazi attacks on West German Jewish cemeteries in order to claim moral superiority for the socialist part of Germany. The bewildered witness had tried to respond to this political, ideological attack on his positive commemoration of the GDR past, but the organizers quickly ended the debate.

This intervention had suddenly expanded the focus of the evening from the Nazi to the GDR past and even further into the country's present. A project about a particular past and with a clear commitment to the future had thus been shifted into a contemporarily contested field of the politics of the past. The intervention made the commemoration of the GDR past the sole matter of discussion. The pupils in the hall must have been confused and lost in this incident, the witnesses at the reception presume. The intervening man, as another history teacher told me later, was a West German psychologist who had moved to Hoyerswerda a few years ago. With his intervention, he explicated the contemporary political and moral context in which this project also had to take place.

In our discussion in the Johanneum on the second day of the project, Herr Oswald commented on this incident in a more balanced fashion. Indeed, the whole project was initially a 'red' project, and some of the VVN/BdA were proper 'lefties' (*Linke*). Explaining to me the man's reaction, he pointed out a similar, though reverse instance. At another book presentation, independent of the 'Against Forgetting' project, one of the – as he puts it – local leftist 'everyesterdayians' (*Ewiggestrigen*) had intervened by attacking the then presenting former high GDR functionary as a traitor with the words 'You should have been hanged!' (*Dich hätte man hängen sollen!*). Although a former apparatchik, this man was now very openly critical of the GDR past. It was these kinds of public clashes that apparently led to the institutionalization of another project about the past, as Herr Oswald had indicated at the reception. This was the actual reason why I wanted to talk to him in the first place.

As he explained, this other project is called 'To the Future Belongs Commemoration' (*Zur Zukunft gehört die Erinnerung*) and solely targets the commemoration of the GDR past. It is also funded by the city, but a local liberal MP and a conservative post-1989 Hoyerswerdian Mayor for Social Affairs founded it in the mid 1990s. Both claim to have initiated this educational history project, although according to local gossip both are seen very critically for their own involvement during GDR times. As being embedded in its own politics of the past, the project's foundation sparked several responses from the founders' political opponents. Thus, both were often described to me as 'turncoats' or 'wry necks' (*Wendehälse*). One was even given the nickname 'the man with the winding in his neck' (*der Mann mit dem Gewinde im Hals*) and some of my informants were outraged that he now claimed moral (historical) superiority, adding a few delicate accusations about his professional practices and state involvement at GDR schools. Despite all attempts at moral delegitimation, both founders have very consciously positioned this project as a critical counterweight to the leftist 'Against Forgetting' project. Their project, it seemed to me later, even had to excel the other project in academic terms: not only were contemporary witnesses invited, public lectures given and excursions to former Stasi headquarters and Stasi prisons organized.

Additionally, in a large interschool competition, respective classes were invited to conduct a research project and present their results in front of all other participants and a jury, which would judge and rank their performance. The jury usually consisted of prominent victims of the GDR regime, thereby constituting a new type of contemporary witnesses. In the next section, I discuss in more detail two clashes of diverging forms of temporal reasoning, which occurred in the 2007 competition. With the help of the participating pupils, some of whom Herr Oswald introduced me to on the day of our meeting, I try to extrapolate the temporal politics clashing a year earlier.

Unintended Clashes: Divergent Takes on 'Commemoration' and 'the Future'

In the 2007 competition's public presentation of research results, one of the groups showcased a project on GDR musicians and their relationship to the state. As part of that presentation, the then seventeen-year-old Franzi, whose goodbye party featured in the last chapter, lectured on the life of Gundermann as the most prominent local example for this relationship. Gundermann had grown out of a distinctive Hoyerswerdian local GDR Singing Movement (*Singebewegung*), which originated at Franzi's school, the Lessing Gymnasium, in the 1970s. However, in the early 1990s he was also revealed to have cooperated with the GDR state security service (*MfS* or Stasi), which was why he subsequently became an official *persona non grata* in the eyes of many conservative city officials. With the aim of commemorating Gundermann's case properly, Franzi painted a complex, contradictory and careful image of a man with strong leftist convictions. She described his short party career, detailing how in 1976 he had signed a declaration of consent (*Einverständniserklärung*) to write informal reports for the Stasi; how in 1977 after an attempted candidature for the GDR ruling Socialist Unity Party his relationship with the party changed significantly and the Internal Party Investigation (*Parteiverfahren*) was opened against him in 1978; and how one year later, his exclusion from the party was only at the last minute transformed into an 'strict reprimand' (*strenge Rüge*). She also underlined the fact that he himself had by then already been spied on for several years. She finished her account by indicating Gundermann's own attempts to deal with his past after it was revealed in the early 1990s, for instance in the lyrics of one of his songs.[2]

However, the jurors disregarded Franzi's desire for complexity and deferral of judgement. Their negative response to this portrayal caused anger and disappointment amongst the members of Franzi's group. Even retrospectively, Franzi could not understand why her group's balanced account lost to other groups' more judgemental contributions; as she later told me, in her eyes, the jury's decision favoured black-and-white ideological judgements over historical complexity, thus circumventing any detailed comparison with the present situation. Indeed, their cautious presentation of lived GDR reality and of the ambiguous motivations prominent in becoming an IM (*Informeller Mitarbeiter* – Informal Collaborator) did not entirely condemn the GDR past – to the jury's dismay. Nonetheless, the jury's authority also seems limited, not least because the term 'contemporary witness' loses rigour when applied to a past, which is so recent that everybody at the presentations apart from the students had had privileged experiential access to it. That the jurors were all self-describing victims of the GDR state did not invest them, according to my understanding, with special authority.

Still, as expected by the project's title, Franzi and her friends had attempted a balanced, complex 'commemoration' of the GDR past. They had even tried to apply their historical findings to the contemporary situation. For them, understanding how people in general, and musicians and artists in particular, are lured into relations with the Stasi should help to scrutinize and resist all other kinds of possible allurements of power as well. As she underlined, freedom of speech and expression can also be limited in the contemporary market economies, that is, even if it was not a state institution regulating the art and music industry. For them, this would be a lesson for the future, which could be learned from the GDR past. Such temporal reasoning, which unexpectedly did not condemn the GDR past, but more genuinely dealt with the near future, clashed with the jurors' focus on their past-fixated understanding of GDR commemoration, which – despite the project's title – did not allow for such a balanced comparison.

Another group of the same year, the one from the Johanneum school, pushed this logic even further. Like Franzi's group, they also partially resisted the project organizers' interpellation vis-à-vis the GDR past by focusing on Germany's present and future. Accordingly, Herr Oswald's group of the previous year went through a similar clash of different forms of temporal reasoning. In order to discuss this, he had arranged for me to meet them during their lunch break. The pupils, he prepared me, remained quite angry about the jury's feedback to – and condemnation of – their project. The students still questioned whether, and how far, 'the future' was actually the jury's concern. If it is indeed not the future that was the jury's and the project initiators' objective – as it was not the complex and balanced understanding of the past in Franzi's understanding – then the project title's claim on the future is false and the project instead propagates a distinct understanding of the past only.

In the 2007 competition, this group of Johanneum pupils had a brilliant idea. Instead of 'just repeating everything they had read about the GDR', as they ironically remarked, they wrote a short theatre play in which they combined insights from GDR history with contemporarily prominent concerns about the post-9/11 extensive introduction of CCTV cameras and other surveillance apparatuses. Their play depicted a conference at which state officials from the Federal Office for the Protection of the Constitution (i.e. Germany's own Ministry for State Security) and from the Ministry for the Interior try to convince the Johanneum's fictitious future headmistress and her deputy to allow the installation of up-to-date security devices at their Gymnasium. This installation would be part of a pilot project for the total surveillance (*totale Überwachung*) of all German schools. As one of the officials in the play explains, such new security measures have become necessary in order to prevent the further growth of the already frightening numbers of politically radicalized youths, who are perceived to be hostile to Germany's constitution. In the play, only the character of the philosopher-cum-adviser and the headmistress' deputy resist the secret state project's convincing logic that was captured in the play's title 'For Your Own Security!' (*Zur eigenen Sicherheit!*).

The author of this well-written sketch, Niko, pre-emptively defended himself in our discussion. He was far from being nostalgic, he proclaimed, and was very critical of the GDR. For instance, in his response to the jurors' reproach that the pupils had misunderstood the freedoms of our current democratic system, he cleverly underlined that it is only because they nowadays had a lawful state and the freedom of speech that he could write such a play. He knew and exercised his freedom with confidence. He also reassured them that he very much agreed that the future must be a particular concern for his generation. However, for him, learning from the past meant scrutinizing the present and being aware of the repercussions that contemporary decisions might have for the future. As he understood the project title and as they were continuously told, they should be critical of everything that could reintroduce elements of what is often referred to as the second German dictatorship. For him, it is clear that any nondemocratic system would nowadays be even more dangerous with all the new technologies at hand. He also very much agreed with the jury by seeing the GDR as a 'totalitarian' rather than only an 'authoritarian' dictatorship and furthermore also despised any form of GDR nostalgia. Nonetheless, he also thought that there was more to the GDR than he was taught in his history lessons at school. In history classes, his friends agreed, there was only limited time for the topic, as history teachers from all local grammar schools confirmed. This is especially so because it was the last topic covered before final exams and hence was hardly ever comprehensively taught. Furthermore, everything they learnt about the GDR in those lessons happened to be negative.

Their play, all the group members emphasized, was in no way criticizing democracy, as the jury, outraged over the play, had claimed – rather the opposite. All they had wanted to achieve was, in Niko's words, 'to defend democracy'. Niko proved this with the play's script. In it, the philosopher comes closest to Niko's stance by saying before he leaves the commission in protest: 'According to you, the only way to defend democracy is by restricting it!' Despite repeating the same ideological logic the jury favoured, Niko used it in a rather unexpected way. Statements by the fictitious philosopher such as 'I am shocked – the German past, the two dictatorships and their systems of control and surveillance seem to be, again, ever more present' would normally cater to the jury's taste, predicaments and expectations. However, uttered in a fictitious future context, they were quickly perceived as an attack on democracy. Some of the jurors apparently felt utterly offended, expressing disbelief and total incomprehension. In particular, one jury member, a famous GDR oppositional, could only express her anger in a very agitated and loud manner. Others verbally attacked the pupils, who in turn felt even more misunderstood. The pupils' reaction, as Herr Oswald had already told me, was surely not very balanced either. Accused of a lack of commitment to democracy, and especially of blurring the boundary between the GDR's past dictatorship and Germany's free and democratic present/future, the students found themselves in the situation of having to publicly account for their moral-political standing.

To my surprise, Niko told me that on the night before the jury's final decision, he had written yet another play – which mirrored the first in plot, setting and structure – out of anger over the jurors' initial reactions after their presentation. This time, the play was named after what he predicted to be the jury's main reproach:

'The Topic was the GDR!' (*Das Thema war DDR!*). It depicted and, indeed, fairly accurately predicted the jury's final assessment of the pupils' play. It is again one protagonist, a particular juror, who critically expresses the author's own thoughts in this intelligent analysis: 'Have you ever thought about the project title "To the Future Belongs Commemoration"? Isn't "Future" and "Commemoration" exactly what this play rightly connects and strives for? That we have to arm ourselves for the future by commemorating what this German [not GDR] past means?'

In reality, the tensions and misunderstandings between this group of pupils and the jury, the organizers decided, were to be resolved in an extra meeting between the jury and the pupils, which was arranged by the organizing Saxon Office for Communal Political Education (*Bildungswerk für Kommunalpolitik Sachsen e.V.*). At this meeting, it was (absurdly) the former opponents to GDR state surveillance who defended contemporary surveillance procedures (uncannily mirroring aspects of Niko's first play). The fictitious good jury member in Niko's second play had pre-emptively responded to such defence thus: 'I dare say, you do not want to understand that this most urgent new wave of surveillance is, also and especially in regard of our history, to be questioned, and you thus don't accept any form of critique other than the one directed against the GDR. Believe me, these pupils have understood, what history should mean for us today.' The clash in forms of temporal reasoning became even more apparent in another fictitious jury member's reaction: 'I am shocked – all of you seem to be unaware of what it means to be critical of history. Perhaps you should yourself get to grips with what our history, our past means to us. You should stop calling yourselves experts, if you cannot see the connection between the GDR and this play!'

What, then, was the jury's differing understanding of the future and its relationship to the past? As the project's title suggested, it is to secure that the future (i.e. the next generation) remembers the GDR past properly. This commemoration is to happen in a very particular way, by wholeheartedly condemning the GDR past and focusing on the Stasi victims' suffering. Other forms of commemoration are seen to endanger the present. Presumed East German tendencies to *Ostalgie*[3] (i.e. a specific East German and postsocialist form of nostalgia) seemed in the jurors' eyes to increase the need for this right form of commemoration. In Hoyerswerda's local political landscape, this threat also comprised the organizers of the 'Against Forgetting' project, former party members and cadres of the GDR's security apparatus. In contrast to them, the Educational Institute for 'Newest History' (*Bildungswerk 'Neueste Geschichte' e.V.*), a post-reunification, state-funded political organization close to the German Conservative Party, would in its various projects and public events propagate the jury's preferred take on 'newest history'. A clash between members of these two associations had, as mentioned above, initially sparked the 'To the Future Belongs Commemoration' project's inception. Hence, locally, it is an *ongoing* and still *contemporary* conflict with a specific local genealogy that remains at the heart of the second project. However, the organizers emphasized disputes about the GDR past, whereas the pupils misunderstood and actually focused on the future.

Based on this analysis, it is interesting that the contemporary, though longstanding politics of the past are played out on the backs of the problematized future generation. The problematization of youth seems to constitute a more general trend in public attempts of 'working through the past' (*die Aufarbeitung der Vergangenheit*) and the 'education for democracy' (*Demokratie-Erziehung*). Furthermore, the pupils are also drawn into specific forms of commemoration by way of introducing a competitive element in the quest for historical truth. This brings certain formal restrictions to the projects. In those preparations for the 'To the Future Belongs Commemoration' project, which I could attend during fieldwork, pupils remained fairly detached and rather bored. It was only the competitive aspect of the projects' presentation that stimulated further interest and passionate involvement. Also, the competitive presentation of knowledge ended up involving many concerns about entertainment and aspects of performance rather than contents. Acquired and produced knowledge suddenly had to fit a particular format and cater to the presumed needs of a certain audience – and jury.

Interestingly, the correlation between age, experience and true historical knowledge did not just structure the relations between pupils and jury; even *within* the jury it had an effect. In August 2008, the famous GDR oppositional Angelika Barbe reproached a comment by a fellow jury member, who claimed that one group had exaggerated the extent of scarcity in the GDR. Barbe immediately raised her voice against this critical remark and inquired about this juror's age in 1989. Her response – then nineteen years old – was followed by a smile and the reply: 'Nineteen? Well you see, I was thirty-nine and for me queuing [in front of the chronically understocked GDR shops] was a big problem.' For Barbe and others, any discussion beyond these generational differences was only possible with an agreement on the qualitative difference between dictatorship and democracy, the East and the West, the GDR and the Federal Republic Germany (FRG), and the past and the present. Critique of the present was taboo and quickly silenced. For the pupils, many of the older generation's concerns remained incomprehensible. The overall interpellation of the youth into this particular historical logic was perhaps partially successful, but it did not produce the intended relation to the GDR past. However, it suffices to say that the third and victorious group did stick to the jury's expected script without lingering on any creative play with the temporal order (as did Niko's group) or any urge for complexity and balance (as in Franzi's case).

To sum up this section, as these two clashes indicate, the young participants approached the GDR past in different ways than the organizers wanted. The project's emphasis on this past was intended to educate these pupils in order to avoid the older generations' proclaimed tendency to forget GDR injustices. It was aimed at problems with the past, which the organizers had defined as crucial. Most participants followed this problematization, but in different ways than the organizers had intended. For the youth, however, problems with other temporal domains were of similar or even more importance. Both commemorational projects hence failed to impose their respective temporal concerns on local youth. Such expressions of local temporal complexity emphasizes the open(-ended)ness of according processes of social negotiation. It explains why interpellations into particular forms of temporal reasoning continue to be indeterminate. Distinct forms of temporalization remain heavily contested and strongly embedded in local sociopolitical conflicts. Like other people in other times, sites and places, Hoyerswerdians have the ability to access and evaluate multiple, sometimes even contradictory, temporal domains and logics at the same time. The multiplicity of temporal references and the clashes of different temporal orientations open up a space for strategic manoeuvre. People use this space in flexible and heterogeneous ways, resisting, redefining or challenging dominant forms of temporal reasoning, and creating and propagating their own critical temporal insights. Importantly, the youth's own internal distinctions are imbued with references to an even more distant – and less experienced – past.

Past Politics of Local Youth

At the end of the day of my interviews with Herr Oswald and his pupils, I attended the Open Day at the Lessing Gymnasium, the city's oldest grammar school. The Open Day is one of the main tools to attract new pupils, who after finishing primary school get to choose which secondary school they want to attend. As in every other Hoyerswerdian school, the format of such days was basically the same: some cultural performances indicative of a vibrant school community were presented live on stage; all classrooms were dedicated to particular subjects and invited the fourth graders (as much as their parents) to some topical games; food and drinks were served in the corridors; and visual and audio material as well as school trophies were exhibited everywhere in order to convince particularly the parents to send their kids here. All of this was conducted under the guidance of friendly teachers and passionate pupils, helping the little ones to feel at home already. However, what was originally intended exclusively for attracting fourth grade pupils suddenly turned out to be a highly symbolic event in quite different terms. The unexpected interventions, which I discuss now, were indicative of a conflict that dominates German youth, that is, the next generation whom the above-mentioned projects targeted so intensely with their moral and commemorative concerns. Interestingly, it is not the GDR past, but the time before that which still structures the young generation's temporal and social relations. The German youth born just around 1989 was in many ways not concerned with the GDR past. As in many postfascist societies, local youth was instead divided in reference to the Nazi past into what were locally referred to as 'left-wing', 'normal' and 'right-wing' factions. Each young person had to choose on which side of the political spectrum she or he belongs.

I was attending the programme on the main stage, whilst looking forward to the school band's performance. At a concert earlier that week, I already heard some critical references to Hoyerswerda in some of their songs, so I wanted to find out more about their critical relations to their hometown. I was initially not paying much attention to a group of young people in their mid twenties, all dressed in black, entering the hall. I only noticed them when one of them hissed an aggressive 'Ah, there they are. All of them. This is our chance tonight!' whilst pointing at the stage. As I looked closer, I saw white letters on this young man's black hoodie. They read 'ANH – Autonome Nationalisten Hoyerswerda' (Autonomous Nationalists Hoyerswerda). As I found out later, this particular local neo-Nazi group had already appeared at other Open Days. Seven or eight of them were led by an older man in his forties, who – in contrast to them – was dressed all in beige.

The openly leftist people in the room had quickly put on their hoodies as well, preventing them from being photographed by the right-wing intruders. They tried not to react to the insults and threats directed at them. Other people, some teachers and parents and the younger pupils in the hall had not realized this very tension in the room. Since there were too many adults and children around, presumably nothing serious was to happen. But it was clear to everyone involved that violent things would take place later outside. The verbal attacks continued. Some other youngsters from the nearby GCSE school, wearing Hip Hop outfits, shook hands with the neo-Nazis and joined them in hissing insults at the left-wingers.

As I approached two of the attending schoolteachers to ask what would be done, the neo-Nazis had left the hall. For the sake of not drawing too much attention to this incident, a courageous group of teachers together with the school's caretaker followed the group, who continued to target left-wing-looking pupils with further insults. They also went to the room for history lessons. The assembled history teachers affirmed afterwards that they had not noticed anything, but others had observed that the material dedicated to the city's new museum exhibition of the former nearby World War II detention centre was disparagingly commented on. A few minutes later, the young neo-Nazis were finally asked to leave the school on the basis of consuming alcohol on school property. One younger pupil had already called the police when he felt threatened. Before the police arrived, the right-wing group lined up in front of the school's main entrance, vociferously waiting for their anti-Fascist adversaries. The police documented their identities and required them to leave the site.

Despite sharing a reference to fascism and the Nazi era (as neo-Nazis and anti-Fascists), these two local youth factions exhibit very different forms of temporal reasoning. Whereas the right-wing groups linked the Nazi past to the distant future by aggressively intervening in commemorational practices and predicting a fatal German future as long as the democratic system endures, local members of Hoyerswerda's anti-Fascist movement (*Antifa*) altogether refrain from references to dystopian/utopian pasts or futures. The only historical references that I encountered the *Antifa* productively citing were the short-lived period of anarchism in Catalonia before the Spanish Civil War and the Mexican Zapatista movement. The GDR past and state-socialism were as despised as contemporary forms of capitalism. Similarly, the Nazi past only structured their fight against local neo-Nazi groups in response to contemporary problems. The young anarchists instead emphasized that Hoyerswerda's officials did not actively enough commemorate recent xenophobic violence and argued for a more immanent official stance against contemporary local fascism. Their main concerns remain in the near future and in proper anarchist practice (see Chapter 5). It is in these groups' many and always potentially violent clashes, such as the one described above, that these differences come to play a role in local practice.

Being Drawn into the Politics of the Past

I came across this neo-Nazi group several times during my field-work. Since I was befriending Hoyerswerda's anti-Fascist and leftist youth, there was soon no chance for me to get in touch with them.[4] I nonetheless tried to indicate their attempts to intervene in, and dominate, local life, which were often not properly noticed by older generations. I focus on the way in which they instrumentalized the Nazi past for what I refer to as their politics of fear.

The Autonomous Nationalists of Hoyerswerda (ANH) became aware of me through a couple of newspaper columns, in which I critically discussed their political interventions in the city. The first time we really clashed was at an incident that took place nine months after I had seen them first at the Open Day. The incident was a flyer distribution at the main shopping centre, informing shoppers about a certain right-wing brand sold in one of the centre's shops. The distribution was organized by the local Civil Courage Initiative (*Initiative Zivilcourage*) and the *Antifa*. Although I had worked with both groups in preparation for this event, I did not participate in the flyer distribution itself. The Nazi group usually guards the entrance of Hoyerswerda's main shopping centre. There, on the Lausitz square, Neustadt's central square, they often assembled, drank beer, smoked cigarettes and listened to music. Once in a while, they would walk through the centre and search for left-wing youngsters or foreigners. If they found any, they would verbally – sometimes even physically – assault them. Many leftist youths therefore avoided going to the centre altogether or at specific times. The reclaiming of this space during the flyer protest accordingly constituted a severe attack on the ANH's spatial politics of fear and evoked in response the assembly of approximately twenty neo-Nazis, who shouted and mocked the flyer distributers. From my point of view, I had not realized that one of the right-wing youths was taking pictures not only of members of the *Antifa* and the Initiative, but also of me. The next day, pictures of several people and myself were posted in a flyer all over the city. My leftist friends joked about this, whilst I first had to confront the fear resulting from these particular threats. It took a long while to regain confidence. However, on which grounds did the neo-Nazis manage to infuse this fear?

Hoyerswerda's right-wing groups capitalized heavily on the politics of the past in order to explain – and claim power for – their position in the present. Local neo-Nazis continuously linked the Nazi past to the national future, for example, by violently intervening in local public commemorational practices and ceremonies. A few days after the Open Day in the Lessing Gymnasium, they disturbed the annual official wreath ceremony for the Liberation of Auschwitz. The city's political and administrative elite was assembled together with the pupils partaking in the 'Against Forgetting' project. The neo-Nazis walked by the central memorial whilst continuously uttering words like 'lie' in denial of the Holocaust. They also enrolled a banner reading 'Stop the Self-Acclaimed Democrats' Propaganda!' The commemorating citizens were taken by surprise. Police forces were doubled for the ceremony in the following year. However, it was at such occasions that they loudly imposed their own interpretations of the present and displayed their aggressive banners and slogans, simultaneously resembling both the shadows of a terrible past and precursors of a similarly terrible future.

In addition, they also publicly commemorated the former Nazi official Rudolf Hess as a martyr in an annual Germany-wide commemorational week and worshiped German soldiers, who fell in the World Wars, as 'heroes', distributing stickers with SS slogans such as 'In Loyalty Strong' (*In Treue fest* – an abbreviation of the oath to Hitler) at the National Day of Sorrow (*Volkstrauertag*) throughout the whole city. On that day in 2008, another sticker depicted an Iron Cross with the slogan: 'You for us, we for you!' These constant historical references reinforced a particular relationship to what they perceived as a glorious German past, which was to be resurrected in the future once power was regained. The path to this future nonetheless remained empty or 'evacuated'. Instead of reappropriating the temporal dimension of the near future, neo-Nazis pointed to the fatal distant future, which they imagined Germany would face if the democratic system had continued to exist – recurrently drawing a comparison between their hometown's misery and the nation's doomed downfall. Slogans like 'Future Instead of FRG' (*Zukunft statt BRD*) pressed for the installation of National Socialism. Their internet presence and their continuous enforcement of fear and violence in the city functioned as ways of claiming, marking and defending space vis-à-vis their anarchist anti-Fascist opponents in their continuous political fights.

Conclusion: Towards Different Futures

In the set of practices presented in this chapter, four groups of people, divided into two different generations, have at different times and in different ways dealt with specific problems of particular episodes of the past. The older people, divided by political faction, were, in relation to one another, primarily concerned with the GDR past. They still shared a commitment to fight the Nazi past's legacies, but they diverged in their understanding of the qualitative distinction between the Nazi and the GDR past. In contrast, the younger generation was not so much concerned with the GDR past. Whereas their (grand) parents' generation unanimously condemned the Nazi past and were more interested in the historical GDR period, the youth surprisingly took the Nazi past as a common structuring principle. For left-wing and right-wing youth, the future, in turn, mattered in very distinct and opposed ways: right-wing youth used old-fashioned Nazi jargon about the nation, purity and race, while leftists instead searched for a new vocabulary (using, for example, English terms such as 'heteronormativity', 'gender' and 'polyarmour'). In their focus on issues of practice and lifestyle, they also used far fewer historical references than their right-wing opponents. Although both older generation groups agreed on their duty of imposing their moral-historical understandings, the targeted youth had their own set of temporal preferences. The past, although often negotiated in Hoyerswerda's present, was thus approached, understood and strategically deployed in very different ways. It is therefore too simple to subsume the differences in temporal reasoning under the analytical umbrella of some form of German past-fixation, a prolonged exercise in typically German 'mastering of the past', or any other presumably national, East German or postsocialist culture or mentality. Rather, we should concentrate on the actual confrontations between different people and groups, and their respective practices, institutions and interests in defining the past in the present. For most of them, the past is a very particular resource. Analytically, social and temporal negotiations of this resource take place in the present.

In this city's present, marked by a problematized future, one might not expect the past to be used as a resource to help solve problems relating to a difficult present. Still, any analysis of the role that the past plays in the present has to account for a multiplicity of temporal understandings, political agendas, ethical norms and specific forms of practice. It is in practice that temporal and historical understandings are activated and negotiated as they are made to have an impact in the present akin to the reformulation of Adam's quote given at the beginning of this chapter. In my analysis, practices related to the past served as access points to the longstanding politics, fissures and social tensions of Hoyerswerda that were continuously maintained in situations like those depicted above. This presentist strategy helped me to indicate how, in very different ways, people continued to situate their practices and moral claims in time. The manifold forms of temporal reasoning, which I extrapolated ethnographically, allow for different temporal understandings of – and approaches to – the past. In their variety, they point to a less dominant and less locally unified temporal regime. Different understandings of the past, evoked in different settings, groups and situations of conflict, also translate into different perspectives on the present and future. Very different (temporal) spaces for the imagination of the future, much needed in the process of shrinkage and its seemingly predetermined negative futures, are thus opened up. Accounting for temporal heterogeneity, I hope, helps to reconfigure our understanding of the way people exist – and situate – themselves in time and to elicit my informants' flexibility in applying different temporal references.

Forms of temporal reasoning are neither predetermined nor spontaneous nor arbitrary, but are embedded in continuous social, political and epistemological processes. Their expression or application is influenced by current socioeconomic changes. Temporal complexity is upheld against powerful dominant public narratives – for instance, of East German nostalgia – by the flexibility, simultaneity and multiplicity, in short by my informants' temporal agency. One way of approaching this complexity is to concentrate on the differences in the way in which particular temporal aspects were specifically and divergently revalued or devalued. Whereas the older conservative elite problematized the GDR past in order to claim moral and political authority in the postsocialist present and future, the right-wing youth faction allied itself with the Nazi past and with a similarly totalitarian distant future. Their anarchist opponents from the same age group countered them without any references to distant pasts and futures. Finally, the older leftist elite predominantly distanced themselves from the Nazi past and claimed their position in the present and their moral authority over the future by sidestepping elaborate discussions of the GDR past.

The analysis of a few local temporal practices has already unearthed local pluralities of, and links between, references to different pasts and futures. Especially with regard to a problematic future, different (groups of) actors engaged in temporal and thereby social 'bricolage' (Crapanzano 2007), developing specific senses of the self and of one's social and temporal existence, both of which were influenced by local temporal politics. This fosters new insights into contemporary forms of temporal reasoning in 'postsocialist' environments, where, with a commonly devalued socialist past, many different temporal periods come simultaneously into play. Our discipline can recast these diverse and unpredictable processes of temporalization in their complexity and show how the future, a powerful experiential dimension especially in times of change, is differently imagined by a whole repertoire of conflicting temporal narratives.

Finally, I want to add yet another ethnographic vignette in which the imposition of a particular form of temporal reasoning produced a rather different outcome than initially expected. I take this last example as an outcome of temporal flexibility, which I investigate in more detail in the following chapter. I refer to temporal flexibility, that is, the ability of connecting distinct temporal dimensions in novel and unexpected ways and against dominant understandings, only at the end of this chapter in order to underline which other temporal politics were potentially at stake.

I attended a twelfth grade history lesson at the Lessing Gymnasium Hoyerswerda. It was the fourth lesson of the day. The topic was the GDR. The teacher wanted the pupils to investigate different definitions of dictatorship and ascertain how the GDR fitted into them. This was prompted by a recent debate in German media about a social science study, which concluded that the majority of contemporary East German pupils were unable to distinguish between democracy and dictatorship. In the break before this lesson, this had been passionately debated amongst this grammar school's history teachers in the teacher's lounge. As many teachers indicated, journalists of several media outlets had reported that East German pupils – then the last generation born in the GDR – failed to know the truth about the GDR's past. Indeed, the majority of East German pupils did not reproduce what turned out to be a specific truth, namely that the GDR was a totalitarian dictatorship. As one teacher passionately pointed out, what went unnoticed in the reports' further accusations against East Germans as a particular group failing in its attempts at moral (self-)education was that most West German pupils also did not know much about the GDR past. However, the duty to know about such matters was exclusively bestowed on East Germans since they had to learn from *their* past – even those children born after the fall of the Berlin Wall. Pupils from the East of Germany were presumed to be also more at risk of falling back into predemocratic attitudes. Self-reassuringly, many West German journalists were happy to point out that even with less duty to know, Bavarian pupils excelled all East German results. Many media commentators found the reason for this lack of knowledge in the presumed failure of East German history teachers to educate their students properly. Supposedly, these teachers were trapped in their own history and hence lacked a critical distance, which is why they could not convincingly teach this topic. Also, the children's families themselves often had, so it was assumed in the reports, not yet distanced themselves enough from their pre-1989 existence. Most teachers of this school were outraged by such allegations. In contrast to the journalists' expectations, the history teacher in the class I was attending was quite apt. She stuck to the official history book, but also often critically engaged with the issues at hand in debates with her students.

In class, the pupils' task was to reproduce the distinction between democracy and dictatorship by a comparison between the GDR and the periods of fascism and Stalinism vis-à-vis contemporary democracy. Indeed, the GDR – self-defining as a proletarian dictatorship – qualified for the category of dictatorship. However, as one definition underlined, it was only questionably to be perceived as a *totalitarian* dictatorship. Still, in one political cartoon on a working sheet, major continuities to the Nazi past were depicted and awaited the pupils' analysis. Basically, the pupils were to understand that only in the West, in a proper lawful state, were essential freedoms and rights granted and guaranteed.

Whilst the class engaged in a final discussion of today's lesson, seventeen-year-old Benni, the young singer-songwriter mentioned in the previous chapter, suddenly raised his arm and asked the following question:

> If the principle of democracy is so fundamentally important for everything political – the right to elect people in and out of power, issues of transparency and responsibility in the organization and decision making process of issues with public relevance, etc. – if that is all so important for the realm of the political and since we all should partake in these processes as we depend on their consequences, why, then, is our economy not more democratized? Why is the economy not more subject to the same democratic principles?

Benni's intriguing inquiry about the democratization of the economy envisioned a future in which practitioners of and in economic processes were institutionally accountable for the public good. It left the teacher temporarily as much without a good response as me. Importantly, it deployed a different form of temporal reasoning, which recaptured the future – not in conscious reference to a particular past, but rather freed from the temporal framework, which should have disallowed this epistemic investment in the democratic capitalist present in the first place. As was the case at the end of Chapter 1, I again end a chapter with a moment of surprise, a notion to which I will return theoretically at the end of the book. I now turn in more depth to the temporal domain of the future as a major aspect of human existence.

Notes

Earlier versions of parts of this chapter were published as F. Ringel. 2012. 'Towards Anarchist Futures? Creative Presentism, Vanguard Practices and Anthropological Hopes', *Critique of Anthropology* 32(2): 173–88.

1. Throughout the chapter, I use the term 'generation' both as a locally significant social category and a heuristic device. I do not essentialize difference between these age groups (see Kertzner 1983), but rather present material in which their experiential differences are used to legitimize particular politics and practices. Still, different 'generations' remain differently affected by the repercussions of the process of shrinkage, especially regarding issues of economic security and mobility (for similar examples, see Cole 2004, 2005; Cole and Durham 2007, 2008; Durham 2004, 2008). For instance, the elderly are financially secured by state pensions and can stay; their children and grandchildren respectively are often forced to leave because they need a job to sustain themselves. However, this is a matter of their present position in society, not of their biographical experiences, and even these positions alter; increasingly elderly people felt the need to follow their children to West Germany or elsewhere in order to secure the care they soon might need.

2. For that, the group played a song, which Gundermann had written for his IM (informal collaborator), that is, the person who had reported on him. The song is called 'Sieglinde' and bears as its title the IM's female code name. It ends with an invitation to contact him: 'They say, you overheard me / apart from you, however, nobody has ever listened to me /... They say, you shadowed me, / and I am thankful for your shadow / because too much sunshine on one's head / only causes a sunstroke /... Good old

Sieglinde,/ whenever I'll find you / it will be my turn / please, give me a call, please, please, give me a call! (*Sie sagen, Du hast mich belauscht / doch außer Dir hat mir nie jemand zugehört / ... Sie sagen Du hast mich beschattet / für Deinen Schatten danke ich / denn bei zuviel Sonne auf die Platte / kriegt man leicht nen Sonnenstich / ... Ja, ja, ja Mensch, Sieglinde, / wenn ich Dich finde / dann bist Du dran / bitte, bitte ruf an / bitte, bitte ruf an!*)

3. For more on *Ostalgie*, see Esbenshade 1995; Bach 2002; Boyer 2006; Berdahl 2009.
4. However, for a comprehensive study of a similar right-wing milieu in East Berlin, see Shoshan (2016).

3

'Hoyerswerda...?' –
'...Once Had a Future!'

Temporal Flexibility and the Politics of the Future

> ... people generally ignore human agency when it suits them to do so.
> —Herzfeld in H. Miyazaki, *The Method of Hope*

Between the Old and New City – along the river that divides them – we find Hoyerswerda's equivalent of the famous Berlin Info Box.[1] Whereas the red Info Box on the grounds of the capital's former death strip documented and forecasted the construction of Berlin's new centre around Potsdamer Platz, the Orange Box (henceforth *O-Box*) in Germany's fastest-shrinking city was supposed to accompany a fundamentally different project: that of a city's deconstruction.

The building's name gives its shape and design away. It was a bright orange cube of 7.2 cbm, built with material donated by the Hoyerswerdian citizenry. It was erected as the only outcome of the City Workshop 15+9. This temporary workshop was a previously unthinkable cooperation of Hoyerswerda's administrative elite and some elected local experts on architecture and urban planning. The '15' of the project's title referred to the predicted number of 15,000 inhabitants of the New City (henceforth *Neustadt*), which anticipates a further drastic decline in population from the formerly more than 60,000 and – during my fieldwork – already only 26,000 *Neustadt* inhabitants. '9' indicates the stable, even slightly growing figure of 9,000 Old City inhabitants. These numbers were the officially valid demographic forecasts in 2008. They constituted the planning horizon (*Planungshorizont*) for those in charge of managing the repercussions of shrinkage in their respective fields of expertise. There was at least some hope amongst Hoyerswerda's citizens that by 2020 or 2025, the process of shrinkage might slow down or stop altogether. But nobody knew for sure. Hoyerswerda's future remained unpredictable – on any planning horizon.

Out of three project ideas emerging from this workshop, only the *O-Box* as the 'Communal Centre for the City's Reconstruction Process' was realized – too late, as critics remarked. These critics claim that most of the damage to the cityscape, and thereby to the inhabitants' future prospects, had already occurred in the years preceding the Box's opening in 2008. That the city officials were finally attempting to include the public in the decision-making process was thus, for some, nothing more than a late empty gesture. The often-proclaimed absence of the public's local commitment, on the other hand, was seen by city officials as one of the reasons why people continued to leave Hoyerswerda. Did the *O-Box*'s exhibition still provide a new vision of the local future? Did it reintroduce new ideas and – finally – some trustworthy knowledge about the city's future, which would help to reappropriate a future that had otherwise been evacuated in most official discourses?

This chapter follows and questions the evacuation of the local (near and far) future. It focuses specifically on public debates concerning urban planning and introduces some of the local challenges to this evacuation. I use the term 'evacuation' in the sense that Jane Guyer (2007) has introduced it with. In order to explain differences between distinct forms of temporal reasoning, Guyer separates linear time into the near and distant past and future, respectively. She uses this analytical tool in order to detect a dominance of a particular form of temporal reasoning in the contemporary neoliberal temporal order, especially in worldwide religious and economic practices. She describes this dominant form as a combination of 'enforced presentism' and 'fantasy futurism' (Guyer 2007: 409f). Accordingly, the temporal domains of the present and the distant future, she argues, are currently emphasized or refashioned, whereas the near future, the main focus of post-World War II modern planning practices, remains devalued or evacuated. As the dominant form of temporal reasoning in the postmodern era of 'flexible accumulation' (Harvey 2000), enforced presentism and fantasy futurism have succeeded the post-World War II, modernist era's wholehearted colonization of the near future. Instead of five-year plans, Fordist production and the expansion of the welfare state, the new temporal regime tells a 'shock-therapy' story about unmanageable market forces, the need for constant adjustment and an acceleration of involuntary change, which is driven by the expectation of growth, wealth and salvation in the distant future.

In response to Guyer, Crapanzano criticizes the notion of the dominance of a particular postmodern form of temporal reasoning. As he puts it, there is no consistency to be expected 'in the way people respond to conflicting temporal experiences' (Crapanzano 2007: 423). Rather, he identifies a form of temporal agency deployed by those opposing such dominance. The ethnographic material presented in this chapter supports Crapanzano's emphasis on what I call temporal flexibility. Deploying it to this shrinking fieldsite will help scrutinize the temporal regime of shrinkage and the postindustrial era. One of the questions I try to answer is whether we can actually speak of an evacuation of the near future in the first place.

My material supports such a perspective regarding one particular group: the city officials in charge of managing shrinkage and deconstruction. However, this group's evacuation of the near future was recurrently challenged. Alternative temporal politics thereby opened up spaces in which people could intervene in the temporal regime of shrinkage. For some of those advocating a new temporal framework, the officials' evacuation seemed more like an active disguise of knowledge about the near future, that is, as expressions of their own temporal politics. Along the lines of Herzfeld's observation about human agency from the beginning of this chapter, this raises the question about agency, specifically temporal agency in local planning practices. Crucially, the detrimental consequences of the local government's inability to provide Hoyerswerda's inhabitants with a convincing idea of the near future led to the further production of insecurities, due to which personal decision-making could not align itself with any reliable predictions. Given this urgency produced by the failure of contemporary forms of urban governance, one particular task of this chapter is to show how the dominance of one form of temporal reasoning could be effectively challenged by deploying alternative ways of relating to the future. This chapter is dedicated to exploring the local politics of the future as indicative of Hoyerswerda's specific knowledge economy as well as the forms of citizenship emerging in a postindustrial city in decline.

Three groups of people ethnographically lead through this chapter: those nominally in charge of the city's deconstruction; the former architectural GDR elite; and the contemporary sociocultural elite. At first I follow the city officials, especially the conservative Lord Mayor, in order to indicate his reasons for refraining from more concrete references to the near future. As I will show, he did not so much evacuate the near future, but rather shifted register in relating to it. Instead of concrete planning and detailed knowledge, he deployed a more affective language. In order to explain this shift, I propose two different readings. The first one follows Guyer's slightly genealogical approach and tries to map the local history of the future, indicating out of which epistemic tradition the Lord Mayor's approach results. This allows me to again raise the question of what happens when different temporal regimes coexist or overhaul one another. The second, more presentist approach embeds the Lord Mayor's strategy in contemporary temporal politics and social dynamics. I depict these political dynamics by analysing a particular moment of confrontation between different architectural elites concerning the locally important discourse on shrinkage and urban planning. Official local planning practices, traditionally providing the most trustworthy and prominent references to the future, were the most significant public arena in which the repercussions of shrinkage were debated.

In the last section of the chapter, I show how yet again other registers, this time stemming from the city's sociocultural milieu, successfully produced a new and convincing vision of Hoyerswerda's near future. Despite the drastic challenges that Hoyerswerda faced more generally, I depict the strategic and concrete ideational investments in the local future as one example of how, contrary to Guyer's analysis, the contemporarily dominant evacuation of the near future was questioned and partially overcome. This contributes not only to a deeper understanding of local temporal politics, but also of what I introduced as temporal flexibility. I end the chapter by asking how the temporal order of shrinkage as the successor to the temporal regime of postsocialist transformation can itself be overcome – for which the ethnographic material already indicates some promising answers. With its help, I emphasize that Hoyerswerda's present is *not* determined by the temporal regime of shrinkage, postindustrial decline and 'no hope and no future'.

Importantly, all of the people mentioned in this chapter demonstrated a surprisingly passionate commitment to their hometown and exemplified the citizenry's impressive and unique daily investment of thought, time and creativity – indeed, their proper reasoning – into the city's difficult present and its many probable bleak future scenarios. However, this chapter only covers the reflected side of relations to the future in a shrinking city amongst widespread deconstruction. Aspects of material, affective, more experimental and artistic engagements with the future in times of shrinkage as well as its ethical revaluation will be discussed in this volume's remaining chapters.

Figure 3.1 *Façade, WK 5e, Hoyerswerda* Neustadt, *2008*

Evacuating the Future

The *O-Box*'s first exhibition was a documentation of Hoyerswerda's postsocialist architectural achievements. It listed and depicted the last two decade's new constructions, costly renovations and all other built signs of growth, progress and the future. These buildings once materialized the realization of the promised postsocialist future; they symbolized the initially unquestioned fact that something was changing for the better. In 2008, *any* new building, renovation or visible investment still had the potential to embody promises for the city's as well as one's personal future simply by guaranteeing this particular building's endurance in time. In a shrinking context, shining facades, renovated rooftops or brand-new doors and windows incited renewed trust in Hoyerswerda's future prospects. However, expectations of the general longevity of built structures were at the same time severely challenged by the ongoing large-scale physical deconstruction of Hoyerswerda's *Neustadt*. Whereas ordinary houses in Germany are usually planned to exist for at least eighty to one hundred years, as an architect friend from Hoyerswerda once explained to me, most of those *Neustadt* houses originally erected throughout the 1980s existed only for ten to twenty years. The city council's as well as the two main landlords' decisions in which buildings to invest the decreasing resources became existential for those living or working in them. Living in a not-yet-renovated apartment block always entailed some insecurity about the building's future. As much as the houses, their inhabitants seemed to be trapped in the present. Apart from the apparent dilapidation, it was the constant status of waiting for a decision about the future that annoyed the inhabitants most. The landlords' policy was to send a notification letter only one year in advance – and only the ominous letter guaranteed financial support for removal. Similarly, most social institutions like kindergartens, schools and sociocultural associations depended on the city's infrastructural support. Each strategic urban planning decision thus affected many people in their professional and personal lives. However, the two main landlords (one communal, one cooperative) as well as the city council and the city's administration all refrained from openly and concretely discussing the future. Because of this evacuation, inhabitants of apartments still awaiting renovation were stuck in the present.

The visible emphasis on new developments in the *O-Box* exhibition attempted to counterweigh the dominant imageries of demolition. However, this architectural documentation made up only one-half of the exhibition, filling the downstairs area. Upstairs, exhibition space was dedicated to the city's future. For that, the visitors were asked to contribute their own ideas by writing them on little square orange sheets of paper. Despite the downstairs proof that the future had continuously been planned in Hoyerswerda, one visitor only commented bitterly on his experiences of decay throughout

Figure 3.2 *The City's Development Plan, vague visual version,* O-Box, *autumn 2008*

Neustadt, saying that 'many people have lost their hope that it will become better'. In a more cynical vein, another visitor envisioned the city's future with a more dramatic, violent image: a dinosaur-like fight involving a bulldozer and a brown coal excavator in the emptied *Neustadt* centre. In the middle of the room, the curators exhibited the official future green space design plan. This plan underlined that even the fallow lands remaining after the deconstruction of by then 7,000 out of formerly 22,000 flats – with 6,000 still to be demolished – had to be given a new urban function.

The most essential document of the city's deconstruction process covered the upstairs part of the wall above the entrance: the city's official and effectual development plan. This plan depicted in detail the politically consented and legally binding spatial ordering of Hoyerswerda's future until 2020. It precisely indicated which areas of the city were dedicated to demolition, industry, commerce or new developments. It was a big struggle, the curators told me, to get the official permission to put it up in the first place. Officials alerted that people should not be frightened by the planned deconstruction of their houses, schools or kindergartens, first, because they should not be lost to the city and, second, because the plan itself might sooner rather than later lose its validity. As a compromise, the legend to explain the plan's different colourings was hung up very inconspicuously and remained hardly visible. The curators kept on joking about the fact that despite its importance, this simple but powerful plan remained both hidden and unexplained. The local future, despite being exhibited, remained effectively evacuated; no public imaginaries catered to the officially guiding reappropriation of the near future. But how did Hoyerswerda lose its future in the first place?

From Planning to Hope

The Lord Mayor's take on the city's future was rather vague. In fact, it involved a vocabulary markedly different from the one used in modernist planning practices. In 2008, he started his speech at the traditional New Year's reception with a quote from *The Little Prince* by Antoine de Saint-Exupery: 'If you want to build a ship, don't assemble your people for collecting wood and don't assign them tasks and work. Rather teach them to long for the endless immensity of the sea.' While this quote contradicted the very raison d'être of modernism, it proposed a very particular take on the near future. However, this purely affective longing for the future did not straightforwardly produce concrete knowledge about it. Nevertheless, it at least offered a relation to the future, which constituted a much-needed good in a city presumably 'without a future'. Why would a Lord Mayor of a shrinking city retreat to such a strategy?

In an interview about his visions for Hoyerswerda's future, the Lord Mayor underlined several times that he, in that regard, had learned from mistakes made in the past. In order to avoid any further disappointments, he refused to give any promises, predictions or other affirmations regarding Hoyerswerda's future. His predecessors had made this mistake many times: they had sparked glimpses of hope by assuring people that a better future was to arrive soon – whether in the form of the erection of a solar panel factory or the opening of the Karl-May amusement park, as had been promised in the mid 1990s. Having seen many officials lose their reputations by not keeping their promises, he refused to give such hopeful prophecies altogether.

The only prediction the Lord Mayor dared to recurrently formulate was the one that Hoyerswerda was, is and will remain to be 'a loveable and liveable city'. This vague trope promised a good future without having to provide details about how this future would actually look and how it could be achieved. It was the fitting response to shrinkage's general and similarly vague dystopian fore-shadowing of a future that could only ever be worse, not better than the present. In the temporal regime of enforced presentism (with only a few invocations of fantasy futurism), there was accordingly not much leeway for concrete references to the future. Rather, as the Lord Mayor said: 'In regard of the local economy and the general infrastructure, our development targets are purely to ensure its survival. We have to keep what we have and *can only hope* to improve or better it' (emphasis added). In his eyes, this was 'actually not the time to follow the slogan "Growth, growth, growth!" anymore; for the city's contemporary inhabitants only questions of "the now" count – and these pressing questions deserve our full attention!' However, because of his unassertive strategy, many Hoyerswerdians saw him as not being a man of action who could actually solve these current problems. These critics claimed that Hoyerswerda needed a strong Lord Mayor with a vision. Everybody, including himself, attested that he did not have this kind of 'prophetic' charisma.

A few months after my fieldwork in Hoyerswerda, the Lord Mayor tried to change this with the help of an external marketing agency and its new marketing measures: the city-magazine *AHOY*; a new design for the city's website; and the use of novel communicational strategies. However, these new imports from the marketing sector also failed to secure a more detailed representation of Hoyerswerda's future. Instead, they catered to the idea of longing proposed in de Saint-Exupery's quote. Their professional advice was hoped to equip the Lord Mayor with a simple message about – and image for – Hoyerswerda's future, something that could convincingly be sold to local citizens as well as to the outside world. Such message should have strengthened Hoyerswerda in the contemporary competition between different regions, cities and towns for new investments, new visitors and – most importantly – new inhabitants. Still, a concrete *Leitbild* (leading image or vision) for the future was impossible to create with these measures.

One of the Lord Mayor's personal concerns was that he knew that in the future he would be remembered in Hoyerswerda's chronicles as the 'Deconstruction Lord Mayor' (*Abrissbürgermeister*). Since he could not reverse this process, his contribution was to bring back into sight his citizens' basic needs: 'it is the citizens who count in a shrinking city'. His vision of a more harmonic path towards the future included 'moving closer together again', 'less throwing dirt at each other' and in the best-case scenario more 'experimental bravery'. The

Lord Mayor's evacuation of the near future accordingly appeared to be a conscious decision for a different register – a vague, affective register, which seemed more promising given the unpredictability of the process that he needed to administer, and the ephemerality of any official plan. In turn, his lack of other conceptual tools might have been indicative of a typical case of enforced presentism. One might use such an argument for explaining the Lord Mayor's shift in temporal reasoning, but what had actually happened to the postsocialist expectations of a better future after German reunification?

Temporal Regimes in Time: A History of Hoyerswerda's Future

Jane Guyer, to repeat, defines temporal reasoning as 'the reach of thought and imagination, of planning and hoping, of tracing out mutual influences, of engaging in struggles for specific goals, in short, of the process of implicating oneself in the ongoing life of the social and material world' (2007: 409). She has been criticized for her exclusive perspective on worldwide economic and religious practices as well as for the daring notion of a dominance of certain forms of temporal reasoning: the postmodern global temporal order of enforced presentism and fantasy futurism. As Wilk (2007) in response points out, this claim misses several other practices of everyday life, which follow a very different form of temporal reasoning, such as particular consumption practices, personal career patterns and discourses on climate change. His critique poses the multiplicity of forms of temporal reasoning against the idea of a hegemonic temporal culture. Even though temporal complexity abounds in Hoyerswerda, I do not want to overstate the agency of actors in the field – as if they could pick any arbitrary temporal aspect or reference out of a random temporal toolbox. However, when artificially constructing a history of Hoyerswerdian futurity, this agency should also not be forgotten. In a Foucauldian framework, I detect a particular problematization at the core of local practices targeting the future. As Rabinow clarifies (2003: 55), problematizations are according to Foucault of a longstanding nature. The future is such a longstanding problematization. It has continuously been problematized throughout socialist and postsocialist times, although in distinctively different ways. Although it is easy to presume a continuity in epistemological investments into the future, this investment currently seems to be ruptured because of the city's perceived loss of the future. Can we therefore speak of a new dominant temporal regime – that of shrinkage?

In Hoyerswerda's past, one can detect a variety of temporal regimes. Only the notion of change prevails throughout the last one hundred years. Change itself did not pose a problem, but crucially its directionality to the future did. Since the 1950s, Hoyerswerda had been subject to accelerated change as a site of socialist-modernist intervention. A huge coordinated project of actual and social engineering shaped life in the whole region. This was mirrored by a vanguard stance, that is, the genuine understanding that one's life is part of history's march to the (this time communist) future. Despite increasing economic scarcity and the lack of political reforms, until the early 1990s, the city was permanently under construction and visibly growing. Yet by the 1970s, grander plans for the city had already been abandoned. The never-realized district WK 11, as part of the third expansion plan of *Neustadt*, would have pushed Hoyerswerda's population over 100,000 inhabitants. But as much as the initially ambitious plan for *Neustadt*'s city centre, it remained unrealized with the state's attention refocusing on projects elsewhere.

During the time of the *Wende* (turn) in 1989/1990, new fears, but also new chances and possibilities shaped local expectations of the future. As a 2010 book project commemorating the twentieth anniversary of these changes showed, for many citizens everything seemed possible during this transitional year before reunification. The contributors, all local citizens, exhibited a tender and nostalgic attachment to this short-lived window of freedom, opportunity and hope. However, their critical assessment of their life in the GDR, which had initiated the changes, was quickly accompanied by experiences of the disadvantages of the new system. Retrospectively, they expressed a disappointment about the subsequent and unexpected loss of the hope for a better future.

For some contributors, this hope had initially envisioned a better GDR, which was to combine the positive aspects of socialist *and* capitalist Germany. Its loss meant the loss of the belief in a better future altogether. Gundermann's widow Conni, for example, remembered how after a concert on 2 October 1990 – the night before reunification – she and her husband were heading home from a gig quite far away from Hoyerswerda. On the autobahn, they listened for the last time to the traditional midnight-airing of the GDR's national anthem. As she recalled, both of them started crying, knowing that all third-way attempts to reform this historical project of socialism were by then obsolete. 'A dream had just disappeared', she said (quoted in

Decker et al. 2010). The programme Gundermann was touring with during this transitional time bore the telling title 'Memories of the Future'. This future, after all, was *Neustadt*'s founding idea. As the GDR's second socialist model city, it had been built to materialize and facilitate a better future. Following socialist-modern rules of construction and social organization, it housed a young and enthusiastic population. Hoyerswerda was the GDR's city with the youngest population and with the highest percentage of children. These children shaped the cityscape. The district schools determined the size of each living complex. If there was ever a place in the GDR where the socialist future seemed to emerge with all its splendour and visionary excitement, it probably was Hoyerswerda *Neustadt*, at least for a few years.

East Germans more generally often experienced and expressed disappointment throughout the early 1990s (Esbenshade 1995; Boyer 2006; Berdahl 2009). Promises of reunification did not materialize. In contrast to the promised 'blossoming landscape', former Chancellor Helmut Kohl's infamous vision for East Germany's future, the actual feeling of being materially, but also morally, legally and politically 'second-class citizens' emerged strongly. East Germans commonly felt a form of dissatisfaction with 'the West'. Envisioning one's personal future in the new era was influenced by the distorted dream of a Western future that never really materialized (Borneman 1992; Yurchak 2006; Berdahl 2009: 90f), and by transitional insecurity and the evacuation of the future. As claimed by some East German intellectuals (Engler 1999, 2002, 2005; Kil 2004), in the postsocialist period, modernity itself seemed to be reversed in places like Hoyerswerda. Whereas modernity at large continuously invoked fantasies of growth, acceleration and expansion, the process of shrinkage introduced the opposite vocabulary: decline, deceleration, and retraction. A certain loss of confidence in a better future transformed affected communities into a very specific kind of Beck's 'risk societies' (Beck 1992). In Beck's eyes (compare Rabinow 2008), risk is modernity's dominant form of temporal reasoning and relating to the future. However, modernity's probability calculations and strategic risk assessments do not add much knowledge to the predicted bleak developments of presumably superfluous, dispensable and redundant cities like Hoyerswerda.

This loss of the socialist-modernist future became most apparent in a shift from concrete planning and construction practices of socialist modernity to the large-scale demolition of *Neustadt*. As Mirko, a local journalist, told me, it had all started 'with the elaborated celebration of the State Festivity "Day of the Saxons" [*Tag der*

Sachsen] in 1998. We Hoyerswerdians had thought, we finally were relieved of the burden of the 1991 past.' Instead of starting anew in the postsocialist period without the reputation of being a Nazi town, a new obstacle for the future suddenly emerged. 'It was only a few weeks later', Mirko remembered, 'that the first building in *Neustadt* was deconstructed: the Z2, a high building in *Neustadt*'s centre.' The images of its demolition constituted a new iconography. Previously, deconstruction was associated with the war and its aftermath. In contrast, socialism and Hoyerswerda were all about the construction of the future. 'To see the Z2 fall, came like a shock. It was only erected thirty, perhaps thirty-five years ago.' The shock even increased gradually when, as in many later cases, the promised replacement building was never even started. For the following eleven years, nothing happened to the remaining fallow land, which – uncannily – marked in the very centre of *Neustadt* that the present had taken an unexpected road to the future (cf. figure 0.2, centre left).

In this context of epistemic (temporal) insecurity, a local architect first introduced the term 'shrinkage' (*Schrumpfung*) to public debates on the future, finally acknowledging a process that had already become obvious. The architect Dorit Baumeister was often described to me as 'a prophet in her own land', a German figure of speech that describes a person who speaks the truth, but is purposefully not heard by her contemporaries. She initially deployed a rather bleak rhetoric strategy by describing this process as one of 'terminal care' (*Sterbebegleitung*). As she retrospectively explained, she wanted to underline the existential threat posed to the city's survival. 'This city is dying!', she said in several regional and national newspaper articles and television reports. For her, this alert was the honest and necessary basis for proceeding towards new futures: the recognition that something dramatic, unforeseen and existential is happening. Without an accurate acknowledgement of the present situation, she argued, one cannot create, form or construct the future. Hence, she openly reached out into the future more forcefully than anybody had done before her. Her intervention, one could argue, at least recaptured the future-dimension, even if in pessimistic terms.

Invoking the city's potential death caused a huge outcry. Dorit was called a 'nest-soiler' (*Nestbeschmutzer*) and was accused of creating even more problems for Hoyerswerda by damaging its – in any case problematic – reputation. In response to her public invocation of the process of shrinkage, Dorit's architecture office was neglected for a considerable time in public assignments, which almost forced her office into bankruptcy. Additionally, some of her friends were asked to end their friendships with her. She was publically shunned at several occasions and often felt like she was running the gauntlet when she walked through the city. Others experienced similar forms of mistreatment after they commented critically on the city's future. For instance, René Dassler, the head of Hoyerswerda's Sport Association in 2008, told me about how, in the late 1990s, he was prohibited by a high-up administrational official from commenting on Hoyerswerda's demographic development. As he recalled, he had intervened in a political fight about the establishment of a new sport's ground at *Neustadt's* outskirts. This idea by the politically conservative West German Chief Planning Officer was opposed by René with the more reasonable and cheaper proposition of restoring existing old facilities, which was also favoured by the then oppositional leftist political fraction. Politically unaffiliated, he had intervened because of the demographic knowledge he had gained from his post-1990 university degree. He said it was obvious that this kind of investment into new facilities would in the long run be needlessly expensive. As he drew attention to this fact, the then West German conservative Lord Mayor, he recalled, smugly asked him: 'Do you want to tell that to Hoyerswerda's citizens!?'

In the meantime, Dorit developed a different vocabulary with which to relate to the future by conducting local communal art projects. Curating the art project SuperReconstruction 2003 (*SuperUmbau 2003*), worldwide – or at least nationally – the first art project on the topic of shrinkage had preceded her condemnation. With the 2005 'I was Born Here' project (*Hier bin ich geboren –* a quote from another Gundermann song) and the 2007 Future Laboratory (*Zukunftswerkstatt*) of the 'The Third City' (*Die dritte Stadt*) project, she regained a position from which to comment on the future. Her vocabulary had changed by then to a more precise and optimistic tone. I will discuss the content of this reinvestigation into the future at the end of this chapter. It suffices to say now that Dorit has changed her rhetoric from a vocabulary of 'terminal care' to the creative and active approach of shaping the process of shrinkage (*Schrumpfungsgestaltun*g). She is one example of how the city officials' lack of a vision of the future opened up a space for 'normal' citizen's temporal interventions. The next ethnographic and more presentist vignette illustrates a clash of different forms of temporal reasoning, which embeds the evacuation of the near future in contemporary local temporal politics rather than in their historical context.

Local Clashes and Temporal Flexibility

In the context of a widespread feeling of loss of the future, most Hoyerswerdians did not retreat to the otherwise expected phenomenon of *Ostalgie*, the East German version of postsocialist nostalgia. However, some of my informants very creatively used references to the GDR past in order to challenge the city's contemporary evacuation of the near future. As the anthropology of East Germany has shown, references to the socialist past are less a matter of a longing for the GDR past. Rather, they express concerns about the present (Berdahl 1999, 2009) or even a longing for the future (Boyer 2001a, 2001b, 2006, 2010). In that vein, Daphne Berdahl (2009) interpreted seemingly nostalgic local expressions as remarks on the future because of the past's distinct feature that it – in contrast to the unpromising postsocialist present – had a future. Furthermore, she claimed (Berdahl 2009: 87ff), the socialist past continues to provide a rhetoric and ideational resource for imagining a different future. It remains capitalism's former 'big other' in terms of temporal politics. In her eyes, the past's futurity serves particular political and epistemic purposes. It assists attempts to recapture the quickly evacuated future, and I am sure the same logic applies to references to the industrial-modernist past in other postindustrial areas and cities. In Hoyerswerda, the evacuation of the near future can be countered by references to the GDR past whilst sidestepping the latter's ideological devaluation.

The Art Club Hoyerswerda (Hoyerswerdaer Kunstverein e.V., henceforth *Kunstverein*) was one of the many institutions to intervene in the local debates on Hoyerswerda's future. It had a long tradition of doing so, beginning with the club's foundation in the 1960s, when it voiced critical remarks on state-socialism's plans for the city. Brigitte Reimann, the famous writer mentioned earlier (see e.g. Reimann 1998), was one of these voices. In previous years, the *Kunstverein* took on her legacy. Reimann had in the 1960s during her time in Hoyerswerda actively intervened in the public discourses on the construction of the second socialist model city. Especially in her unfinished novel *Franziska Linkerhand*, she had critiqued the increasingly bureaucratic and technocratic character of the plans for the city during this decade.[2] In public lectures, discussions and literary tours through *Neustadt*, the club tried to keep her ideas about Hoyerswerda's (past) future alive during times of shrinkage. A 'Research and Meeting Venue' was established in her honour in *Neustadt*'s oldest living district WK 1. At its entrance, a plaque quoted Lewis Mumford with a sentence cited by the protagonist of Reimann's novel, the young architect Franziska Linkerhand: 'The city is the most valuable invention of civilization, which, as a mediator of culture, is only superseded by language.' With its impressive variety of cultural events, continuously put on over the last fifty years despite all political changes, the club impressively followed the author's promise of culture and urbanity. Reimann's urge for a 'more human(e)' layout of the city which would better cater to social and cultural needs of its inhabitants rather than to the 'sole functions of sleep, hygiene, heating and nutrition', as one of the club members had it, was applied to current imaginaries of how to deal with the city and its increasingly perforated cityscape.

In August 2008, the *Kunstverein* organized a lecture on *Neustadt*'s architectural history. Christine Neudeck, a former construction engineer and currently one of many dedicated *Kunstverein* members, had prepared a very comprehensive PowerPoint presentation. In her talk in the Old City's castle, the *Kunstverein*'s preferred venue, she linked *Neustadt*'s vanguard history to the larger tradition of the German and international Bauhaus movement. For that, she repeated the theories of Mies van der Rohe and Le Corbusier, and reiterated the epoch-making agenda of the famous Charta of Athens, in which Le Corbusier and others already in the 1930s argued for – amongst other things – the separation of work and living spaces, the introduction of living complexes with reduced traffic, and wide green spaces in new functional cities. Under the approving glance of the remaining architects and engineers from GDR times assembled at this lecture, Neudeck underlined that Hoyerswerda *Neustadt* could indeed be seen as an almost perfect realization of precisely this pioneering modernist agenda. She continued to explain in great detail the technological innovations that were either realized or invented in the GDR's prime architectural and urban planning project of the 1960s. There were so many of them because *Neustadt* was the first city worldwide to be erected solely by industrially prefabricated concrete units. In the early 1950s, its predecessor, the GDR's first model city of Eisenhüttenstadt (literally, Iron Hut City, officially Iron Works City, built for the workers of the GDR's main iron mill), formerly known as Stalinstadt (Stalin-City), was still erected in the traditional brick-on-brick method. Its Stalinist design differs tremendously from *Neustadt*'s sober vanguard modernist architecture.

Most members of the auditorium nodded knowingly since several of them had played an active part in *Neustadt*'s erection. The technical language is compelling: 'The 1967 prefabricated roof-element covers 3.70 m … The development of in-factory façade-plastering solved the problem of isolation that had demanded costly, time-consuming scaffolding … The 1980 WBS 70-series, following the older P2 type, was only a short-sighted response to the financial constraints and increasing material scarcity so prevalent in the last decade of the GDR.' Still, the strict implementation of the rules of Bauhaus guidelines endured and was only in later years distorted. Previously, per capita living space, population density, issues of hygiene, social services and general infrastructure solutions were all addressed with, back then, most progressive standards.

The discussion following this thoughtful presentation was unexpectedly emotional. The head of the *Kunstverein* expressed his joy about the rare gathering of so many local experts. He particularly had the old socialist architects in mind, who would usually not attend events organized by the *Kunstverein* due to personal and political differences. He then explained how the idea for this lecture had come about. A small group of people, all part of the current, conservative elite governing Hoyerswerda, were seriously considering proposing Hoyerswerda *Neustadt* to the UNESCO World Heritage Committee for world heritage sites as a prime example of modern industrialized (i.e. prefabricated) architecture and urban planning. The promise of new prestige and novel touristic opportunities related to such a title obviously incorporated yet another strategy to secure Hoyerswerda's future. However, it was ironic that a few members of this group were some of the most active protagonists in *Neustadt*'s initially chaotic and still very damaging deconstruction process.

The construction engineer hired by Hoyerswerda's administration to write the General Integrated Urban Development Concept (*Integriertes Stadtentwicklungskonzept*/INSEK), a concept necessary to receive state funding for further demolitions, spoke on behalf of the group. Although in charge of producing the main framework through which the (admittedly complicated) deconstruction process was to be managed, he started his remarks in all modesty. He said he was only 'a small wheel in the whole machinery' and, like the Lord Mayor from above, 'really just a practitioner, not a visionary'. 'Others might take over the visionary aspects', he claimed, and he welcomed their contributions. As he had already emphasized in a previous interview with me, as the city's main planner he had to adhere to political and economic restrictions as well as practical constraints that made the decision-making process ever more difficult. Still, as he underlined in front of many former architects and engineers, he believed in *Neustadt*'s architectural uniqueness and extraordinary value, and hence was fully committed to proceed with this UNESCO application.

A former *Neustadt* architect in his late sixties – a generation older than this engineer – offered a very critical response to this proposed undertaking. He was, he initially emphasized, 'the last to deny the worth of the architectural and technological achievements of the *Neustadt* planners and architects'. However, he continued, the engineer's statement was most unacceptable. 'Now', he disconcertingly stressed, 'after more than ten years of deconstruction and twenty years of often mediocre postmodern restorations, people in charge of the city's urban reconstruction finally start to acknowledge the treasure that was materialized at their doorsteps! Only now, when more than eighty percent of the initial plan is either deconstructed or, by poor restoration, essentially distorted?' For him, the application was nothing but a farce. The whole post-1989 planning process was conducted incorrectly, as he passionately argued. It was 'headless' and 'without any plan, concept or vision'. In fact, *Neustadt* would have deserved its own urban planner, a professional expert managing and uniting the complex interests at play, preserving its urbanity and modern character as an architectural entity. 'Instead we find especially the city-centre maltreated and torn apart.' In his eyes, the two main landlords' short-term economic interests had ruled the decision-making process for far too long. One result of this was that current planners still do not implement the far preferable deconstruction strategy to 'unbuild' the city from the outskirts towards the centre. In contrast and due to a lack of concerted planning, *Neustadt* and especially its centre were becoming increasingly perforated. In order to preserve the city as an architectural world-class heritage site, other decisions should have been made years ago. To finally pursue its rescue now was much too late.

The atmosphere in the hall became intense. This passionate intervention produced immense awkwardness on all sides. The architect's son tried to concretize his father's ideas, which were quickly refuted by the attacked planning engineer. The son listed the following three points to clarify the mistakes his father intended to address. First, the living complexes' individual characters had been destroyed. Instead of officially imposing a WK design and thus retaining their unity, they now appeared as a hotchpotch of different colours, designs and materials. Second, for economic reasons the city centre's eleven-storey apartment blocks had been most prominently targeted by deconstruction. Overall, they were cheaper to demolish: similar deconstruction costs, more flats deconstructed. This 'razing of the city's crown' seriously questioned Hoyerswerda's material integrity as well as its urban character. The loss of urbanity, for him, was also linked to a fear of a further reduction in quality of life.[3] Nowadays, they could have provided much-needed suitable flats for the growing numbers of elderly inhabitants, who depend on lifts and easy access – a major concern for a shrinking city whose population's average age had almost doubled in the last four decades. Third, the whole process should have followed its founding modern principles, which deserved a centralized and visionary, but also transparent, open and democratic regulatory planning elite. Instead, there was no master plan, nor were there architectural guidelines, and most of the decisions were made without any incorporation of citizens' opinions and other experts' ideas.

In return, the engineer defended his planning strategies and solutions with further practical concerns and the assertion that the people did not need such 'elitist' aspirations. He proclaimed that they *want to live* in individualized apartments – not in the standard blocks of uniformly renovated modernist living complexes. The individually restored buildings, as official statistics apparently indicated, were very popular. Indeed, inhabitants had left the high blocks in the city centre for good reasons. They had thus, as a German phrase has it, 'expressed their opinion with their feet'. Furthermore, there were economic and financial concerns that simply could not accommodate unrealistic visionary ideas like those proposed by the architect and his son. Suddenly, there was no sign of the openness to the visions of others, which the engineer had so dearly underlined before, and it probably did not help that the architect and his son were Dorit's father and brother. He also disguised the fact that people preferred renovated houses simply because such houses promised not to be deconstructed in the near future, not because of their colourful façades. Also, the people living in the centre's apartment houses, as was explained to me later, were of the younger (and thus more mobile) age groups. Finally, the economic argument against other ways of reconstructing the high eleven-storey apartment houses – such as partial deconstruction by only dismantling a few storeys or creating gaps in these otherwise monolithic structures – had been disproven by successful renovation projects in other, more experimental urban regeneration projects (compare Kil 2007).

The head of the *Kunstverein* tried to mediate between the conflicting opinions for a bit longer, but he finally gave up and defended the engineer's cautious strategy. The next day, a critical letter by the architect's son was published in the local newspaper. Apart from that, the UNESCO plan was quickly forgotten. Several months later, in the new version of the INSEK, all mention of the application disappeared. Neither the critique nor *Neustadt*'s proclaimed architectural values were in any particular way taken up again in the months and years thereafter. Despite all conflicts and emotional intensity, the city's urban near future remained evacuated.

This clash amongst Hoyerswerda's architectural experts did not only spring from the confrontation of the old and the new elite, and their diverging deconstruction strategies for Hoyerswerda's shrinkage. It also entailed the confrontation of two different forms of temporal reasoning. Respective groups differ in their relation to – and problematization of – the future, or rather the strategies with which to fabricate or approach this future. As represented by the planning engineer, the new conservative elite then running the city followed a pragmatic approach to the near future, which mirrors Guyer's 'enforced presentism'. This approach positions one's own agency in a network of financial, legal and practical restraints. It is cautious and reactive, and complicates planning practices by circumventing any concrete discussion of the future. Interestingly, in Hoyerswerda, it neglected both the recent postsocialist and the socialist past as well as the near future. In contrast, the former GDR architectural elite built up a more continuous relation between these different periods and were thus able to (re)colonize the city's evacuated near future. They utilized recent traditions and shortcomings of GDR experiences in order to apply them to Hoyerswerda's present problems as well as their potential solutions in the near future. Due to their former expert status, they were confident and competent enough to respond to the city officials' powerful representational as well as material and factual evacuation of the near future. Others would be hardly in the position to challenge this evacuation, which was so convincingly depicted as resulting from given restrictions. In other instances, those currently in charge of the deconstruction process continued to delegitimize citizens' expressions of anger, loss and disagreement with a remark on their 'too personal approach'. These critics were accused of lacking the proper knowledge about the wider context – as I experienced, for instance, with regard to the guidelines for the federal Urban Redevelopment East (*Stadtumbau Ost*) programme, which subsidized deconstruction costs under very specific conditions, such as a detailed INSEK plan. An actual vision, as demanded by the old elite, did still not exist. It had thus far not been discussed in public. Its absence continued to produce new insecurities by leaving the near future as an epistemic domain empty.[4]

With the increase of the visibility of the deconstruction process in almost all parts of *Neustadt*, the term 'shrinkage' finally became widely accepted in 2008/2009. It started to provide an epistemic framework for more critical remarks on the city's management of shrinkage. Critical interventions, like the one described above, started to pose new problems regarding the future. They also revived the local politics of the future. Another architect summarized the problem nicely with the help of a historical example: in the early 1990s, the urban planning decisions implemented by the West German Chief Planning and Construction Officer did not endorse or continue the modern tradition. Rather, she explained, they inscribed 'a post-modern playfulness onto the formerly modern surfaces'. By that, the Chief Planner revealed that he not only failed to understand – or even rejected – the past of these buildings; he was also, on that very ground, incapable of envisioning a future for them – and for the whole city. To voice a critique of the people on power and their evacuation of the near future, based on a different form of temporal reasoning, can be seen as an outcome of temporal flexibility. It shows a certain flexibility because it does not follow the dominant temporal framework. Such alternative forms were often found in Hoyerswerda. Not least because of its evacuation by city officials, the future remained problematized in many different social arenas.

Reclaiming the Future

Gerhard was a former mining engineer. Although over the age of seventy, he was probably one of the most active and jaunty people I met during my fieldwork. He was a member of at least five different clubs and associations, including the *Kunstverein*, the Seniors' Academy and the sociocultural centre. Every time we met, he came up with new ideas on how to improve the world in general and life in Hoyerswerda in particular. Most of his reflections were captured in his countless although often unpublished letters to the local newspaper. His self-understanding found best expression in the often half-ironically repeated old miners' slogan: 'I am a miner – who is better than that?' Gerhard embodied the vanished pride of the GDR's once-official City of Miners and Energy Workers (*Stadt der Berg- und Ernergiearbeiter*). The passionate dedication to the city, to which he had moved in the 1960s, resembled many of my informants' commitment to their hometown. Letters to the newspaper's editors were only one form of expressing it. They were carefully fabricated reclamations of hope, hardly nostalgic, but often as pragmatic as visionary.

Gerhard was a member of *Neustadt*'s *Aufbaugeneration*, that is, the generation that was responsible for the construction of a socialist *Neustadt* in Hoyerswerda, a group of now retired residents who as young adults in the 1950s and 1960s came to Hoyerswerda in order to build the GDR's Second Socialist Model City and the nearby brown coal industrial complex. They saw *Neustadt* growing day by day, waited for their apartment to be finished and helped to erect the city as well as the region's industrial infrastructure. This first *Neustadt* generation later had to witness how the outcomes of their courageous achievements were abandoned, left to decay or demolished. Still, like many other Hoyerswerdians, Gerhard linked the city's contemporary problems to a variety of practical, philosophical and temporal considerations. His main critique of the people in charge of Hoyerswerda's deconstruction process (*Rückbau*) might be summarized in a powerful claim he often ponders on: 'A human without a utopia is not a human!' This claim is a serious challenge to the new, postsocialist elite's non-utopian stance. Gerhard's quote generally implied the somewhat anthropological importance of well-established relationships to the future, maybe similar to philosopher Ernst Bloch's work on hope. Something like Guyer's enforced presentism was thus acknowledged by people like Gerhard. However, it was also – if you wish – *temporally* countered. *Qua* being human, he claimed, we depend on a proper investment in(to) the future – and Gerhard thereby challenged the then-dominant temporal regime of postindustrial decline.

Indeed, if anything, it was the locally shared problematization of the city's arguably still distant future that made up Hoyerswerda's temporal regime of shrinkage, not the evacuation of the near future. Hoyerswerda's future was not only at risk with regard to its cityscape. Shrinkage affected all citizens' future prospects. Due to the fact that the social, cultural, medical, political, educational and economic infrastructures also faced deconstruction, all inhabitants were forced to think about their city's and their personal future. As a result of this, I encountered multiple forms of new future and shrinkage expertise. In all kinds of everyday practices, a variety of strategies of survival and particular tactics of securing a certain quality of life were deployed. Gerhard's demand for a continual investment in the time-to-come was a powerful tool to give such strategies a (new) direction.

Like so many of my friends and informants, he became an expert in this form of temporal agency, especially in his passionate involvement in many sociocultural clubs and associations. The term 'shrinkage' enabled people like Gerhard to name the changes and thus not only passively endure, but also actively reappropriate and manage them. This reappropriation could take many forms, but it always had to target the future.

As part of his strategy of reclaiming a future for Hoyerswerda, Gerhard, for instance, was a founding member of the association Subversions (*Subversionen*) Hoyerswerda, later renamed Urban Redevelopment and Civic Participation Hoyerswerda (*Stadtumbau und Bürgerbeteiligung*, henceforth SuB HY). This association consisted of a small and dedicated group of former architects, planners, engineers and committed citizens. To the Lord Mayor's expressed dismay, it criticized the city officials' deconstruction strategies. However, it also tried to produce new ideas in order to support their work. SuB HY recurrently published contributions to the local newspaper, submitted written suggestions to the Lord Mayor's office and opened a little temporary office and archive in an abandoned shop in *Neustadt*'s city centre. Still, the main reproach by the local government capitalized on the fact that SuB HY had failed to activate the Hoyerswerdian citizenry. Its plans to inspire more inhabitants to actively assist in imagining a future had indeed not taken place in the way intended. This fact ended SuB HY's existence in 2007 after only three years of existence, which Gerhard still remembered with much disappointment. The club challenged the official evacuation of the near future, but without much effect. However, was there really nothing else at stake than an elitist expert argument? Or was the Lord Mayor right in shifting his registers from modernist detailed planning (which was SuB HY's redeployed strategy) to a more affective, but vague vocabulary? To claim like some city officials that Hoyerswerda's general public was simply not interested in Hoyerswerda's future misses the point.

The Future Laboratory (*Zukunftswerkstatt*) of the 2007 'The Third City' project similarly intervened in the public debates about the city's future. It convincingly claimed that Hoyerswerda's future could only be found in consequent redevelopment strategies springing out of its modernist past. Hoyerswerda's former architects and the alternative cultural elite had initiated this art and local history project, whose title refers to the Hoyerswerda emerging after the first presocialist Old and the second socialist New City. In the Future Laboratory, twenty-five young Hoyerswerdians and Dorit, the local architect mentioned above, re-evaluated the socialist past in order to produce a detailed urban planning vision of the near future. This vision entailed several midterm projects developed over the course of a week. It detailed the realization of new forms of communal living and architectural, educational and sociocultural strategies for Hoyerswerda's *Neustadt* – all derived from its socialist-modern heritage. For instance, the project AWaKe (*Autonomer WK* – Autonomous WK) envisaged a whole living complex dedicated to alternative forms of living and the continuous experimentation with social, cultural, architectural, economic and political forms. The inhabitants of this WK were envisioned as being committed to discuss and implement, and if necessary debunk, new ideas about how they wanted to live their lives, organize their community, design their communal spaces and sustain their WK in an experimental way *beyond* restrictions of property rights and potential deconstruction. The project used the distinctively socialist form of a WK and communal property, and gave it a new meaning in and for the future.

The members of the local youth participating in this workshop developed very concise ideas for Hoyerswerda's future as a, yet again, experimental vanguard model city. This demonstration of temporal flexibility – that is, of freely connecting distinct temporal dimensions ('authoritarian' socialist past with 'democratic' postsocialist present) – fostered an otherwise unimagined and unimaginable vision of the near future. The city's socialist past became a resource for approaching the local future in unconventional ways. It helped to re-envision the former socialist-modernist, industrial residential settlement as a new model 'city for living' (*Lebensstadt*). It proposes giving Hoyerswerda a future by transforming it yet again into a city, in which new ideas and forms of life are practised and tried out in – not beyond – the context of shrinkage. The participants hoped the city would be attractive for those working in the region's few remaining industrial hot spots because of its modern functional infrastructure and the possibility for experimenting with new social forms. For them, Hoyerswerda should become a place where the future is continuously created.

In the course of this project, Dorit yet again shifted her rhetoric strategy, this time from 'shaping the process of shrinking' (which followed the one of terminal care) to proactively 'foregoing economic growth' (*Wachstumsverzicht*) – a profoundly different, in the best sense alternative approach to the future. As she said in a 2010 television interview: 'Still, nobody knows what the future will bring here in Hoyerswerda. For sure, we will still and even more prominently shrink and age. These are the pure facts and they don't stimulate much bravery. Nonetheless, we should start to develop a new "culture of life", so that people say, here, in this city, things take place, which do not happen in other, healthy cities!' The inspired television reporter ended the report about yet another Hoyerswerdian art project targeting the city's difficult present with the summary that the prejudices against Hoyerswerda as a city 'without jobs, without people, without culture', indeed without a future, were not true after all. In contrast, 'so much free space for ideas is not to be found anywhere else – and the inhabitants seem to have started to appreciate that'. So did members of Hoyerswerda's citizenry finally develop a new form of temporal reasoning and regain its future?

Conclusion: The Future after Shrinkage

During my fieldwork, Hoyerswerda's future remained a problematic topic in most public discourses and private conversations. However, the local administrative and political elite refrained from recolonizing the city's near future. The concern with the immediate and the constant adaptation of what is left of a plan did prevent particular milieus from reaching out into the future. People in charge, as the Lord Mayor emphasized, did not want to make false promises. They were afraid to dispel people even quicker from the city by revealing what might happen to Hoyerswerda in the near future. The evacuation of the near future produced further insecurities, since personal decision-making could not align with any temporal guidance or directionality.

I nonetheless encountered manifold clashes over – and politics of – the future. Hoyerswerda's former architects and the alternative cultural elite deployed markedly different forms of temporal reasoning and thereby exhibited their ability to evade powerful temporal regimes and move more flexibly in time. They re-evaluated the otherwise disregarded socialist past in order to produce an urban planning vision for the future. This happened, for instance, in the Future Laboratory. However, the efficacy of temporary reappropriations of the near future remained limited. Most of the Laboratory's young participants still left the city and started their higher education elsewhere. None of their daring and concrete ideas has thus far been realized in practice. They remained unheard (or willingly ignored) by Hoyerswerda's current planning experts. Still, they indicated a shift in the approach to the process of shrinkage, a very powerful challenge of the temporal regime, order or framework imposed by drastic postindustrial decline, and in parts executed by the current administrative elite. The challenges against this official evacuation provided examples for the emergence of new and unexpected temporal references, cracks in the broader temporal order dominant in this particular context. This temporal agency or 'bricolage', as Crapanzano (2007) calls it, was the condition for a successful reappropriation of the near future. It gave the present a new direction and thereby allowed for an analysis of a present, whose main character is that it is not enforced.

Accordingly, this chapter has examined different forms of temporal reasoning, which clashed with regard to the evacuated near future. This constitutes one way of opening up the future as an ethnographic object. However, I have thus far not approached the solution to the problem of the future regarding the efficacy of these alternative forms. What can we do about the very low numbers of visitors to the *O-Box*, the lack of public support for SuB HY and the non-realization of the ideas of the Future Laboratory? Clearly, all three of these projects were essential in explicating and establishing a different stance to the future – a stance that was, indeed, new in Hoyerswerda's recent history. And by doing something about the future, that is, in concrete practices targeting the future, these people had, irrespective of their practices' outcomes, indeed reappropriated the future in the present.

I also claim that the reappropriation of the near future and the process of shrinkage was only the first step. The next step was the even more crucial question: what comes after shrinkage? This entails the question about how to deproblematize the future rather than to build up a new enforced relationship to it. Dominic Boyer (2006) grants us insight into the first step. By following the works on post-reunification Germany by Borneman (1992, 1997) and Glaeser (2000, 2001), Boyer detected two significant phases in inner-German national temporal politics: first, the total devaluation of the East German past by West Germans; and, second, the Western gift of a particular form of rehistorization. He then explains that both strategies deny East Germans a say on their own and the nation's future. In turn, he demands a more self-determent 'sense of mastery over one's past and future' (Boyer 2006: 379; also Boyer 2010: 26). In addition, I have shown that due to its novelty, the process of shrinkage remained in itself an East German affair for which there was not much conceptual support to be expected from West Germany. It constituted a very different, uniquely East German postindustrial temporal regime.

Second, and more importantly, in order to regain one's position in the present, my informants had to avoid both enforced presentism *and* what could be seen as the main temporal logic of shrinkage: enforced futurism, the focus of the next chapter. Whereas the former aim was accomplished by reappropriating the near future, the latter aspect could only be changed by going beyond shrinkage's constant and all-pervasive concern with the future and return anew to the present, as shown in Chapter 5. To ask what comes after shrinkage overcomes the dominant temporal regime of decline. The Future Laboratory accordingly proposed concentrating 'on a good life' independent of future concerns; this would be a true 'forgoing of growth', as Dorit had it. For such a strategy, it does not suffice to 'make people passionate' about their city and its future, as the Lord Mayor described it. Rather, the elaboration of present and enduring solutions to very mundane problems of life, ethics, social relations and education were able to shape the process of shrinkage differently, and at the same time concretely pointed beyond it. Many Hoyerswerdians, especially the city officials, did indeed exercise the agency described in Herzfeld's quote from the beginning of this chapter: they denied their and others' agency when they could have fostered it. But the maintenance of their evacuating (non-)take on time and the future ultimately failed. Instead, other Hoyerswerdians exhibited temporal agency by challenging the locally dominant temporal regime with their own, and often surprising, relations to the future.

Notes

1. The quote from the title of this chapter translates as *Hoyerswerda...? – ... hatte mal `ne Zukunft* and is a quote from the 2009 communal art project 'PaintBlock' (*Malplatte*), in whose temporary cafe three big squares painted on the wall invited participants to comment on the following three topics: 'youth', 'Hoyerswerda' and the 'future'. In the square dedicated to 'Hoyerswerda', the only remarks were the one quoted in this chapter's title and '...looks from above like a huge forest with some little houses in it', which criticizes the process of deconstruction and the subsequent decline of urbanity. The comments in the youth section were also telling: '...which youth after all?', '... escapes as long as they can' or 'I stay here!!!' (*Ich bleibe hier!!!*). The future box was suspiciously left empty altogether.
2. One of her most telling interventions was a much-acknowledged newspaper article entitled: 'Is it Possible to Kiss in Hoyerswerda?' In her eyes,

this is what a newly built socialist city should provide: splendid spaces of social interaction, enjoyment and love – not the ever-taller typified apartment blocks then emerging in *Neustadt*.

3. Two female friends in their thirties once remarked jokingly to the loss of urbanity: 'These days, Hoyerswerda feels more like a village than a real city – one can't even properly cheat on one's partner anymore without the whole city noticing immediately.' The loss of population, by the way, also resulted in the closure of the local brothel as it is legally required in Germany when a city's population falls below 50,000 inhabitants.

4. This led me to a remark to the Lord Mayor whilst we were discussing Hoyerswerda's future. I said that it would not even be important what his exact vision of the city's future was. Rather, the simple fact that he had one at all would make a decisive difference. Even if people could then potentially disagree with him, they could still orientate their own thought and practices accordingly.

4

Enforced Futurism/Prescribed Hopes

Affective Politics and Pedagogies of the Future

The Future dimension contains what is feared and what is hoped for.
—Ernst Bloch, *The Principle of Hope*

Following Ernst Bloch's philosophical approach to the 'not-yet' (Bloch 1986 [1959]), this chapter continues the exploration of human relations to the future and focuses on local beliefs in their efficacy. It extrapolates the role affects play in Hoyerswerda's postindustrial economy of knowledge. In contrast to previous chapters, I do not solely focus on explicit forms of temporal reasoning. Rather, I claim that the anticipation of the yet-to-come comprises particular investments of reason *and* affect. These investments are my ethnographic point of access to study the relations between affect and the future. This chapter will scrutinize the transformative logic and actual efficacy of such affective relations. However, analytically, I will use my informants' explicit reasoning about particular affects, the hope they invest in them and their presumed efficacy. Following Nigel Thrift, I embed affects in a thoroughly epistemic framework: I circumvent methodological problems of studying affects by focusing solely on reflections about – and strategic uses of – them as yet another, non-reflective 'form of thinking' (Thrift 2008: 175) about Hoyerswerda and its future.

My concern with affects and the future stems from the common assertion that Hoyerswerda had lost all hope for a better future. This loss was repeatedly expressed in public proclamations such as 'We need a vision for Hoyerswerda!', 'Hoyerswerda does not have any

Figure 4.1 *Graffito, WK 10, 'I love you – Don't go', summer 2008*

future perspectives!' or 'Young people cannot imagine any future here!' In particular, local youth – for many the incorporation of the city's future – were seen to leave the city either because of the proclaimed efficacy of pessimistic representations of Hoyerswerda's future or because of the lack of optimistic knowledge. In response, particular youth projects explicitly targeted the affective character (rather than the concrete contents) of the young generation's knowledge about the city and its future. In a project problematically called 'Youth Has Visions!' (*Jugend hat Visionen!*), local pupils were asked to develop, formulate and publicly present their own optimistic future fantasies and planning visions. In another youth project, 'Letters to Franziska Linkerhand' (*Briefe an Franziska Linkerhand*, in reference to Brigitte Reimann's novel, which has already appeared in the previous chapter), the participants were invited to create visual and textual representations – images, maps, models and literary texts – of Hoyerswerda's future. In what follows, I want to analyse these projects in relation to yet another, intimately related, set of practices dealing with hope.

Intriguingly, with regard to the city as a whole, the Lord Mayor also sought to represent the city's relation to the future more forcefully in affective terms by hiring a marketing firm, which was in charge of producing advertising material such as tourist brochures, leaflets and a city magazine as part of a more elaborate marketing concept. The self-proclaimed aim was to sell Hoyerswerda's future potential more successfully to external investors and to Hoyerswerda's citizens. All of these attempts to win back Hoyerswerda's future aimed at affective effects in order to overcome the current lethargic and pessimist situation of 'no hope': a local youth optimistic about the city and their future in it; thrilled investors; and happy citizens. They thus followed Miyazaki's insight into the method of hope as a method for the 'reorientation of knowledge' (Miyazaki 2004: 5), in this case of affects about Hoyerswerda's future. However, this potentially redirected affect was left unchanged and empty, and the concrete near future therefore also remained evacuated in affective terms. This particular set of actors continued to refrain from the creation of any precise new knowledge and only repeated standard announcements about how Hoyerswerda was a place worth living in. To put it crudely, in this case and in contrast to Miyazaki's account, hope itself was invested with hope. Diffuse affect – not concrete knowledge – was seen as the most promising of tools to secure the city's future. Given the omnipresence of such problems with a representational and/or affective grip on the future, I felt confronted with a form of enforced futurism: a plethora of incitements to produce knowledge about, and affective relations to, the future.

With the help of my ethnographic material, I explore the different ways in which politics, pedagogies and affects interact in specific situations or expressions of enforced futurism. In the first section, I introduce the ethnographic moment, which initially sparked my interest in the politics and efficacy of affects of the future. This discussion of one incident of the local politics of fear is followed by some theoretical remarks about academic conceptualizations of the relationship between affect and the future. Thereafter, I present the two aforementioned pedagogic projects in order to detect a similar logic concerning the efficacy of affective relations to the future in professional marketing and planning practices. I end the chapter by asking whether it is possible to sidestep both enforced presentism and enforced futurism altogether.

Imposed Threat: Affective Politics of the Future

On 27 January 2008, in the first month of my fieldwork in Hoyerswerda, the local administrative and political elite, members of the Association of the Prosecuted of the Nazi regime/Federation of German Anti-Fascists and several pupils from Hoyerswerda's schools gathered at *Neustadt*'s central memorial. The day marked the sixty-third anniversary of the Liberation of the Extermination Camp of Auschwitz and people had assembled for the city's official wreath-laying ceremony. I approached the scenery with fearful anticipation. A couple of weeks before, I had encountered problems with local neo-Nazis (as laid out in Chapter 2) and I was still assessing the actual risk they posed. Due to this commemoration's historical and ideological relevance, I expected some form of right-wing intervention.

I walked around the memorial site, trying to take pictures with my mobile phone for my own documentation. I positioned myself sometimes inside and sometimes outside of the group of those attending the ceremony. Since many of the group did not know me, I felt the need to be seen with the main organizers in order to clarify that my picture taking was of a purely documentary kind. As the pupils partaking in the 'Against Forgetting' project began to recite poems and citations by Holocaust victims, I encountered through my mobile phone's display other observers of the official commemorators. The local neo-Nazis had entered the stage. In groups of three or four, they paraded around the memorial site, hissing statements like 'Lies!' and other proclamations of Holocaust denial. As I turned around, I saw two of them unrolling a large banner, which read 'Stop the Propaganda of Self-proclaimed Democrats!', subtitled 'For Our People's Right of Self-Determination'.[1]

Only Werner Gertler, a courageous citizen in his mid eighties, dared to intervene. He approached the group and asked them politely to leave. The Deputy Mayor had rushed away to inform the police.

All others pretended not to notice them, proceeding as normally as possible. The arrival of police forces made the neo-Nazis leave the grounds, but not before a last encounter between one of them and one of the attendant citizens. Having noticed that a neo-Nazi started taking pictures of those attending, the citizen, a committed school-teacher in his late forties, quickly got out his own mobile phone and started 'shooting back'. This encounter puzzled me: a weird digital fight of a young neo-Nazi and a teacher taking photographs of each other. I was to understand later that a potential reproduction of the representation of the respective other entailed an inherent claim of power over the opponent's future, an affective imposition of threat.

Let me unpack the logic of this peculiar event in order to show the affective power that was claimed via the storage and poten-tial future use of (personal) knowledge. Importantly, the neo-Nazi wanted to document the lay-participants, not the persons of official standing whose personal details were easily publicly accessible. This was part of a wider strategy to assemble information about political opponents.[2] Having secured this visual information, the neo-Nazis would then search for the names and addresses of those depicted and publish them online together with the picture, as one technique of their politics of fear. In the worst-case scenario, the depicted ends up being listed on some website list of their main local enemies – including details such as telephone numbers or one's car's number plate. Several of my informants had already had to deal with such threats. One anti-Fascist friend of mine faced a huge graffito showing his full name and the menace 'We will get you!' The logic of threat grants the knowledge collected in the present a certain efficacy in the future. As a source of fear over those whose information was held, this knowledge should make them afraid in the future and should stop their anti-Fascist actions. Otherwise, they had to confront the possibility of harm being inflicted upon them – anywhere and at any time in the future. It rendered the affected people vulnerable, violable and assailable at any future moment. The brave teacher was in this moment visually captured as a targeted person and encountered the initial act of harm, of being constituted as a subject to potential future neo-Nazi violence.

The teacher's own reasoning in 'shooting back' follows a similar logic. As I understood him in subsequent discussions, he did not want the neo-Nazis to succeed in their claim to power over the par-ticipants' futures. As a second thought, the pictures he took could help as evidence if state institutions were to prosecute the neo-Nazis. They could do so, he presumed, on the basis of Holocaust denial, which is prohibited by German law. He and another citizen were seriously debating bringing forth such charges. The threat he produced whilst reclaiming situational agency was also aimed at building up an atmosphere of fear by claiming power over the opponents' futures, their activities, thoughts, senses of security, feelings, etc. A method of fear drove these practices, enforcing a redirection of future actions. How did this logic of the neo-Nazis' politics of fear differ from other affective claims on, and relations to, the future? What is the specific relation between knowledge, affect and the future?

Affect and the Future

As laid out previously, Barbara Adam's presentist claim that '[a]ny reality that transcends the present must itself be exhibited in it' (Adam 1990: 38) underlines that in any present the future – perhaps even more so than the past – depends on being represented. Affects are an essential part of this representational work, even if they are by definition nonrepresentational. As Thrift claims, affect is just another 'form of thinking, often indirect and nonreflective true, but thinking all the same' (Thrift 2008: 175). For him, it is 'a different kind of intelligence about the world' (ibid.), not just a matter of the irrational or sublime. Even though affects 'are largely non-representational' (ibid.), they were still an integral part of Hoyerswerda's local economy of knowledge about the future. On the one hand, affects like hope and fear exhibit a certain futurity, that is, the specific ways in which they related to the future (for example, hope wishes for a future being better than the present, whereas fear is afraid of the future being worse than the present).[3] On the other hand, affects were often intimately linked to particular representations of the future, being part and parcel of their qualities, social meaning and efficacy.

In recent social science literature on the future, hope played a significant role (for example, Anderson 2002, 2006a, 2006b, 2007; Crapanzano 2003; Miyazaki 2004, 2010; Kleist and Jansen 2016). Although my interest was initially sparked by the aforementioned example of the politics of fear, I subsequently concentrated on the role that hope (rather than fear) was to play in the city's negotiations of the future. Although the dramatic socioeconomic changes of 'shrinkage' translated into a loss of hope and the future, the local imaginary remained indeterminate about how it did so, and in which order. Some Hoyerswerdians said that at first the future was lost (no jobs, closures of public institutions, friends' or relatives' outmigration) and then hope disappeared; others underlined that actually at first people gave up their hope and stopped believing in Hoyerswerda's future, then, in the form of a self-fulfilling prophecy, they decided to leave and thus accelerated the city's decline. The latter logic, or local theory of hope, was usually deployed when explaining the youths' emigration, bequeathing to the loss of hope the primary explanatory power of the process of shrinking. Such presumed loss in affective attachment to the city sparked a variety of affective responses, which I describe subsequently as the imposition of hope. Local hopes in good affect mirror academic hopes about the efficacy of affect in general and hope in particular (compare Hemmings' 2005 critique of Massumi and Sedgwick). Local practitioners targeted the production and dissemination of hope in a variety of practices. They intended to 'engineer' (Masco 2008) and distribute[4] affect in relation to particular representations of Hoyerswerda and its future. In local 'affective economies' (Ahmed 2004), specific affects were the explicit targets of particular practices, in which their 'transmission' (Brennan 2004) was not just happening as such, but was intended and socially negotiated.

However, the imposition of affect did not always work as straightforwardly as intended. As shown in the previous chapter, the actual substitution of the concrete modern and reasoned reappropriation of the near future for an affective, nonconcrete hopeful outreach into the distant future might suddenly become dominated by dystopian affects of fear and despair rather than hope. In such cases, affect's potency was not just a hopeful, liberating one – which is the one usually given to it by scholars such as human geographer Ben Anderson, who sees hope as disclosing 'a point of contingency within a present space-time', producing 'a renewed feeling of possibility' (both Anderson 2006a: 744; see also Bloch 1986 [1959]; Anderson 2002). Conversely, in Hoyerswerda hope was foremost a technology of power, a tool, which was put to political use. Hence, the affective (re)appropriation of the future took the often straightforwardly engineered form of what I call enforced futurism or prescribed hope. In such cases, hope failed to foster the new, the emergent or not-yet-become – and thus strongly contradicted current academic hopes such as that of Anderson. I approach hope and other future-orientated affects as objects of social negotiation, underlining the politics and pedagogies they comprise. As Hemmings (2005) underlines, affect is not the autonomous force some theorists wanted it to be and it should never be thought of as existing outside of social meanings (compare also Thrift 2008: 176). How then was affect produced, circulated, negotiated and brought to bear in a city of 'no future' – and with what consequences?

In Hoyerswerda, a constant, recurrent and omnipresent concern with the future produced an endless variety of epistemic and affective relations to the future. Since the future does not – or, in Bloch's determinist framework, does 'not yet' – exist, the relationship between the present and the future is often somewhat awkward.[5] As Rabinow states: 'Although our times abound in futurologists, prophets, and prognosticators, it is hard, Luhmann sarcastically observes, to take them seriously as we actually have very little sense of what a future not yet visible in the present would look like in any detail' (Rabinow 2007: 57). In modernist times, the relationship that people were supposed to have to the future was one of risk and calculation, of rational reasoning. In postmodernist times, the matter of affect gained further prominence worldwide. This is one of the reasons why the Lord Mayor endorsed and evoked affects instead of providing clearcut plans and strategies, following the aforementioned Antoine Saint-Exupery quote: 'If you want to build a ship, don't drum up people together to collect wood and don't assign them tasks and work, but rather teach them to long for the endless immensity of the sea.' Accordingly, anticipatory representations of, or powerful claims on, the future not only involved specific knowledge practices (forms of explication, the rhetorical use of particular tropes and narratives, and the deployment of discursive and visual modes of representation), they also entailed particular affects, feelings and emotions (hope, fear, suspicion, concern and boredom, vague gut feelings, sentiments and expectations). The politics done with such affects, I argue, established what I refer to as enforced futurism.

As Anderson underlines, distinct anticipatory practices produce 'different epistemic objects through which future possibilities and potentialities are disclosed, objectified, communicated and rendered mobile (such as scenarios, trends, forecasts, predictions, signals, plans and roadmaps)' (Anderson 2007: 158). In the ethnographic example given at the beginning of this chapter, a powerful claim on the future entailed pictures taken with mobile phone cameras. The following examples comprise touristic material, urban development plans and particular artworks. I investigate their specific politics and pedagogies of hope and optimism as well as their actual and acclaimed efficacy. The efficacy of representing a not-yet-better future, apparent in these youth projects and marketing strategies, depended 'on affect because of its capacity to self-cause a change in a body's capacity to affect and be affected' (ibid.: 159).

Knowledge per se would not or had not done the job thus far. But there was more to that: affective politics and pedagogies targeted defined groups of people (political opponents, local youth, the electorate and potential investors) and aimed to bestow specific affects/ knowledge on them. They activated the affective dimension and meanwhile reduced actual and practical future contents to superficial, feelgood slogans. The following sections ask what happens if that imposition of affect fails in enforcing a particular relation to the future. What happens when these impositions of affect fail to establish intended affective predispositions?

Prescribed Optimism: The Pedagogies of Enforced Futurism

The annual wreath-laying ceremony was only one of the many ways with which the youth project 'Against Forgetting' attempted to educate the local youth about the Nazi past. Other pedagogical techniques included the encounter with historical witnesses and day trips to concentration camps and thematic exhibitions. With their help, the organizers intended to bestow knowledge *and* affects about the past upon the future generation. This involved certain strategic implementations of consternation, compassion and sympathy, perhaps even shame and guilt. The memories of these pedagogical events should have guaranteed that the participating children remained critical, precautious and vigilant. Having experienced such affectively loaded places, situations and representations of history, it was hoped that the participants would resist future neo-Nazi atrocities, and their contemporary lures and false promises. By acquiring and internalizing the right knowledge, the local youth should learn from the past for the future. However, the belief in pedagogy – that is, here a belief in the efficacy of knowledge – was not limited to projects targeting the past. There were similar youth projects in Hoyerswerda concerning the future and following the same affective logic. Their organizers believed that once the youth is endowed with the right knowledge and subsequent affect about their hometown's future – not the bleak demographic forecasts of regional and national media – they would be able to finally imagine their personal future in Hoyerswerda. With new hopes and proper knowledge of their chances, they might be prevented from moving away and solely imagining their future elsewhere. I present two projects that each capitalized on the efficacy of affective representations of the future.

The club The City's Future (StadtZukunft e.V., henceforth *StadtZukunft*) consisted of approximately a dozen local entrepreneurs. On their website, they described Hoyerswerda's dramatic demographic changes rather pragmatically as a 'loss of regional human capital' and local youth, in turn, as a decisive 'economic factor'. As they often debated in their weekly meetings in one of the restaurants in the Old City, most members feared that their city, as much as the whole of East Germany, would soon even more forcefully face the predicted shortage of qualified trainees and employees. They were increasingly anxious for young people to stay and support their businesses. In their meanwhile traditional annual youth projects, it was in particular the well-educated youths who were encouraged to envision their local prospects and thereby stop Hoyerswerda's further decline and shrinkage. Since the region's future was usually – if at all – depicted in dystopian terms, this was not an easy endeavour. With the help of this youth project, participants should have acquired positive knowledge about and affective relations to the local future. The least the organizers wanted to achieve, as one of their most committed members emphasized, was that the participants gave Hoyerswerda a chance as a future option. They wanted to counter the self-fulfilling prophecies of negative visions about Hoyerswerda's future and their transformative effects.

The project was insistently called 'Youth Has Visions!' (*Jugend hat Visionen!*). In it, the organizers asked young people to develop ideas for Hoyerswerda's future – for their hometown's sake as much as for their personal futures. This strategy pursued two aims: first, the production of *Heimat*-feelings – a feeling to be at home in the region, which the local youths presumably lacked; and, second, an understanding of the actual future chances they had in Hoyerswerda. Each year in autumn, the organizers approached local schools. In the years I attended the preparations, there was, unfortunately, already a poor turnout and schools were not easily persuaded of this project's worth. For their respective contact teachers, the members of the *StadtZukunft* thus developed a variety of project proposals in case the pupils needed some help with their ideas. In 2009, the pupils were asked to choose one of the following subject areas: regional touristic futures; renewable energies; marketing and external communication; Hoyerswerda's industrial past; *Hoyersfiction* (i.e. descriptions of fantasies of the future with what the organizers referred to as 'real roots' in the city);[6] and attractive future jobs portraits, for which personal help by the *StadtZukunft* members was explicitly offered. The individual projects should have each targeted only one aspect of the local future. The desire was that each project should evolve around novel touristic products, marketing strategies or visionary practices. In this entrepreneurial approach to shrinkage, ideally, product developments happened in cooperation with local business partners in order to connect – as stated on their website in similarly economic terms – the future 'job supplier' (employer) and 'job consumer' (employee).

The project was part of a more elaborate network of regional vocational orientation projects, which tried to position school leavers more quickly and efficiently in the regional economy. This required indicating potential personal paths into the future. To name just a few events emerging from this network: Girls' Day and Boys' Day took place around 8 March, International Women's Day, at which pupils of both sexes were encouraged to explore jobs traditionally perceived as jobs of the other gender; at least once a year at a job and vocational training fair (*Zukunftsmarkt* – Future Market), most regional companies as well as nearby universities and technical colleges advertised their offers; one of the local grammar schools had a Pupils' Agency for Early Job Orientation (*Hoyerswerdaer Schüleragentur zur Beruflichen Frühorientierung*); and, finally, there was the longstanding, scientifically supervised project for transitional management called Fit For Life (*Fit fürs Leben*), which was supervised and conducted by the West German Freudenberg Foundation and the Regional Work Team for Education, Democracy and Life Perspectives (*Regionale Arbeitsstellen für Bildung, Demokratie und Lebensperspektiven e.V.*). Transitional management, in their understanding, tried to ease the transitions from one life phase to the other by actively assisting respective children, youth and young adults.[7] Arguably, as long as the economic situation did not change, there would not be more job perspectives, despite the grand pedagogical efforts being put into place. Nevertheless, these efforts aimed at affective outcomes and a more general change of attitude. As a self-proclaimed 'exile-Hoyerswerdian' had it in one of the (then only two) entries in the *StadtZukunft*'s online guestbook, the 'Youth has Visions!' project is 'important, and perhaps it really does help … I left Hoyerswerda in a time when there were no visions for young Hoyerswerdians'.

The entrepreneurial take on providing young Hoyerswerdians with concrete knowledge about and affective relations to their own future in the region initially deployed – expectedly – the instrument of competitiveness. One could claim that it did so in order to affectively create more commitment, passion and dedication. At the first 'Youth Has Visions!' projects, the groups' results were therefore evaluated and ranked. Since this seemed to have caused too much disappointment, rankings were later abandoned. Still, the projects' result demonstrations were the main event, at which all groups tried to stand out in front of other participants, their teachers, friends and the *StadtZukunft* members. In the 2008 competition, the presentations included a virtual promotional tour through the emerging Lusation Lake District, whose 'heart' Hoyerswerda officially claimed to be(come) (as the head of *StadtZukunft* said in his moderation of the project presentation: 'This group already allows us a glimpse into the much desired future'); a musical about the immediate future after leaving school and finding one's way in life; and a short film about the locally much-endorsed inventor of computers, Konrad Zuse, and his years in Hoyerswerda, which was to be put on sale for future visiting tourists. The year before, there was a similarly diverse range: the installation of sculptures as an artful regeneration of the old city's high street to make it more attractive for shoppers; new business communication strategies involving new technologies and an overall outreach to the local youth; the 'DreamCity Hoyerswerda' project, which assembled a variety of concrete wishes for the city's desired future in the form of visual and textual material; and the musical *Hoywatch 2027*.

The last contribution was a witty thought experiment about a school reunion in 2027, depicting the performing class on a return to Hoyerswerda twenty years after their prom. The play simultaneously deployed and ironically mocked a dystopian vision of Hoyerswerda's future. It started by showing the former pupils standing around a lawn, which marked the place where their (by then) closed-down and demolished school used to be, chatting about the good old days, of which no material remains existed anymore. They then went on a city tour, on which they had to move their – by then already quite senile – former teacher around in a wheelchair. *Neustadt*'s central square looked deserted and the shopping centre was empty. On their way, the class encountered a young anarchist punk handcuffed to a former socialist apartment house. He was protesting against its demolition. It was – as a banner clarified – 'the last of its kind'. After their tour, they had problems finding a local bar for a farewell drink. The one bar remaining in town only served water, since the severely aged population could no longer drink alcohol due to their ridiculous amounts of medication. At the end of the play, the former pupils went on their way to their new homes, leaving Hoyerswerda as a sleepy small town behind. Dystopian in character, this play drew a quite concrete picture of Hoyerswerda's near future. The constant use of irony countered its pessimistic contents, but it remained a pessimistic vision. The 'Youth Has Visions!' organizers thus could still pride themselves on inspiring future visions, although whether this kind of vision was the one they aimed for remains questionable. What, then, if the pedagogy of the future, this enforced futurism, failed to produce the intended outcome?

The pedagogical logic of 'Youth Has Visions!' did ensure that the participants in one way or another related to the local future. Apart from the projects' imaginative contents, this was intended to happen via the imposition of a sense of hope. The power that was (rather defiantly) claimed over local youths' imaginaries, affects and ideas promised a change in their predicted decisions, and hence a chance of the city's long-term survival. If it could not prevent them from going, the project would at least, as the club's chairperson once put it, 'make their return mentally possible'. The second youth project followed the same logic, but used different techniques – derived from the realm of art and literature – to spark similar affects of hope and other affective relations to the future. Both projects were embedded in the all-pervasive problematization of the future, for which the emigrating youth had become the main symbol by literally embodying the endangered survival of the city.

The triennial project 'Letters to Franziska Linkerhand' was first initiated in 2008. It commemorated Brigitte Reimann's seventy-fifth birthday, as well as her life in and work around Hoyerswerda, where she had moved as a young writer in 1960. The organizing *Kunstverein*, introduced in Chapter 3, underlined her work's timeliness and importance for contemporary debates on the city's future. The organizers proclaimed that her most famous novel *Franziska Linkerhand*, which depicts a young architect and her problems during *Neustadt*'s construction period, 'moves each young generation anew'. Hence the project's title: participants were asked to engage with this young, courageous and critical protagonist, perhaps in the form of letters. Due to Reimann's passionate, committed and intelligent approach, the organizers thought that what was valid for the time of 'construction' (*Aufbau*) could be as valid for the period of 'deconstruction' (*Rückbau*).

As in 2008, the participants in 2011 were asked to use Reimann's literary texts in order to create a new stance on their hometown's present and envision new possibilities for its future. The tasks given to the participants were strictly hopeful and optimistic. They included writing letters, poems or other texts about 'one's favourite place in Hoyerswerda' or about 'one's own thoughts, wishes and expectations of cities and urban life' more generally. Participants could also paint, draw, assemble a collage or construct three-dimensional models of Hoyerswerda's future. As anticipatory objects, they materialized the immaterial relationship to the future. During a public presentation, an independent expert jury selected the best works. The winner was awarded a voucher for the main shopping centre, which hosted a temporary exhibition of most of the submitted art objects.

However, the project's inherent logic can be challenged in manifold ways. As became apparent at the 2008 award ceremony, participating youth did not always present optimistic, feelgood images of the future. Instead, negative images of Hoyerswerda's present as much as dystopian visions of its future were regularly produced. The project thus only partially and temporarily succeeded in prescribing a newly emergent, positive content in contrast to the widely mediated negative imagery.

One reason for this could be that the youth's ideas for Hoyerswerda's future sometimes simply mimicked already-established and very common notions of the city's future potentials. For example, a miniature model of Hoyerswerda presented by ninth-grade pupils uncannily followed the city's official economic development strategy with its (postmodern and neoliberal) focus on shopping and tourism. It depicted an even bigger shopping centre, a variety of new touristic attractions and extensive accommodation for tourists, repeating the city administration's own hopes for Hoyerswerda's future as 'the heart of the Lusatian Lake District'. With a similar focus on tourism, Nadja, another participant, composed a poem describing her relationship to the future as it developed in this project thus: 'We people of the twenty-first century are very curious / because we think full of optimism and hope / about an even more beautiful and inhabitable Hoyerswerda and / the miracle of the Lusation Lake District'. Other participants even exceeded official demolition strategies regarding the New City by suggesting the complete deconstruction of all higher buildings and replacing them with smaller private property developments: a suburb as city centre. They also – like official urban development plans – argued for the creation of more parks and green spaces, which they believed would attract tourists as much as shoppers to Hoyerswerda. Even the project's logic was wholeheartedly embraced and reproduced. Saskia, for instance, stipulated: 'The city council should encourage local youth to produce more ideas, so that more people decide to stay in Hoyerswerda.'

The young participants also advocated more meeting points for local youth in the form of a new youth clubhouse or a bowling centre (which both already existed, but remained unacknowledged). Otherwise, they proclaimed, 'there is simply nothing that keeps people in Hoyerswerda'. In the elaborate explanation of another future model of the city, the young participants even reproduced older generations' reproaches against local youth, describing the typical Hoyerswerdian teenager as 'constantly loitering on the streets'. In turn, another group's idea of a recreation centre was explained with a statement about the old generations; in such a centre, 'even the old people would find fun in life again'. Despite the hopeful accounts of Hoyerswerda's touristic future, I also encountered much bleaker anticipatory accounts of the city's future, such as 'nobody wants to live in our city anymore' or 'Hoyerswerda is a doter's city. What is going to happen when all those old people are dead in a few years time? What will then happen to Hoyerswerda?' The participants' represen- tations of the future replicated already-existing tropes, speculations and proclamations about the city's present and future – pessimistic and optimistic, fearful and hopeful ones. Positive ones mirrored the city's official take on the future; negative ones were common currency in most public discourses. Both are reproduced in this project. However, what did the project then finally enforce: 'hope' or 'no hope'?

Perhaps the answer is 'both', as the following reaction to the project underlines. The head of the local Municipal Enterprise for Culture tried to seriously implement the critical and unhopeful contents of the youth's statements into the city's official Cultural Development Plan. She turned the participants' pessimistic, critical and dystopian takes into a source of hope, underlining the project's actual efficacy. As she put it in a work meeting after the project's grand finale: 'All submitted works bare witness of an intensive examination of the topic. They reassure us in regard of Hoyerswerda's future, because these youngsters are everything but disinterested. Alert and self- confident young people grow up here, who also articulate unpleas- ant truths; truths which hurt, but whose articulation only makes the future possible.' Instead of countering the youth's pessimistic rep- resentations of Hoyerswerda and its future with the production of polished positive accounts, she included them as valid toolkits for fostering a better future, despite the fact that some dystopian rep- resentations left hardly any space for such a constructive approach.

However, as a matter of fact, the 'Letters to Franziska Linkerhand' project's aim of 'detecting or retrieving prospects for Hoyerswerda's future', as one local journalist put it, still factually failed: young people continued to leave the city. As he rightfully put it (even if still in favour of the project's pedagogical logic), 'future ideas cannot be forced into existence. They have to be encouraged and fostered in an age as young as possible'. The local theories about the efficacy of affect remained the same as in this chapter's first ethnographic example of the local politics of fear: knowledge about and affect for the future promised power over it. As this statement implies, this imposition should even start earlier. The kids should ideally be taught all through their childhood about the worth of living in Hoyerswerda – an ongoing imposition of the right affect about and relationship to Hoyerswerda and its future

As the *StadtZukunft*'s 'Youth Has Visions!' project, this literary and art competition aimed at the creation of *Heimat*-feelings, of a deeply engrained belonging to Hoyerswerda (compare James 2012). Whereas ideas of marketing strategies and product developments dominated the 'Youth Has Visions!' project, the Brigitte-Reimann-Competition deployed forms of writing, painting, sculpturing and photographing, as well as formats derived from architecture and urban planning. Both projects incited the creation of knowledge about and affective relations to the local future, securing the propensity of participants to change their own view on Hoyerswerda, that is, to affect their hometown's internal reputation against all external prejudices. The efficacy of proper future knowledge was seen to open up the possibility for – and even potentially secure – their remaining in or return to Hoyerswerda. Influenced by vastly depoliticizing logics of marketing and advertisement, the 'Youth Has Visions!' organizers described their strategy as changing all citizens' self-perception, which had long suffered from the widely mediated derogative perceptions of Hoyerswerda. To prevent the latter's negative performative effects, both clubs proposed the production of other images, visions and representations of Hoyerswerda's future, which they claim were more accurate, more real, and more positive and optimistic. Interestingly, the *StadtZukunft* members' project ultimately failed. It was cancelled in 2009 as many teachers and the organizers themselves were dissatisfied with its outcome. One feels forced to conclude that either they had lost their own hope in their future pedagogies or the youth had altogether lost its visions.

The project organizers of yet another project targeting the youth and the local future, the Future Laboratory (compare Chapter 3), had come to deploy a different logic in their attempt at influencing the local youth's relationship to the future. They redefined their initial aim of making the youth stay into an acceptance of their necessary decisions. As one of them put it: 'We have accepted the process of shrinkage and we know we cannot reverse it. But if the young Hoyerswerdians irrevocably have to go, then it is our duty to provide them with an inspiring adolescence and with as many opportunities as possible, so that they in their own futures elsewhere will be able to look back at where they came from with pride and self-confidence.' This rather presentist approach deproblematizes the youth's future decisions and thereby the process of shrinkage. Although its logic still worked on an affective level, it granted the knowledge of, and the affective relations to, Hoyerswerda and its future a very different efficacy.

In the following section, I present a last format of affective impositions regarding the city's future with a special focus on the deployment of discursive visual tropes. These tropes embodied the hopeful wish that if one had the right knowledge for and about the future, one could solve the city's contemporary problems. In this example, the hope in knowledge was more a hope in the right planning strategies, expert knowledge, development plans, and marketing and advertisement efforts. Before, I used my ethnographic material to make the links between affect and its social production, dissemination and imposition, and to look at the pedagogies of future affects; now I return to the relationship between affect, the political and urban governance.

Advertising for the Future: The Efficacy of 'Affective Images' and Hopeful Knowledge

> The irony is that the [East Germans] apparently took these dreams of a better and more prosperous world more seriously than the [West German] state ever expected, so much so that the [German] government was ultimately sued for false advertising.
> —Paul Betts in D. Berdahl, *The Social Life of Postsocialism*

In Hoyerswerda, it is widely believed that if it had not been for the 1991 xenophobic attacks, the city would have faced a different future altogether. Although people know that the technological modernization of the nearby brown coal industrial complex and the resulting dramatic loss of jobs in the region were the actual reasons for Hoyerswerda's unprecedented shrinkage, there was still some belief that the media coverage of the atrocities of 1991 had prevented an economic recovery by keeping external investors away from the city. Hoyerswerda's reputation – or *Image*, as Germans say using the English expression – as a Nazi, prefab and shrinking city was seen to be detrimental by all accounts. The same efficacy, in contrast, is granted to a better image/reputation, but with hopeful implications: a better image might solve the city's problems with the future. It could make people stay and attract external investments, tourists and new citizens. What was the logic attached to this belief in the efficacy of a city's image? Miyazaki (2010) has already drawn attention to the link between hope and neoliberalism. I want to extend these insights with an exploration of local theories of the efficacy – as well as the official impositions – of hopeful knowledge. I at first unpack the bad reputation Hoyerswerda is seen to suffer from.

The terrible events of September 1991 produced a plethora of articles, photographs and other media coverage that not only travelled all across Germany, but also gained some prominence worldwide. The visual combination of socialist apartment houses, frightened asylum seekers and drunken, bawling normal citizens proved to be more than convincing in shaping Hoyerswerda's new image as a *Nazitown*. It was quickly accompanied with visual material from other xenophobic attacks in East Germany. Since Hoyerswerda was the first city of the former GDR where such right-wing violence occurred, it quickly became the symbol for what was taken to be typical East German intolerance and xenophobia. In effect, people from Hoyerswerda faced all kinds of negative reactions when meeting people from other places in Germany. One of my informants mentioned that just a few months after the event, she was refused service at a petrol station near Leipzig when the owner saw the number plate showing the initials HY for the district of Hoyerswerda. Twenty years later, people still earned derogatory remarks and immediate references to 1991 when mentioning their hometown. As a result, many of my friends refused to name Hoyerswerda as their hometown and instead claimed their origin to be 'in Lusatia', 'near Dresden' or 'in Eastern Saxony'. Despite its obvious superficiality and reductive nature, Hoyerswerda's negative image had not lost its efficacy. As a powerful representational form, it endured in time, continuously (re-)activated in media and other practices. More positive and accurate representations of the city, more akin to most Hoyerswerdians' personal experiences, were hard to position against it. The image of 'right-wing Hoyerswerda' became part of the expected, unquestioned knowledge about Hoyerswerda. Only further negative images could claim a place alongside it.

One of the other negative reputations attached to Hoyerswerda was that of the East German *Platte*, the socialist apartment houses made out of prefabricated concrete units. As seventeen-year-old Mira in the 'Letters to Franziska Linkerhand' project put it: 'Isn't this, what the city needs: people who are interested in her and her citizens, and who offer a possibility to (re)present her beautiful sides. A chance to get away from the Prefab-image.' The socialist apartment houses and settlements more generally suffered from a bad reputation post-1989, especially since dominant West German discourses associated them with social housing and its corresponding negative connotations. After the Berlin wall came down, the national government preferred to fund the building of detached and semidetached housing, promoting, as it was called, 'more individualized forms of living'. Those able to afford it moved out of their flats and into private property. The effect of this concrete and widely propagated bad image was the accelerated social differentiation and disintegration, contributing to an ever worse reputation of the *Neustadt*'s prefab houses and living districts.

In Hoyerswerda, the bad image of prefab housing was combined with a sense of being stuck that came to characterize many small cities, towns and rural regions all over the world. In contrast to urban centres, life at the periphery suddenly seemed less 'liveable' (*lebenswert*). This third 'image' included repercussions of the process of shrinkage and of a presumed lack of urbanity. The problems of social decline, demographic change and physical demolition all questioned Hoyerswerda's existence as a city. The current negative visual images of dilapidating socialist apartment houses, abandoned playgrounds, the infamous group of grey-haired pensioners with their walking frames, and bored and loitering youth were widely disseminated throughout Germany. As 'affective images',[8] they fostered the sense of 'no future', 'no hope' and utter decay.

Hoyerswerdians were acutely aware of the affective danger posed by media coverage. They were therefore extremely suspicious when it came to interactions with external journalists. Although journalists (as much as academics) were greeted with the hope that their potentially good representations would have positive effects upon the city's future, there was also always the fear that journalists would yet again reproduce old stereotypes and misrepresentations, and that these misrepresentations would yield further negative consequences. Every translocal article was therefore carefully scanned for such images of decline and accordingly judged for its potential harm or benefit for the local future. At the end of my fieldwork, several journalists of international and national newspapers and TV stations flocked to the city on the occasion of the public announcement of Hoyerswerda being Germany's fastest-shrinking city. In response, one informant, who was recurrently interviewed and represented in such articles, remarked: 'Well, who cares. All these articles don't change anything to the better for us after all, do they?' Indeed, for the practical concerns of his everyday and professional life, there was no immediate benefit from even the most positive reports. However, the valid critique of the efficacy of these media pieces did not eliminate broader representational concerns. Why then all the affective fuss, all these future concerns and presumptions about their efficacy?

German discursive tropes explicate the intimate relations between knowledge and the domain of the anticipatory, the expected and the feared. There was hope invested in such tropes and their efficacy. For instance, in the 'Letters to Franziska Linkerhand' project, seventeen-year-old Saskia suggested that 'the city council should choose another city as an exemplar, which has already stopped or at least positively altered outmigration'. The word she uses for exemplar is *Vorbild*, literally a 'pre-image', an image held before oneself with the intention to follow it. German governmental planning technologies deploy a different 'image', which is to relate to the future: the *Leitbild* (a 'leading image' or general master development plan). All cities in East Germany had to produce such a *Leitbild* in order to be eligible for federal funding. Many Hoyerswerdians claimed that their city's government had not yet created a coherent *Leitbild*, otherwise Hoyerswerda would have regained its future prospects already. The most recent draft for the *Leitbild Hoyerswerda 2025* concept confirmed the definition of a *Leitbild* as a 'long-term strategic conceptual action plan' (*langfristiges Strategie- und Handlungskonzept*). In order to underline the affect invested in such knowledge (mostly cloaked in visual tropes), I describe its 2011 version, extrapolating its strong marketing logic.

As the *Leitbild*'s editors underlined (with all emphases added), the *Leitbild* answered crucial 'future-questions' such as 'How is Hoyerswerda going to *look* like in 2025?', which, they presumed, required a 'primary city-idea and -*vision*'. This vision would be created using '*focus* groups', which create 'modules of *visions*', including 'trend-based future *images*'. A Leit-'*bild*' was therefore '*visionary*' and realistic at the same time. It consists of '*visions* and guidelines'. This visual approach to knowledge was intertwined with marketing rhetoric. For instance, the editors asked: 'Is there an integrative leit-idea to make our city interesting for citizens, tourists and investors?' They claimed that the *Leitbild* will help 'limber up the city *and* the business location for the challenges of the future'. For them, 'urban and economic development' were one and the same. The difference between citizens, investors and tourists disappeared.

In modernity, such belief in knowledge and particularly in knowledge about the future (i.e. a form of knowing in imaginary, representational and visual form) was dominant, as was the belief in its efficacy. Anna Tsing frames this characteristic of modern knowledge practices as follows: 'Stories of the Enlightenment often pair knowledge and vision, in two senses: the privileging of the sense of sight, and the importance of planning' (Tsing 2005: 81). For example, the iconic vision from space onto the blue planet 'has energized knowledge of the globe by condensing it in a friendly visual icon and normalizing its futurist aspirations' (ibid.). In postmodern times, visual representations influence the efficacy of knowledge by increasing its affective potency. In a similar vein, Brian Massumi states that 'affect is central to an understanding of our information-and-image-based late capitalist cultures' (quoted in Anderson 2006a: 733). For him and other affect theorists, such affects like hope allow 'an over-spill of virtual in actual' (ibid.). If we follow that line of thought, then affects, which are related to the future, spill over into the future from the different presents, in which there are deployed, in form of the effects they have on the future. How can future affects have concrete effects?

Crucial for the advertisement firm's strategy was the redirection of the city's marketing concept. For that, they urged for more and better knowledge and its more efficient communication: 'we have to know in Hoyerswerda how we position ourselves internally and externally'. As they put it, mirroring the pedagogical projects' logic discussed above, this included internally a 'better communication with the youth about which economic potentials in the region are in place for vocational training, staying here and coming back'. For external communication, the 'city-marketing' also promised short-term success. This underlines that, for the firm, urban development was 'not just planning and construction', but that it was all about giving an 'urban *identity*'. For that, Hoyerswerdians had to do a proper analysis of their market value and were asked: 'How are we perceived and how do we want to be perceived from the outside?', 'How do we differ from other cities?' and 'What could bring us competitive advantages?' Accordingly, representations of Hoyerswerda's present and future potentials should underline the city's unique selling points in order to foster a new identity and a new reputation and (self-)image.[9]

The concern with reputation as a particular form of knowledge not only pervaded political and administrative planning practices, but also gained prominence in many other local forms of representation. The local media was seen to have a crucial role in this. Members of social clubs and associations, which all faced new fears and challenges in relation to the demographic and economic changes in the city and in their respective institutions, were very concerned about their standing in the city and about their reputation and image amongst their fellow citizens. A good internal reputation incited hopes and promises of a better and secure future; a negative local image produced further fear and insecurity because it could impede the future developments of one's association.

One of the most contested fields was Hoyerswerda's education system. Due to the decreasing numbers of pupils, primary and secondary schools competed for this scarce resource fiercely. One instrument in this fight was the school's image. Since the children – or rather their parents – could choose their preferred school freely on 'the educational market', the schools basically turned into small firms with their own marketing and public relations units. In most of them, next to the entrance, a bulletin board displayed recent newspaper articles in which the corresponding school was positively mentioned. This fostered school identity (as every marketing expert would attest – the pupils were after all the best advertising medium) and impressed visitors. Accordingly, the local newspapers' representations were followed carefully. Like other professions, the teachers took the media into consideration for the sake of their institution's survival. Once the targeted Hoyerswerdians – especially parents of potential future students and the political and administrational elite – had acquired the right knowledge about a particular school, it was believed that they would align their future actions correspondingly: parents would send their children to this school and not to another one, and city councillors would do their best to prevent this particular school's closing by allowing new investments in its buildings, sports halls or computer cabinets. Therefore, pupils were encouraged to take part in different kinds of competitions and creative activities because they could potentially earn good media coverage for the school. All local schools also arranged the aforementioned open days (see Chapter 2), at which they tried to advertise and sell their school to potential future students.

What preoccupied local schools and kindergartens also prevailed amongst other social, cultural, economic and political institutions. The recognition by potential participants, clients, investors or club members was desirable in such a context as a form of getting a hold on the future, and securing one's financial and actual institutional survival. Social and sport clubs compete for members; cultural organizations for audiences; entrepreneurs for clients; and political parties for voters and active members. Local journalists were often asked to report on particular events, or they received complaints about missing coverage and faced criticism of having favoured respective competitors. Out of this hope in – or fear of – the affective and actual power of knowledge in form of local reputations, most local institutions produced leaflets, a website, corporate design and a growing list of more creative ways of reaching out to the public. Once either of these institutions had sponsored a local social event, it was ensured that the logo appeared on all printed material. These concerns about image could obviously be criticized for their superficial surface representation and their reductive form of representation (see Kemper 2001; Pfeiffer 2004). More importantly, the introduction of methods of a different field – here that of marketing and advertisement – produced new work, obligations and preoccupation on top of the institution's normal running and maintenance. Teachers increasingly spent time advertising their school, social workers had to sell themselves to the youngsters they were supposed to care for, and sport club representatives had to work on media strategies in order to attract new members. Apart from the decreasing financial resources, it was especially the dwindling member numbers that most clubs in Hoyerswerda struggled with. As the average age of club members increased, all the institutions I worked with expressed severe concerns about their club's long-term survival. Attracting new people was of the utmost importance. In fact, for some of my informants, the work on their institution's image took up more time and effort than the job's actual contents.

The *Leitbild* debates catered to the same logic. Self-knowledge paired with affects of the future was the key element for claiming a hold on or, indeed, power over the future. As the *Leitbild* manuscript had it, such knowledge answered the question 'Do our citizens *know* in which direction the city is going to develop in the future?' People in Hoyerswerda, the text continued, should be encouraged to know more about their city's past and future, about themselves – 'Who are we and who do we want to be in the future?' – and about the *Leitbild* as the main idea of what the future should look like. Citizens shall '*understand*', '*altercate*' and 'finally *identify with*' the 'path-breaking' 'primary city-*idea*', enabled by 'intensive' and 'strategic city-*communication*' (all emphases added). The appeal to the affective dimension of knowledge about the city's future was apparent. An older *Leitbild* from the late 1990s had already captured the link between the future and knowledge with its challenging marketing slogan 'Hoyerswerda wants to know it!' (*Hoyerswerda will's wissen!*), a defiant self-encouragement and a claim to belong to the knowledge-based future economy. How did this logic differ from the logic exhibited in the encounter between the young neo-Nazi and the local teacher or the youth project's pedagogic logics?

As I have indicated above, the belief in the efficacy of any representational take on the future – whether in form of a *Leitbild*, a project presentation or a photograph – entailed the hope (or fear) that knowledge about the future had power over what was to come. A *Leitbild*, however, was not a plan, that is, it did not produce a detailed, concrete representation of the future. It only offered guidance into it – like 'a compass', the Lord Mayor said. Its relationship to the future was vague and purely affective, intending to provoke a feeling of security, optimism and other feelgood emotions and affects, especially hope. The hope for a better future was seen to be inherent in one's own stance towards the city's future, so people were encouraged to wholeheartedly embrace the notion of a better future and work on themselves. However, the power to actually change the future was still located in the hands of external powers: the market, ominous investors or endless numbers of future tourists. The *Leitbild* thus evoked and incorporated a form of a depoliticized hope, similar to that which David Harvey has convincingly described as one repercussion of global capitalism's 'flexible accumulation' with his example of urban development in the city of Baltimore (Harvey 2000): state and citizenry increasingly compete for foreign investment and grant most hopes to the investors, who are seen to be almost the only guarantor for new jobs, and thus for the future. These investors, in turn, have to be convinced to come to a particular city and not go to any other competitor. Since all towns, cities, regions and countries compete for these investors, they have to sell themselves to the global flow of goods, people and finances.

Like so many other small- and medium-sized cities worldwide, Hoyerswerda failed in that competition – and blamed itself and its wrong image for it. To counter the affects/effects that the city's image supposedly had on external investors, potential tourists and shoppers as much as on internal hopes and future prospects, many Hoyerswerdians ventured to produce and disseminate new images and other forms of knowledge. Such representations reduced complexity in order to sell the city, internally and externally, in positive and attractive affective terms. Otherwise, it was presumed, this knowledge's efficacy would not work. As Nikolas Rose pointed out, the 'politics of conduct at the end of the twentieth century is conducted, at least in part, through the selective amplification of passions, anxieties, allegiances and identities intrinsic to the commercial struggle to sell goods and maximize profits' (Rose 1996: 344). The role of forms of knowledge and affects of the future could be seen to be part of a wider 'instrumentalization of passion' (ibid.), including the imposition of hopes and fears on singular persons, particular groups or whole cities. An even stronger point has been made by Thrift, who detects changes in politics of affect 'which make affect an increasingly visible element of the political' (Thrift 2004: 64). He also emphasizes that new knowledges 'construct power in a number of ways (indeed, it is often the force with which passion is delivered which is more important than the message)' (ibid.).

A *Leitbild* as a vague technical utopian vision of the future is one example of a performative claim on the future. Having knowledge *about* the future does not mean one has power *over* the future; rather, it entails a claim to power in the present. This idea of power, that is, the local belief in the efficacy of these affective politics and pedagogies, is fascinating. I conclude this chapter with a discussion of the non-efficacy or powerlessness of representational claims on the future. The fact that the neo-Nazis rarely lived up to their threats, that local youth continued to leave because they still could not find a job in the region and, finally, that Hoyerswerda's shrinkage was not stopped by a proper *Leitbild* or image does not deny the potential efficacy of aforementioned relationships with the future. But how can we criticize forms of enforced futurism and prescribed hopes?

Conclusion: From Hope to Serenity

As somebody who has never seen Hoyerswerda in its early, vanguard days, I can hardly comprehend how it feels to experience the many changes by which Hoyerswerda and life in it were affected during the last two, almost three decades. The city I encountered had undoubtedly retained some of its charms. It was still a loveable city. Therefore, I sometimes asked my informants the following question: if anybody had suggested twenty years ago that your city was going to lose half of its inhabitants by 2010, how would you have reacted? This dystopian knowledge, they agreed, could have had detrimental effects. Accordingly, visions of the future could have accelerated the process of shrinkage. However, in 2008/2009, when the halved population was a fact, people were still full of hopes and dreams as much as of fears and sorrows. They tried to enjoy life and worked passionately with the given situation's problems. Then facing the same challenge yet again, since a further population cut by 50 per cent was predicted by 2030, the dystopian logic again evoked fears of a decline and 'no future'.[10] Such fearful anticipation stemmed from official demographic predictions of a further decline due to an ageing population. But the accuracy and efficacy of these predictions remained questionable. They worked as superficially as the marketing representations from the previous section. Their representation of the future did not allow for detail, change or much temporal agency. As dystopian expressions of enforced futurism, they denied in the present the human capacity to be able to react to future challenges regardless of how drastic they would be. It also does not account for the indeterminateness of any present, despite the fact that it was totally unexpected and unforeseen changes that have initiated Hoyerswerda's decline in the first place. As a matter of fact, in 2015 Hoyerswerda's population rose again for the first time in approximately three decades due to the arrival of several hundred refugees in the city.

So what if these representations of the future in the end fell short? What if their inherent claim to power over the present and the future was nothing but pretence? The pictures taken by the neo-Nazis were, after all, creating more fear (in the present) than actual risk (in the future). Their efficacy was based on a fear effected by a pretence to power. This was how they had an impact on the future. Similarly, the knowledge the young Hoyerswerdians were asked to produce might fail in making them stay. However, their efficacy was a formal anticipation of the future, an exercise in future thinking, which opened up spaces not for the intended representations, but for new images, ideas and criticisms. Finally, the *Leitbild* also proclaimed performative power over the city's future, and its formal relationship to the future might be more important than the content it purveys, particularly when we understand it, despite its affective logic, as a serious attempt at recolonizing the previously evacuated near future.

For me, the promises of loose affective relations to the future were replaced by the simple hope for *concrete* solutions answering to *particular* 'demands of the day' (Rabinow and Stavrianakis 2013) – for example, the concise hope for the maintenance of a particular institution, building or set of social relations as discussed in this book's last chapter. This form of anticipation does not work with respect to vague affects regarding the future, but in relation to the *specific* effects these relations to the future should have. It expresses a belief in the efficacy of practice, not of knowledge per se. This practical approach can be called anticipatory presentism, a presentism directed and open to the future, but also concerned with already laying out specific steps towards it. This approach's take on affect is not based on hope, but on serenity, on a certain groundedness in the present. Instead of false hopes, enforced futurism and enforced presentism, which in Hoyerswerda seemingly prevailed as the political and epistemic repercussions of current forms of postindustrial urban governmentality, such a presentist strategy, always with an eye on the future and people's actual agency, related to the future without falling prey to petty politics, cramped pedagogies or short-term, superficial marketing logics.

Notes

1. In German: 'Stoppt die Propaganda der selbsternannten Demokraten!' and 'Für das Selbstbestimmungsrecht unseres Volkes'.
2. For that reason, young anti-Fascists in Hoyerswerda cover their faces at public demonstrations and wear inconspicuous clothes when entering territory claimed by the local neo-Nazis (foremost around the main shopping centre) in order to avoid attention and prevent knowledge being gathered about them.
3. As Frederic Jameson underlined in reference to Ernst Bloch, 'in the realm of existential emotions and affects, it is clear that we ... have at our disposal two different ways of visualizing the future' (Jameson 1971: 126). Bloch introduced the distinction between expectant and filled emotions. Whereas hope, fear and desire have a relationship to a future, in which the future is different from the present, filled emotions such as greed, envy and adoration 'also ask something of the future ... Yet ... filled emotions project their wish into a psychic space which is properly unreal; they project what Bloch calls an "inauthentic future"' (ibid.). The future that filled emotions (help to) envision is 'at all points identical to that of the present' (ibid.), which arrests all possibility of change and of imagining a radically different future (see ibid.: 127).
4. Some analysts even deploy the logic of the commodity in analyses of affect. In their accounts, hope can thus be circulated, distributed and consumed (Anderson 2007; Miyazaki 2010). Miyazaki (2010) even frames hope as a scarce commodity, and neoliberalism as unevenly distributing hope over the world and thereby creating places of hope and places of no hope. Hoyerswerda being presumably an example of the latter, I focus on the manifold and intricate social production and forceful imposition of hope. Instead of the economy of hope, I concentrate on the politics of affect: the seduction by and application of sentiments, emotions, feelings and affects.
5. Reinhard Koselleck (1989) famously asserted that whereas the past constitutes an 'experiential space' (*Erfahrungsraum*, a spatial metaphor), the future is a more intangible 'anticipatory horizon' (*Erwartungshorizont*).

The metaphor he uses to describe human relations to the future is visual and entails the notion of distance. A horizon is something one can never touch, feel or experience apart from seeing it from afar. As is the case with the future, one will never be able to actually arrive at it. This explains its dependence on being represented in the present. Gell defines the future as 'inaccessible except as a representation, an imaginary present' (Gell 1992: 288; compare 237–41).

6. This was introduced in the official letter to the teachers with the slogan 'We need positive visions. Hence, no fear of utopias!' (*Wir brauchen positive Visionen. Also keine Angst vor Utopien!*).

7. A more playful incentive to imagine the local future was given in January 2011 by the Economic Initiative Lusatia, which conducted an Innovation Game for the pupils of a local grammar school. This game was intended to help imagine the future of Hoyerswerda's main employer, the hospital, in 2025. The pupils role-played to manage the virtual company AidTech Industries, providing the hospital with its future products, such as the AidPad (as part of a electrical health network), flying ambulances, automatically moving beds and a new health garden. The desired result of that stimulated imagination is summarized by one journalist collaborator thus: 'Perhaps we'll succeed during the course of this project to also give some incentives for staying here.'

8. My understanding of affective images follows Masco (2008) by focusing on images that are engineered to have certain affective effects.

9. Only one statement overcomes the market logic inherent in the concerns with the city's image and its self-representation: 'In times of change, long-term goals become increasingly important' (*In Zeiten des Wandels werden langfristige Ziele immer wichtiger*) – a call for sustainability and long-term investment, which marks the *Leitbild* still as a policy instrument, but infused with economic logics.

10. One form of local reasoning had it that the actual danger of a further wave of shrinkage is that once the city loses its still present urban character, more people will outmigrate. The term used to explain this is the idea of a 'critical mass'. Once a certain, though undefined, population number is undercut, the city will irreversibly have lost much of its urban qualities, and with it its essential quality of life, entering a phase of rural rather than urban decline.

5

Performing the Future

Endurance, Maintenance and Self-Formation in Times of Shrinkage

No matter what is given to see, we persist in seeing alternatives –
often very possible ones that are implicit in the forms we see as dominant.
But why can't we be realists and demand impossible hopes
– in different times?
                                    —Bill Maurer, 'Chronotopes of the Alternative'

Bill Maurer's 2005 finishing lines of a conference paper on 'Chronotopes of the Alternative' might seem out of place in an introduction to a chapter on practices of maintenance, permanence and endurance. His urge for alternatives is a very common trope among contemporary social scientists; it is part of our own academic imaginaries and personal hopes. However, Maurer gives this common source of relevance an interesting twist by claiming that we should be realists and demand *impossible* alternatives. After recent surprising political developments (Brexit, Trump, etc.), this might be this time's unfortunate presentist lesson to be learned about the unexpected turns history can take at any point. However, it might also entail a new approach to the concepts of change and continuity. Being realist, according to Maurer, means striving for the unexpected. To some extent, this captures the experiences and attitudes of my informants – although in reverse fashion. In fact, in a presentist framework, that something turns out to be a surprise only depends on relevant prior expectations. Faced with a predictably worse future, many Hoyerswerdians continuously held expectations of decline. To fight for the survival of the forms of their social, relational, material and economic environment, then, constituted an act of temporal agency directed to the unexpected. In times of shrinkage, this fight indeed seemed unrealistic: people in my field strove for permanence in a context that was otherwise increasingly deteriorating. They practically and concretely appropriated – indeed, *performed*, that is, shaped and structured – their own near future. Stemming from a certain hopeful and anticipatory, but at the same time pragmatic form of temporal reasoning, my informants maintained what seemed to be threatened. I take this to be in a broader sense indicative of the role that the future plays in human life and experience.

This chapter looks at several different and fairly mundane practices of endurance, starting with some more general observations and thoughts, and then exploring in more depth one communal and one ethical example of the practical formation of the future. The first example concerns the fight over the reconstruction and future use of one of Hoyerswerda's most prestigious buildings. I focus on both the continuous work my informants put into rescuing this building from a very probable future of decay and collapse (or its sale to private investors), and the all-pervasive use of tropes and figures of sustainability instead of progress and growth in local discourses, which seemed to involve a different imaginary of the future. The second example also targets the per*form*ation of the future or, as my informants called it, *die Zukunft gestalten*, that is, giving gestalt, a certain form or shape, to the future. I follow the same temporal logic of endurance in practices of self-formation, that is, the set of ethical teleological practices that in our analytical understanding has certain, if still contingent, performative or transformative effects with regard to the future. Importantly, such practices also depend on their enduring enactment. Despite Hegel's description of the future as 'formless' (cited in Bloch 1986 [1959]: 883), I thus want to show how people in a city with no future engage in maintaining established forms and structures in their lives and practices.

At the end of this chapter, I engage critically with three analytical tools that exemplify how anthropology recently came to understand issues of continuity and change: emergence, becoming and assemblage. The first two appear to be presentist at first sight, but, if they are presentist at all, they are differently so. However, instead of debunking these terms, I want to examine how such emergent and continuously becoming forms are made to endure in time. This focus on the aftermath of emergence reintroduces the question of the efficacy of human practice, that is, the topic of agency, or temporal agency, without denying aspects of its contingency and indeterminacy. I claim that by giving particular forms of practice – communal, ethical or otherwise – a direction to the future, my informants maintained a sense of anticipation, vigilantly as well as hopefully, that was linked to a hope in their own agency. They thus maintained a sense of agency in their deteriorating social and physical environment. This was not simply a matter of survival or a pragmatic approach to life in reaction to the impossibility of knowing the future of an 'everlasting present' (Baxstrom 2012) in times of postindustrial crisis and decline. Instead, they were invoking a form of agency that, in Maurer's words, demanded the impossible – and strove to make it practically real against all odds. They were, if you wish, tricking time, and particularly the future (Ringel 2016a; Ringel and Moroçanu 2016) in their various attempts to 'modify, manage, bend, distort, speed up, slow down, or structure the times they are living in' (Moroçanu and Ringel 2016: 17).

New Traditions and Practices of Permanence

I will begin with a simple observation. During my fieldwork, I often heard people proudly referring to a recurrent event as a 'new tradition' (*neue Tradition*). At most anniversary celebrations of the many post-1989 founded clubs and associations, the Lord Mayor or his deputy stressed the 'by now traditional character' of these social institutions in their speeches. At more recent repetitions, they repeatedly expressed the hope of more of these events to come by underlining 'how wonderful and important this new tradition for the city' was and 'how much it is already essential part of the local sociocultural life'. But even beyond official addresses, people in private celebrations expressed their joy about a recurrent occasion and call it their 'own little new tradition'. The notion of a new tradition was also discussed in the local newspaper, when a local journalist critically responded to the county's District Administrator's opening speech at the *Second*(!) Lusation Lake District Fair. Whilst praising the fair and wishing it good luck for the future, the District Administrator had declared that in these turbulent times, 'everything from three times onward is a tradition' (*Alles ab drei Mal ist Tradition*). In response, the journalist enquires acrimoniously about what should actually count as traditional – one hundred, fifty or twenty years? He favoured at least ten years, but admits that he will have to resign to the now official verdict 'from high up' that puts the mark at three. Despite such ironic remarks, the logic of a new tradition widely prevailed and expressed a certain hope for – and appreciation of – endurance of a valued form of the present.

As a remark on a – itself – traditional anthropological topic, the somewhat paradoxical phrase draws attention to traditions' own 'inventedness' (Hobsbawm and Ranger 1983), but turning their proclaimed temporal claims on the past upside down. Instead of linking a recurrent event in the present to its apparent predecessors in the past, many of my informants using that phrase did the opposite. They linked a recurrent event in the present to its anticipated, desired or intended recurring successors. They hence gave relevance and meaning to this event in the present by granting it the quality of enduring in time. However, they were not only giving their present a future; rather, they were giving these social forms a tradition with regard to the future, not to the past. Their future had pre-emptively been given a past. By looking at the present not as an endpoint or outcome of a tradition (which was thus commonly predicted to endure), they reversed the temporal order by looking at a specific event as the starting point of a 'new tradition'. Is a new tradition an expression of an 'anticipatory consciousness' in Blochian terms (1986 [1959])? Is the hope for something to endure the same as the hope for the not-yet-become, that is, the emergent, virtual and potential, which Bloch and his recent discussants so strongly favour?

For a city like Hoyerswerda, endurance in time was, indeed, a pressing but hopeful concern. Many of my informants (apart perhaps from the anarchists discussed above) would agree that traditions are a good thing and that humans need traditions. However, having lived through the peaceful revolution of 1989/1990 and the following years of dramatic change, their understanding of traditions was less fixed to the past and more open to new definitions. In contrast to the revival of local Sorbic traditions, which fits more easily into the common definition of traditions, the invocation of new traditions dwelled on a strong relationship to the future. Following Olivia Harris' intervention in reference to the temporal logics of tradition (1996, 2004), we should take the investment of people in traditions seriously, and in turn question our own disciplinary and currently very fashionable focus on events, emergence, potentiality and new alternatives. As Harris pointed out, people are not brainwashed or ideologically dominated when they subscribe to notions of tradition and continuity – even more so, I argue, if these traditions refer to the future. The experience of postindustrial decline might, in fact, alter the meaning of the term 'conservative', which is usually attached to the past-orientated notion of tradition. Such practices can be understood as acts of agency along the lines of Mahmood's influential study of ethics among a women's pious movement in Egypt (Mahmood 2001, 2005). Despite their conservative undertones, 'new traditions' can be seen as hopeful practices of the future, which exhibit actual transformative (even if conservative) effects of agency that help to secure and shape my informants' futures.

For instance, the many archiving and documenting practices deployed by clubs and associations in Hoyerswerda seem conservative or past-orientated at first sight. However, they subscribed to the same temporal logic as the new traditions in their own strive for future endurance. Especially in the sociocultural milieu so heavily dependent on public funding, all projects and activities were carefully documented: first, in order to preserve their own memories for the future, and, second, for procuring the club's survival in the future. Such documentaries were used for proving (as much to oneself as) to local authorities or potential sponsors one's worth, right and ability for continuous existence, emphasizing one's eligibility for external funding. They were therefore, in a double sense, techniques to create a future: imaginarily as a commemorative trace of the past that was made to last and actually as the promise of – and basis for – continuity in time. I saw endless folders with pictures, collections of leaflets and posters, internet archives of photos, short movies and collections of media coverage. Whereas some clubs passionately decorated their collections of photographs of the preceding year's events with ruler and felt pens, others excelled in producing little videos that were posted, stored and made available on the club's website. Such documentation entailed the promise of repetition in the future. Similar concerns with the future were prevalent in most clubs, associations, schools or private companies. In particular, media coverage in local and regional news was seen as a highly valued currency to gain public reputation and support for securing one's future. Documenting practices were thus understood as efficacious investments in the maintenance and endurance of one's institution. For most Hoyerswerdians, this construction of a new tradition in material form was one of the many constant investments in the forms that made up their life, requiring time, money and personal commitment. Against better knowledge and bleak prospects, my informants maintained these forms, continuously fighting for their survival. In the next section, I concentrate on the work invested in the survival of one particular building. I also introduce the notion of sustainability in order to elaborate on this temporal and hopeful logic of endurance.

Claiming Sustainability: The Future of Braugasse 1

Some houses in Hoyerswerda were different from others – they carried a high symbolic value in an ever-disappearing architectural environment. The building *Braugasse Nr. 1* (1 Brewing Alley) that is the focus of this section was a very special one. It had been closed by the city in 2000 according to building law: its state of dilapidation posed significant dangers for public use. The building's dilapidation made it look very much out of place in the Old City's picturesque centre, a ruin more than a house that was in fact so heavily invested with hopes, dreams and futures. Many people were awaiting its renovation and reopening. It was one of Hoyerswerda's most central and popular buildings, located directly in the old market square. Since its construction more than a century ago, it had already functioned as a ballroom, a grammar school and a socialist youth club. The city council as much as the local government had repeatedly declared their full commitment to trying to acquire the external funding needed for its reconstruction. However, these wishes had been continuously disappointed over the last decade. In response, a new club – *Braugasse 1 e.V.* – was founded in March 2006 aiming solely at promoting this building's renovation. One of its interventions was initiated by the head of the Cultural Factory (henceforth *KuFa*) Röhli, the building's previous occupant. To do so, as he said one Sunday morning at a cultural brunch in the club's then still 'Temporary Occupancy' (*Zwischenbelegung*), the *KuFa*'s interim exile after evacuating Braugasse 1, he had copied an idea from a Tibetan tradition.

In Tibet, the audience was told, people who go on long journeys attach wishing scarves to holy trees or erected monuments. On these scarves, they write their wishes and hope that the supernatural force related to the place of worship will help them make this wish come true. Accordingly, Röhli suggested, all supporters should take pieces of old linen, tear them into strips, write their wishes for the building on them and attach them to the house's fence. The idea was enthusiastically received and many of the approximately seventy attendants realized the idea soon thereafter. The bands bore on them the wishes, dreams and hopes that referred to the building's future. Some simply read 'Children's Laughter', 'creativity, pleasure, stimulation' or 'A place for our grandchildren, our children and us. A place for everybody'. Others were more critical, demanding 'Some reason in the Mayor's Hall and the City Council'. Literally hundreds of them decorated the fences over the course of several months, creating a

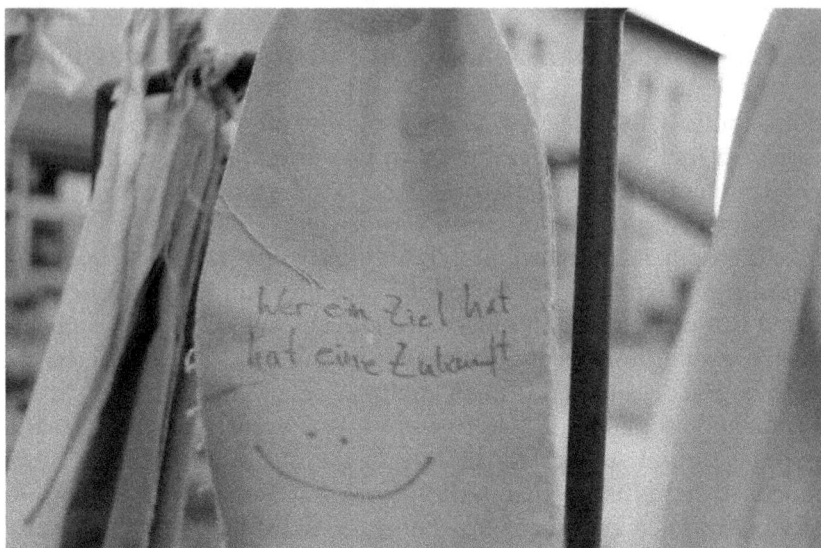

Figure 5.1 *Wishing scarf, Braugasse 1, Hoyerswerda* Altstadt. *'Those who have an aim do have a future' (photo by Mirko Kolodziej)*

colourful and obviously highly political expression of hope and determination (which the city's officials working in the guildhall opposite the Braugasse 1 had to see everyday at least twice on their to and from work). Even after rain and sunshine had faded their colours and they rather sadly adorned the fence, they still reminded passers-by of the hope directed to the future that endured here visibly and in material form. Just before one of the crucial municipal council meetings, the Braugasse 1 club members distributed to all councillors a scarf attached to a sheet of paper stating the club's desired amendments, drawing the councillors into this mode of wishful thinking and concrete anticipation. The amendments, in turn, were the outcome of the city's working group (*Arbeitsgruppe*) Braugasse 1, which was concerned with the practicalities of this building's future that the club members so passionately fought for. An amendment would, however, only ever be the first step in making the desired future happen.

By searching for the places where Hoyerswerda's and this building's future were actually made, one might end up in one of the working group's rather dull, but no less intense meetings in Hoyerswerda's guildhall or the city council. This was where the public imaginary expects binding future decisions to be made. The meeting I discuss below concerned the (re)utilization plan for the not-yet renovated building Braugasse 1. The main quest for all attending was not the question of whether the house would be renovated, but rather, once it would have been renovated (which was still undetermined), who would be using it. In fact, the question was not who would use it, but rather who would be *able* to do so – whose agency could endure to fulfil this task. The presiding Deputy Mayor recurrently underlined that all assembled potential users would in any case face severe problems in the near future, like any other club in Hoyerswerda – lower finances, fewer members and smaller audiences were his undeniable predictions. The Deputy Mayor, who was responsible for all social and cultural matters, opened his statement with a rather discouraging claim that mirrors the official enforced presentism framework discussed in previous chapters: 'Nobody can predict how each club's developments will look in the future.' He somewhat meanly insinuated that those running the clubs would grow older and there would be – no matter what – an increasingly smaller clientele in the future. More serious were his financial concerns: would the city, the district and the state continue to fund these clubs? Would the clubs' own financial future be sound enough to guarantee that they would be able to run the building and pay the maintenance costs, which the city no longer wanted to be burdened with? The quest was, in that sense, not about the emergence of something new and hoped for: the renovation that seemed still as unlikely as before. Rather, of concern in this particular meeting was how this hoped-for future moment could be given an enduring future in the future – a guaranteed maintenance in a future that was predicted to be like the present: full of enforced changes, insecurities, financial scarcity and the perceived unpredictability of its own futures. The house's maintenance was the very practical question that was posed in this round and against this unpredictability.

Contrary to its instrumental character, the debate's subtext was tense. Assembled were the local government's main personnel, including the Lord Mayor and his deputy, the commissioned architect, and representatives of three of the clubs that, following an earlier council resolution, were seen to be running the future building. As potential occupants, they were supposed to discuss the usage of the yet only planned, that is, virtual, new building. The stakes were high. It was only by bringing these three clubs together that the city council reached a majority approval for renovating the building – too many other projects demanded financial provisions too. Although the renovation of Braugasse 1 had initially been decided already a decade earlier, the city had increasingly run out of money, being unable to provide the *Eigenanteil*, that is, its financial equity ratio, which

German communes had to pay in order to gain state funding. As the last decade of deferred renovation promises had already shown, the future might turn out very differently than expected, despite council and governmental decisions. The performance of planning in such working group meetings might as well be empty or just yet another step in mediating between different parties, which all suffered from insecurities prevalent in a shrinking city. However, the main trope and logic used was the one of sustainability with all its promises of secured permanence. It seemed to be the sole reference point and evaluation criterion, covering all other fissures and conflicts. Below I will introduce the three clubs' representatives and their stakes in this meeting.

Frau Nagel, the executive head of the *NATZ* club, the Natural Science and Technology Centre (*Naturwissenschaftlich-Technisches Zentrum*), felt quite uncomfortable in this setting. She used to be a coal engineer in the mines and appeared harsh rather than articulate and diplomatic. Her job was not easy. She had led the *NATZ* for only a few years. The club and her job were mainly sustained with money from the city. The *NATZ* was a typical GDR institution. Founded in the late 1960s in the then heavily expanding socialist New City, its aim was to educate Hoyerswerda's children and youth in their free time about scientific and technological issues. Pupils could come around after school and built their own miniature racing tracks and cars, do experiments in physics, help care for all sorts of pets and animals or, in recent decades, construct and assemble their own robots. Since it was at first sight not ideologically charged, the *NATZ* survived the turmoil of the early 1990s, but during Frau Nagel's time as CEO, the club ran into serious spatial and thus future problems. In the mid 2000s, whilst still being housed in its original domicile in living complex WK 4, its building was hit by an exceptional storm, which led to the evacuation of the building and the club's move to a former school building in WK 9. Located on the outskirts of *Neustadt* in one of the living complexes most severely affected by shrinkage and deconstruction, the *NATZ* faced difficulties attracting its main clientele. For some of the children, or their parents respectively, WK 9 was just too far away from the city centre. Furthermore, the building the *NATZ* was forced to occupy was soon to be demolished too, as part of the further deconstruction of WK 9. Facing future cuts in public funding, a decline in the in any case increasingly fewer children and existential housing issues, the club, despite its very good reputation, encountered existential problems. Moving into the soon-to-be-renovated Braugasse as part of the community centre would solve these issues and, it was hoped, would grant access to a more secure future – with lower maintenance costs, more children and a better standing in the city.

Uwe, the executive of the KulturFabrik e.V. (*KuFa*), was also not very comfortable at these committee meetings. A quiet and arduous worker, he was not a loud and flamboyant strategist. His stake in this meeting was, however, essential too. His club, the *KuFa*, had run the Children's and Youth Centre in the Braugasse 1 building until its closure. Having moved to the Old City's outskirts, it also struggled with attracting its clientele. More importantly, the new location made its formerly very successful café unprofitable, thus decreasing its income and financial security. It was the general perception that the club depended on the renovation of this building for its survival. As was commonly agreed in most of the club's board meetings I attended, there was an economic necessity to relocate from the outskirts to the centre. The club's main clientele, Hoyerswerda's children and youth, but increasingly also older people, might be attracted in higher numbers to a central location. The restoration would make the reopening of a café lucrative and hence guarantee financial income independent of public funding.

But the *KuFa*'s return to the Braugasse after years of conflict, fight and public denunciation was for its supporters in yet another way linked to an issue of the future and, indeed, of survival: this time the survival of the whole city. As several people claimed, without the *KuFa* and its admirable work, 'nothing would keep me here' (*dann würde mich nichts mehr hier halten*). Supporters argued in the name of the public good that the *KuFa*'s return and the establishment of a vibrant community centre would strengthen the Old City. Conflicts arose: adjacent residents feared the noise the club would cause, whereas the nearby shop owners were for obvious reasons appreciating the 'revitalization' (*Belebung*) of their quarter. For those running the *KuFa*, the concerns were both existential and pragmatic. Some feared the loss of their job if no future solution with the city was found. Others knew that the *KuFa*'s current building would also have to be closed soon due to its current material state and with no chances of further investments. Instead of a nomadic future of having to move from one dilapidated house to another, they instead hoped for a secure future in an enduring abode. Moreover, the maintenance costs of their current domicile were so high that once privatized – which is part of the negotiations with the local government and yet another municipal attempt of out-sourcing – they would not be able to afford these for long.

The third club was the former (in English) 'Spirit of Zuse', renamed 'Computer Forum Konrad Zuse' in 2009, founded in memory of the famous inventor of computers, who has done his A-levels in the Braugasse 1 building. Its CEO, the former leftist Lord Mayor Horst-Dieter Brähmig, also had much at stake. Currently, the Forum's technical museum was housed improperly in a mediocre office building at the northern outskirts in *Neustadt's* former industrial area. Therein the Forum's unique Computer Museum occupied several large rooms to exhibit the overall impressive collection of Zuse's and other – by now antique – computers. It also owned a rare collection of items from the then emerging GDR computer industry. Brähmig well knew that the exhibition needed a proper makeover – interactive multimedia-based sections, comprehensive and well-designed explanations, and a good pedagogic concept. Its visitor numbers were underwhelming. Indeed, despite the city officially bearing Zuse's name (as the *Konrad-Zuse-Stadt Hoyerswerda*) for marketing and image purposes, this museum was not an actual attraction. Plans to relocate it had been put forward time and again. A move to the nearby spacious Energy Factory, the museum dedicated to Saxony's industrial history and culture, was more sincerely considered, but finally failed. The Braugasse 1 house, Zuse's former grammar school, soon turned out to be unable to harbour the heavy machines for statical reasons. The construction of a new building adjacent to it could have been a sustainable future solution, but the city was unable to raise enough money for such project. Dreams of some wealthy benefactor, some ominous friend of Zuse or Bill Gates himself were often, but only half-seriously entertained. Finally, the Computer Forum executives, with the help of their many political connections, had demanded to at least be included in the plans for the Braugasse 1 community centre, which in their opinion should carry Zuse's name. A room of more than 120 sqm has been granted to them in recent plans – not for a museum, but for a 'commemorational room' (*Gedenkzimmer*). In the future, visitors could be directed from there to the museum, wherever it would then be housed. Because they intended to equip the room with posters, photos and smaller artefacts in memory of Zuse, competitors for the same space criticized the whole idea as a horribly old-fashioned 'pennant room' (*Wimpelzimmer*) indicative of the club not having to make any contribution to the community centre's – and the city's overall – future. Nonetheless, to bring Zuse back to the heart of the city remained the Forum's aim, claiming that with a prominent Zuse, the city would benefit in the long run, regain identity, attract external investors and thus secure its own survival.

All three clubs were similarly affected by Hoyerswerda's socio-economic and demographic changes and its crucial spatial repercussions. All of them were forced to operate strategically to secure their future. To do so in this meeting, they had to prove their ability to survive (in an almost Darwinian sense) and to endure in the future. In order to be found worthy of state funding, they had to confirm their capacity for enduring existence. Demographics became bound up with spatial and temporal strategies of survival. All three clubs suffered from decreasing external support – less public financial support, lower audiences and a reduced clientele – and decreasing reliability on their own older ranks: what in German is called 'offspring-problems' (*Nachwuchsprobleme*), the result of an inevitably ageing and decreasing cohort of members. To overcome these problems, they tried to adapt to the complicated present with various strategies, one of them being the attraction of constant media attention to proliferate their compassionate work for the common good (in a similar fashion to the case of local schools discussed previously). All of them invested the renovation of the Braugasse building with high hopes to overcome many of the aforementioned problems with their relocation into it. The key for this was to claim the power of sustainability, that is, the ability to endure in the future, which they each continuously did throughout the intense debates.

After fierce quarrels about the practical details of who would get how much space (hence the presence of the architect to update the construction plans), it was finally agreed that the only club able to run the centre was the *KuFa*. The other proposed forms of organizing the maintenance of the building were withdrawn. It was agreed that only through the cooperation of the three clubs would it be possible to obtain the city council's final approval. The *KuFa* was seen to have better professional skills and, over the long run, more resources to sustain the house and its management. This concluded outcome of the meeting would endure until the virtual plan would be realized, that is, the house will be renovated and the clubs will have moved in. As all participants, despite enduring conflicts and tensions, indicated their support, this agreement would most probably only be amended in terms of minor details. However, the actual future after the reconstruction's realization remained indeterminate. As all clubs had underlined after the meeting, one still needed to see what the situation would actually be like. Perhaps the *NATZ* would need less space than required – or, some commentators suggested, perhaps it will no longer exist. Similarly, the Zuse Forum might be busy enough occupying its future domicile (which was indeed opened in *Neustadt* in the winter of 2016). Or the *KuFa* might have, as some viciously predicted, 'grown too old to bother anymore'. As I claimed in the previous chapter, we should transcend the affect produced by such bleak speculations and concentrate on the practical reappropriation of the near future. In this vein, the *KuFa* later won a grant from the Federal Foundation for Culture for a project called 'Training Activity Braugasse 1' (*Trainingsmaßnahme Braugasse 1*). This project involved probing the cooperation between the three clubs before the move in. It also made it possible to try out the idea of a community centre with Hoyerswerda's citizens. Several projects had been conducted in order to secure the smooth running of the centre once it was built in the future (which, I am happy to say, it indeed was, having opened with only the *NATZ* and the *KuFa* in it in 2015). As I have shown with these examples, concerns with and practices of permanence, continuity and maintenance can in a context of shrinkage be seen as reinforcements of agency and a form of reappropriation of the future – against all realistic expectations. In the next section, I want to trace the same temporal logic in a very different form of practice – that of ethics – in order to present another arena in which hope, the future and practice were bound up under the notions of permanence and endurance.

Teleology and Continuity: The Future of Self-Formation

As shown throughout this book, the temporal dimension of the future played an important role in many communal practices in a city that faces constant (involuntary) change. It was the central focus of this urban community's many collective attempts at getting a grip on its problematic, supposedly futureless present. The future, however, also had dominance in other, more individual sets of practices. One area in which such practices have been theoretically dealt with is the anthropological literature on ethics. Ethics, as a set of teleological practices, have been studied in two main strands in anthropology, both following Foucault's late contributions. One group of scholars, mostly from Science and Technology studies, approach ethics as socionormative technologies of governmentality (see Collier and Ong 2005; Rabinow 2007; especially Collier and Lakoff 2005: 25ff), in which ethics appear either as a technology of power (compare Rose 1999; Strathern 2000) or as a form of necessary guidance through increasingly overwhelming changes (compare Rabinow 2007: 62f).

Another strand of research on ethics is more concerned with individual practices of self-formation in religious contexts (Faubion 2001; Hirschkind 2001; Mahmood 2001; Laidlaw 2002, 2014; Zigon 2007, 2009; Robbins 2009; Schielke 2009a, 2009b; Simon 2009). Although Zigon, for example, underlines ethical practices' 'creative participation in the possibilities of becoming' (2006: 75) and thus speaks to a Deleuzian understanding of hope as discussed at the end of this chapter, I focus more on what he calls 'little projects' (ibid.: 72), in which through experience (*melete*) and training in real situations (*gymnasia*), *askesis* is practised and a particular *telos* is pursued. This analytical take on the process of ethical practice with its long-term efficacy contributes more generally to the latter group's insights into the teleological and enduring character of ethical practice. However, I wonder whether it is change or maintenance that is at the root of these practices.

For instance, my anarchist informants' attempts at keeping their anarchist youth culture alive involved in their own ethical practices an urge for maintenance rather than for becoming. As mentioned in Chapter 2, their distinct mode of temporal reasoning focused on the present and the near future. It shaped local anarchists' continuous attempts to remain anarchists *in practice*. In a Marxist critique, anarchists have precisely been reproached for being too practical and not utopian enough (Kumar 2010: 561ff). Despite this, anarchist practices in Hoyerswerda were indicative of yet another way of maintaining something from the present into the future in the form of self-inflicted change that counter-intuitively strives for and produces continuity. Accordingly, hope became in Zigon's understanding more a matter of a concrete 'temporal orientation of intentional and ethical action' (Zigon 2009: 267) than of a diffuse distant utopia. My anarchist friends built up a relationship with the future by continuously following a certain anarchist *telos* in form of what Ernst Bloch would call 'concrete utopias' (1986 [1959]: 579). Such hopeful practices were no less future-orientated than more abstract utopias (as is provided by the theory of becoming discussed below), but they were in important ways focused on continuous practice – and not only, as Zigon has it, on survival in times of existential crisis or breakdown.

For example, Hoyerswerda's anarchists (during the time of my fieldwork) initiated and, more importantly, kept alive against all odds a vibrant alternative youth culture (cf. Krøijer 2015). They continuously organized concerts, parties and art sessions, whilst experimenting with particular styles of clothing, consumption and relationality. In such practices of self-formation, local anarchists maintained their own sense of being anarchist vis-à-vis other local milieus and the broader mainstream, and, despite the constant outmigration of many of their older peers, continued to reproduce it. It was these kinds of practices through which anarchists constructed 'local alternatives' (Graeber 2009: 292). As performances of future-orientated practices, they adhered to the temporal logic of experiments and transformed critical ideas into actual, enduring and workable solutions, which most members of the group kept on cultivating in the places they finally went to, including Dresden, Leipzig and Berlin. In their time in Hoyerswerda, this involved the continuous application, elaboration and experimentation of forms of practice. Anarchist epistemic and more precisely – following Graeber's insights (2004: 6) – ethical practices thus constituted an arena in which the 'not-yet' of viable alternatives was pursued not in the utopian distant future, but in the concrete practices of the present, which, in contrast to the practices discussed in Chapter 3, not only opened up but also continuously recolonized and invested in the near future.

In a late interview, Michel Foucault (1991 [1984]) defined four aspects for the comparative study of ethics. Whilst disregarding *ethical substance* and *mode of subjection* (ibid.: 352ff), I concentrate on what he calls *askesis,* a particular set of self-forming activity, and the similarly defining aspect of the *telos.* The *telos,* Foucault says, answers the question to which kind of being do 'we aspire when we behave in a moral way' (ibid.: 355). That said, the accomplishment of this anticipated goal does not always seem to be the most important part of ethical practice. Rather, the continuous practices – directed by the *telos* to the future – gain prominence. My anarchist informants continuously tried to find answers to the question of how to be an anarchist, but simultaneously occupied themselves with the continuation of established forms of practice in often hostile, adverse or unsupportive environments. The more or less concrete teleological character of their practices was an expression of their inherent relation with a future, which was performatively, bodily and sensually expressed in their practices (Hirschkind 2001; Mahmood 2001). Yet, the application did not work that straightforwardly. The idea of a linear application of moral codes in ethical practice (here those of being a good anarchist) has rightfully been criticized by notions of moral multiplicity and failure (Simon 2009), moral breakdown (Zigon 2007) or moral ambivalence, fragmentation and incoherence (Schielke 2009a, 2009b). All the more interesting was the inherent continuity exhibited in such practices. Below I present two examples that elicit the complex and critical ethical approaches of my anarchist friends to maintain their lifestyle. As with the communal examples above, their concern was not with something new to emerge and to change current circumstances. More importantly, the continuous practices towards this aim proved the success of ethical practice.

One of my host brothers turned vegan in October 2008. Just two months before Christmas, this decision caused culinary dismay on his parents' and grandparents' side. When the many orders from the vegan-wonderland website were delivered at their home and my host brother was experimenting with his new recipes on a daily basis, the family was exposed to a very different world, with its own ideology, objects and forms of practice. His *ersatz*-meat dishes – made from ten-kilo packages of *seitan*-powder – were bravely tried but ultimately not incorporated into the family's consumption patterns. For all involved, it was clear that the refusal to consume animal products (including honey and leather shoes) did not stem from a major concern for animals per se. My host brother's and many of his anarchist friends' conscious decisions to become vegan rather constituted a statement and form of continuous action against the capitalist system, which substantially defined a good anarchist self. They were seen to be both a political and an ethical act. These 'ethics of revolutionary practice' (Graeber 2004: 6) were thus deployed in practices of the self and essentially both create and maintain the aspired anarchist self in practices aiming at permanence. A few months later, my host brother turned vegetarian, and later continued in different ways to monitor and experiment with his consumption practices as one way of remaining true to his anarchist convictions.

A similarly enduring topic as part of practices of self-formation was the issue of gender and sexuality. I describe a chat with M., one of Hoyerswerda's anarchists. I had told him how intrigued I was to find a sticker in Hoyerswerda, depicting a transsexual, red-haired Japanese manga fighter proclaiming: 'Fight Heteronormativity!' I wondered what a saying like that – in English – would actually mean to my informants. As a form of knowledge imported from elsewhere (the academic or activist milieu), did it actually pose a particular inclination to practice or was it just a visible critique of mainstream sexuality? M. convincingly told me that so far he had not managed to overcome his, as he phrased it, 'heteronormative upbringing'. He added that most of his friends refrained from experimenting despite their daring proclamations. They all nonetheless recurrently discussed the links between capitalism, the state, gender and sexuality, thus rendering their own ideas about gender and sexuality problematic. In order to overcome a system that they despised, they permanently rethought their most intimate self-understandings, relations and practices. All members of the group enduringly checked their language for homophobic vocabulary and were ready to correct others for the usage of demeaning words or phrases, thereby continuously working on their anarchist selves.

These were only two examples of the many means of anarchist self-crafting practices. Many Hoyerswerdian anarchists played in one of the several local bands, produced art (from street art to drawings and installations) or composed poems, song texts, audio books or comics. Every concert, film screening or shared cooking session enacted a youth culture that otherwise would probably not exist in a city of Hoyerswerda's size. The constant experimental mode consequentially followed their inherent *telos*. The young anarchists constantly searched for, in their eyes, better ways of living and maintained in practice their own local anarchist micro-utopias through continuous ethical self-reflection. In their enduring concerns and practices, they were creative, experimental, curious and anticipatory – but their hope did not stem from the deferred notion of something new, emergent or potential to arise. Rather, they continuously invested in themselves, their group of friends and their specific and various forms of practice, which comprised social gatherings, art and more intimate ethical aspects, and consciously aimed at keeping the local anarchist youth culture vibrant and alive. Interestingly, as in the previous communal example, for them, endurance was also related to a spatial configuration. One of the main problems for sustaining their practices was spatial: they were constantly searching for a space in which to hang out. They had previously lost their youth club to a group of dubious punks and regarded other places as potentially dangerous due to their right-wing enemies. Like the potential Braugasse 1 occupants from above, they were also perpetually searching for a place where their practices could endure in a safe environment. Midterm plans of establishing their own commune in the countryside created an idea of what such a place could look like. Since most of them, like other youths, were to leave the city, such a place should also become a permanent place for their culture to survive in the future after their certain departure from the city – and thus should also, if unrealistically, provide an enduring place for their potential return.

This section has explored anarchy in practice, drawing attention to the continuous and enduring work that was invested in maintaining a certain way of life and alternative youth culture. In it, the problematization of the certainly insecure future was sidestepped by the fabrication of anarchic selves and spaces, by critical reasoning

Figure 5.2 *Party flyer, 'Coke, Puke, Communism II', winter 2008*

and continuous practice. A certain form of autonomy and independence was constantly and communally reclaimed, reproduced and defended. The promise of anarchy in this context was the continuation of critical and, indeed, ethical practice. It resembled the maintenance work I discussed at the beginning of this chapter, but has focused on the more intimate aspects of this kind of practices of endurance. I am now going to compare these very distinct notions of the hope of endurance with the hope that many academics invest in the promises of change, recently expressed in the analytical terms 'emergence' and 'becoming'.

From Emergence and Becoming to Maintenance and Permanence

The possible, the new and the emergent have long held some promise for change in academic imaginaries. Bourdieu, for instance, once claimed that 'the very specific restrictions on the subjective definition of "the possible" ... is imposed by historicity ... as an intrinsic limitation on freedom' (quoted in Gell 1992: 266–67). As freedom is valued, the hope for expanding the limits of the possible is pervasive for many scholars, who thereby deploy a very particular notion of change and efficacy of human practice. The logic is usually the same: change the virtual limits of the possible in order to affect the actual world. At first, a new idea emerges, then follows its actualization in practice. Utopian writing, for instance, accordingly serves as an 'imperative to imagine' 'radical alternatives' (Jameson 2005: 416), and 'imagination as social practice' becomes a 'collective tool for the transformation of the real, for the creation of multiple horizons of possibility' (Appadurai 2002: 34). The hoped-for outcome of these imaginary, virtual or utopian practices in the scholarly imagination is usually the emergence of the alternative or the new – posed against any notion of predetermination. Such practices rightly add to the sense of the 'multiplicity of possible worlds' in our own temporal maps (Gell 1992: 239) and future promises. However, they differ from the presentist approach deployed in this book by seeing the present in itself as being restricted and only ever to be overcome rather than cultivated.

In this section, I scrutinize such Deleuzian imaginaries of change, especially emergence and becoming. I want to contrast the academic urge for the emergent (compare e.g. Rabinow 2003, 2007; Rabinow et al. 2008) with my informants' concern with the maintenance of the threatened forms that make up their life. For them, hope was not located in awaiting the new as an anticipation of something becoming – Bloch's 'not-yet-become'. Their promises instead lay in the tedious maintenance of things they hold dearly in the present. This was not enforced presentism or simple pragmatism, but a form of anticipation. There was hope in the continuous work that members of the aforementioned clubs invested their committed practices with. For example, in the Braugasse 1 club, the hope of influencing the local administration to support the renovation of the building involved hundreds of club and working group meetings, and endless pins, stickers, raffle tickets and glasses of mulled wine sold at dozens of promotional public events, which had to be continuously organized and attended. But it also involved the constant reminder that all this effort was worth it despite the dire prospects for success. The clubs I engaged with most, the *KuFa* and the Braugasse 1 club, both went through phases when they lost hope and believed they were unable to maintain their efforts. Change for them consisted of the old *not* disappearing – as was predicted. Their practices of maintenance were driven, amongst other things, by a vision of an alternative future paradoxically similar to the present, that is, a sustaining future or sustained present in the future.

Waiting for something to become or emerge, whether as an anthropologist or a citizen of Hoyerswerda, has a certain millennial, messianic flavour. It is also passive. Constant becoming obviously also involves continuous human practice, but it surely lacks form and structure. This can be celebrated for very good reasons as a form of liberation. My informants, however, missed the security and predictability that the absence of shrinkage had provided them with.[1] The efficacy of hope as the anticipation of the 'not-yet-become' according to Bloch's theory consists only of the direction and stimulation of practice: 'the "anticipatory consciousness" … prepares the way for the Not-Yet-Become, the realized material reality of the future which however cannot yet be described, only hoped-for and willed-for. This "Not-Yet" … is … "a directing act of a cognitive kind"' (Bloch 1986 [1959]: 561). That said, hope has this capacity only as long as its contents are actually anticipating the future and are not just contemplative. However, for a presentist to foretell the actual future is not an option.

In Bloch's theory, the truth-value of predictions of the future is not judged by its efficacy, but by whether it correctly predicts the 'yet-to-become'. If so, the content of a particular hope turns into a 'real fragment' or 'pre-appearance' of the future (ibid.: 210, 217f, also 108f), otherwise it fails to 'notice the real tendencies' (ibid.: 479). As Bloch puts it, 'everything real passes over into the Possible at its processual Front, and possible is everything that is only partially conditioned, that has not yet been fully or conclusively determined' (ibid.: 196). Although in Bloch's deterministic philosophy the future often appears as being given, he still caters to a particular fashion in current theories of affect, hope and the future. From such perspectives, hope, as an affective force, activates people and functions like a catalyst, keeping people tuned into the future. It is the guarantor of change. There is much to be said about Bloch's basically Marxist theory not living up to academically prevalent concerns about indeterminacy and contingency, and this book's general take on presentism by remaining partially deterministic. Despite differing from postmodernist scholars' 'performative understanding of moments of hope' (Kraftl 2007: 126), Bloch's take on hope still promises the emergence and becoming of something new.

Ben Anderson (2006a), inspired by Bloch's work, offers a similar example of how emergence is approached with academic hopes. As a postrepresentational geographer, Anderson argues that hope 'heralds the affect and emotive as always "not-yet-become"' (Anderson 2006a: 733) and thus 'discloses the creation of potentiality and becoming' (ibid.). Its affective impact, like in much scholarship on affects, directs action and stimulates the emergence of something new by opening up the present for change. Hope and other affects are seen as the motor of change and against determination since they facilitate emergence and becoming through their inherent affective anticipations. However, becoming in the Deleuzian sense does not anticipate something doomed to come. It has an open, not a predetermined idea of the future and is directed against theories that linger on predetermination. For Deleuze, change accordingly happens to a large extent at random. It results less from intentional practices in the present, as I would see it. The efficacy of the practices I am concerned about certainly does not translate flawlessly into the future, as indeterminacy, contingency and any form of surprise make us aware of each moment's actual potentiality. Some acts, however, are successful in their performance. Moreover, there are areas of life over which people actively claim this efficacy, as in the examples discussed above. Is there a false hope in the academic imagination of a postmodern utopia of 'enduring indeterminacy' (Bloch, quoted in Anderson 2006a: 749)?

The endurance of hope in Hoyerswerda stemmed only partially from a belief in the emergence of something new. It also emerged out of the experience of partial efficacy of continuous practices. How does this relate to the idea that 'hope enacts the future as open to difference and reminds us that the here and now are "uncentered, dispersed, plural and partial"' (Anderson 2006a: 733)? Anderson uses Massumi's theory of affect as the basis for establishing his take on hope, becoming and emergence. Accordingly, affect is always on the 'edge of the virtual, where it leaks into the actual' (Massumi, quoted in ibid.: 737) and hope, more specifically, is an overspill of the virtual into the actual. The virtual thus produces change in the actual: it is the immaterial that creates real material changes. However, the hope for change (for the better) for my informants did not stem from an abstract affective dimension, but was strongly related to particular and actual forms of life and practices, and remained continuously directed towards their own and their city's future. In contrast, for Anderson, hope is not an 'intentional act directed towards the future' (ibid.: 741) and becoming hopeful is 'not an act of transcendence to a good elsewhere and elsewhen', but 'an act of establishing new relations that disclose a point of contingency within a present space-time' (ibid.: 743). For him, actual change depends on disclosing this contingency, not on affecting it. Hope for permanence, as expressed by my informants, counters such a point of contingency. Hope from Anderson's perspective can indeed be cherished as a much-needed response to the widespread hopelessness so characteristic of the postindustrial times in which we are living. However, any virtual idea, which is given form in the actual, still needs to be maintained. Another hope in times of hopelessness can be found in my informants' maintenance work.

Similarly, 'becoming' for Biehl and Locke results from a 'transformative potential' in 'immanent fields of action and significance', which are 'leaking out on all sides' (Biehl and Locke 2010: 317). It is again affect that initiates this leaking. In their eyes, 'desire can break free open alternative pathways' towards 'unexpected futures', especially in contexts like their fieldsites, where people are 'moving through broken institutions and infrastructures in the making' and 'when life chances are foreclosed' (ibid.: 318). Whilst celebrating potentiality, Biehl and Locke claim that their informants in contexts of decline and threatened survival make 'possibility … a crucial dimension of what is/was' (ibid.: 323). In contrast, my informants had very practical concerns and would have been opposed to this idea of fluidity as a source of hope. Rather, they made endurance crucial to their lives and were critical of the present's character of becoming, its very 'element of flight that escapes its own formalization', which Deleuze would cherish (Biehl and Locke 2010: 326), as well as its refusal of 'attaining a form' (ibid.). They precisely wanted things to have a form as a basis for their endurance. Similarly, Locke's informant Maja concentrated on practices 'of small hopes and aspirations, of better maths grades and prowess in snow-boarding' (ibid.: 333). This was concrete and productive. Why not include, then, Locke's ex-Yugoslavian informants' 'much more specific expectations' of politics 'to again provide the kind of social protections and safety nets they recall from the communist era' (ibid.: 332)? They constitute, I claim, one way of how these informants practically and daily 'endure and try to escape constraints and articulate new systems of perception and action' (ibid.: 336) in the 'abiding of intolerable present circumstances' of 'a new kind of day-to-day survival' (ibid.). In contrast, the authors conclude that 'a crucial element of this immanence is the day-to-day anticipation or envisionings of alternative forms of existence' (ibid.: 348).

Biehl and Locke also pose possibility and emergence against the 'anxious uncertainty and open-endedness of life' and the 'routinized urgency and crisis' (Biehl and Locke 2010: 336), thus verging on a distorted celebration of neoliberal ideologies of possibility. Does it help my analysis to perceive my informants as showing 'a passion for the possible' (ibid.: 319), for the new and emergent? By prescribing openness, Biehl and Locke end up accusing others of a 'straitjacketing of the future' (Hirschmann, quoted in ibid.). However, in the sense of Maurer's quote at the beginning of this chapter, it might actually be these practices aiming at straitjacketing the future in which we find 'a little more allowance for the unexpected – and a little less wishful thinking' (Hirschmann in ibid.), as required by Biehl and Locke. Hope in hope's anticipatory and wishful capacity can therefore be found in the improbable continuity of particular forms of life, still functioning as an innovative drive of human action. Such thought might make us appreciate our informants' many creative ways of dealing with the problems they face. I follow the guidelines for judging the future laid out by my informants in this chapter's first section – shifting their own temporal reasoning away from progress towards the logic of sustainability. Instead of installing longing into our informants akin to the Lord Mayor's Antoine de Saint-Exupery quote mentioned in previous chapters, some practical help and support in maintaining their club, association, school or kindergarten would have been more appreciated than an urge for abstract longing. Instead of waiting for emergent new ideas, many people in my fieldsite – as one of my host mothers underlined in Chapter 1 – were busy trying to keep things alive. If they had not made the effort, these forms would have ceased to exist. And some forms did indeed cease to exist once their maintenance failed. For instance, the 'Youth Has Visions!' project mentioned in Chapter 3 ended because most participants – especially the schools – stopped investing in this format. The strength and motivation to maintain this form of crafting and explicating such visions, which first appeared in 2003, was not kept alive.

Another version of analytical preference for the emergent comes from Rabinow's development of Foucault's history of the present into an anthropology of the contemporary. Rabinow starts with the simple but profound question 'what difference does today make with respect to yesterday – and to tomorrow' (Rabinow et al. 2008: 67) and focuses on 'concepts to make visible what is emerging' (ibid.: 64). As Tobias Rees summarizes: 'For Rabinow, "today" – understood as an intellectual category – is a logical and conceptual challenge. The present is a historical, open moment in which what is or has been is, at least potentially, changing. His aim as an "anthropologist of the contemporary" ... is to identify, trace, and name such changes' (ibid.: 9) by focusing 'on events and actualizations that take place in a particular field' (ibid.: 78). George Marcus critiques Rabinow's focus on the present for a lack of historical consideration (ibid.: 56), detecting a familiarity with neoliberal ideology and enforced presentism, preached and practised by 'consultants' and 'advisers of policy makers' (ibid.). However, as Rabinow explains, a focus on the contemporary, inherent in our basically presentist methodology, is not about forgetting the past, but about analytically opening up the present for both the past and the future. He quotes Blumenberg saying that we should remain 'open to the present, against narratives of decline, disaster, and other forms of closure' (in Rabinow 2007: 13), which also captures this book's presentist spirit. For Rabinow, the question is 'as Nietzsche saw long ago, whether historical conditions are everything. And I believe strongly that they are not. There is a great deal of contingency and underdetermination in most situations' (Rabinow et al. 2008: 56).

One powerful critique of such theories of the emergent has been voiced by Miyazaki and Riles (2005: 327–28). They compare its analytical logic with the response of Japanese finance experts to what they perceive as 'failures of knowledge'. The authors claim that for 'the anthropologist of the contemporary, the failure at issue is a failure in the ability to "know" the ethnographic subject. In response to such failures of knowing, the focus on "emergence", "complexity", and "assemblage" implicitly resigns itself to the fact that little can be known about the world except for the fact of complexity, indeterminacy, and open-endedness, since reality, in this view, is always emergent, indeterminate, and contemporary' (ibid.). Although I greatly sympathize with Rabinow's stance, I still find Miyazaki and Riles' argument intriguing. As they continue, in response to the apprehension of the endpoint of their own knowledge, these theorists 'retreat from knowing. And they also retreat from the recognition of the failure of their own knowledge by locating indeterminacy and complexity "out there", as if to be discovered, documented in real time' (ibid.). They note that for 'Rabinow, for example, anthropology becomes "a chronicle of emergent assemblages"' (ibid.) and offer in response the strategy to stabilize (i.e. to know) such failure as endpoints and transform them into new beginning points, which mirrors my informants' attempts not to abandon the forms they care about. What both approaches share is the concern for concrete (knowledge) practices. Rabinow in an anthropological fashion remains particularly attuned to the emergent, meanwhile shaping and sculpting new forms and norms of practice and analytical toolkits in his impressive oeuvre. For him, the contemporary is accordingly where 'older and newer elements are given form and worked together' (Rabinow 2007: 3) – and, I should add, where some of these forms are made to endure.

These last remarks on form have much to say about a potential imaginary of endurance. Yet another fashionable trope – assemblages – seems to entail both aspects: first, that of impermanence found in the only temporary, constantly changing and shifting relation or constellation of different elements; and, second, the propensity to endure as inherent in their formal character. The work on the persistence of particular assemblages, as shown in this chapter, could be seen as one way of *performing* – that is, giving shape to – the future. As Rabinow takes from Dewey: 'the giving of form (whether discursive, logical, artistic, scientific, political, and the like) is a primary task in living in general' (Rabinow 2007: 9). As shown with regard to my ethnographic material, giving particular forms a future (and thus future a form) depends on practice. However, the future, as Hegel famously wrote, is 'the formless ... so no form whatsoever can be viewed in the future' (quoted in Bloch 1986 [1959]: 883). Performing the future (i.e. having performative or transformative effects on future presents) means very specifically attempting to give the future a form. For example, this may include practices of regularization and situational adjustment (compare the discussion of Sally F. Moore's work in Turner (1987)). For Sally F. Moore, writing in the heyday of the struggle between processual and structural approaches in anthropology, such an approach is 'a declaration against indeterminacy' (quoted in ibid.: 30). Regarding her informants' legal and religious rituals, she claims that through 'form and formality they celebrate man-made meaning, the culturally determinate, the regulated, the named, and the explained ... Indeed there is no doubt that any analysis of social life must take account of the dynamic relation between the formed and "the indeterminate"' (in ibid.). Formal features allow a higher probability to endure in time. However, the actual temporal endurance of forms dissolves in their dependence on practice. Particular moments in time are thus quite literally *perform*ed: not in the sense of performance, but in the Latin sense of the word – given form/shape.

In their book on *Global Assemblages*, Collier and Ong underline the importance of the formal character of assemblages, which makes them endure through time and space, and accordingly deterritorializable and reterritorializable throughout the world (Collier and Ong 2005: 11). However, what happens when these characteristics disappear – the aftermath of assemblages – is not explored further. For them, the idea of a constant process of re-formation seems to suffice as a theory of change – without fissures, breaks, gaps or exhaustion (see Povinelli 2011) along the way. Even life in itself, as Collier and Lakoff (2005: 22ff) underline, can be given form by being rendered problematic – as did the future in Hoyerswerda. Collier and Lakoff use the term 'regime' in order to emphasize the 'provisional consistency or coherence' of what they call 'regimes of living', which combine 'principles of ethical reasoning' with 'concrete practices' in 'specific contexts', as well as 'norms of conduct with forms of practice' (Collier and Lakoff 2005: 31ff). They are engaging in 'a form of inquiry that stays close to practices' and 'concrete problems' (ibid.: 17). As I have shown throughout this book, these two things are methodologically accessible by ethnographic presentism since they are the *perform*ed elements of social life, rendered explicit in the present in conditions of presumed instability. People, like my informants, thus give the problematized a form and have a grip on it as an object of knowledge and affect, even if in relation to something as intangible as the future. As I have shown in this chapter, the relationship to such forms (social, communal or of the self) can be a hopeful one. The endurance of these forms through times of change thereby promises as much, if not more a future than the waiting for something new to emerge. Such reasoning does not part from notions of indeterminacy, but links theories of the future, practice, forms and change differently in order to explain the hope stemming from practices of maintenance and endurance.

Conclusion

In this chapter, I have contrasted the logic of permanence as exhibited in my informants' concerns and practices to the imaginaries used in the academy to describe and conceptualize change. Instead of deconstructing notions of emergence, possibility, the virtual and assemblages, I see them as one possible imagination of hope and change – the wishing scarves at the Braugasse 1 building being a colourful expression of such thinking. I am nonetheless advocating taking the second step into consideration that follows the moment of emergence and is somehow threatened by it, namely that of maintenance and endurance. Such practices of endurance produce stability and sustain the maintenance (or survival) of given forms of life – a particular building, a set of social practices, the anarchist self and youth culture. They do not entail less hope or less critical potential. Rather, concerns for permanence, endurance and continuity do not contradict important notions of indeterminacy and contingency, nor should they be understood as inherently old-fashioned and conservative. They are neither less future-orientated nor simply embedded in the past. In fact, they demand and make *impossible* alternatives survive, against all odds, and sustain the future in a context characterized by postindustrial shrinkage and decline.

Notes

A previous version of this chapter was published as F. Ringel. 2014. 'Post-industrial Times and the Unexpected: Endurance and Sustainability in Germany's Fastest-Shrinking City'. *Journal of the Royal Anthropological Institute*, 20: 52–70.

1. For some interesting post-Yugoslavian examples, compare Greenberg (2011); Jansen (2014).

Conclusion

Coming to Terms with the Future/'Zukunftsbewältigung'

Hope must be unconditionally disappointable.
—Ernst Bloch in H. Miyazaki, *The Method of Hope*

One and a half years after I left Hoyerswerda, I returned to my field-site. With all of the frightening predictions in mind, I was not sure what to expect. However, on my arrival, I was suddenly told that the deconstruction process actually seemed to have slowed down. Apparently, the city's two main landlords recently became even more cautious about their demolition strategies. Too many potential tenants had already been lost because they, unexpectedly, could *not yet* be provided with renovated, that is, 'secure', apartments closer to the city centre. Shrinkage seemed to happen too quickly sometimes and at other points not quickly enough, as it seemed.

My first impressions were ambivalent, too. WK 4's famous Y-shaped apartment block, whose survival I had hoped for, already lay in pieces. The colossal structure, of three eleven-storey blocks attached at an angle of 120 degrees (building the shape of a 'Y' as seen from above), had been demolished in less than a week. In contrast, another dominant *Neustadt* building, the eleven-storey Apartment Block 'At the Knee' (*Hochhaus am Knie*), had, again against general expectations, been rescued by its inhabitants. They had successfully formed a citizens' group in order to fight for their house's survival and force the city's administration and the landlord to secure its existence. Some corners of the city looked better than before; others were still not taken care of. At least the restoration of the Braugasse

Figure 6.1 *Former Burger King branch, outside WK 10, autumn 2009*

1 building was on the way. Some new developments also attracted my attention, but I was most amazed by the increasing decay and closure of other buildings erected in the postsocialist era: small shopping centres, supermarkets and business parks at the outskirts of Hoyerswerda, and even the local Burger King branch had all been closed down. The remaining buildings showed clear signs of decay and dilapidation despite their short, postsocialist existence. They were even more quickly emptied than their neighbouring socialist apartment blocks.

However, it was not the physical or material changes that affected me most on my return, but the social ones. The very *sense* of the city had changed from that of the city I had so intensely studied and enjoyed living in for almost a year and a half. Or so it seemed initially. What really hurt on my return was the fact that so many of my informants – virtually all the younger ones – had left the city. Whilst walking through the city, there was no concrete sense of missing them. It was rather a sadness felt for the city itself paired with an awkward feeling one of my host brothers had once expressed to me on the occasion of one of his rare returns: the feeling that as somebody who had left Hoyerswerda, one very soon did not belong here anymore. Indeed, as a group of young artists captured it in the title for their then most recent exhibition in the *KuFa*: 'Nobody, who I know, lives here anymore' (*Hier wohnt keiner mehr, den ich kenne*). As a result of the continuous exodus of citizens, had the long-feared future finally arrived? This question might be misleading. My personal view only mirrored what most of my informants had experienced throughout the last two decades. And in each new present, they still had continued with their lives, against all odds and with much zeal.

The Present of the Future

In the previous five chapters, I have assembled a variety of heterogeneous notions, logics and affects of – and references to – the future. I showed how, conceptually abandoned by state, federal and academic expertise, many Hoyerswerdian informants kept searching for new concepts – epistemological tropes, symbols or narratives – in order to make sense of the changes that pervaded their lives. Most of the examples discussed in this book comprised knowledge practices in which the inhabitants of this shrinking city reassured themselves about themselves, scrutinized their personal and communal pasts, presents and futures, and – most importantly – produced knowledge about what is to come in order to adjust or redirect their own practices, plans, aims, hopes and expectations. Knowledge and affects remained key players in this quest for survival, but the hoped-for visions for the future were not of a curatory, cathartic or salvific kind.

These diverse practices guided my exploration of the epistemic consequences of the process of shrinkage in the city of Hoyerswerda twenty years after the fall of the Berlin Wall. I encountered them in many different public events, conflictive situations and intimate moments, at professional conferences and workshops, at sociocultural and artistic projects, amongst members of social clubs and associations, on screen and on stage, in families and groups of friends, in the city council, local schools, private businesses, *Neustadt*'s shopping centre, bars and restaurants. I discussed them with local youth, retired miners, engineers and architects, with city officials, external experts and local businessmen, with the Kurdish kebab seller in WK 10 and the last tenant of a soon-to-be demolished *Neustadt* apartment house, with local journalists and my physiotherapists, and also with my wonderful host families and many Hoyerswerdian friends. From the Lord Mayor Stefan Skora to every pupil, the city's future was and continued to be of much concern. Even though the city was infused with these concerns, hopes and other future knowledges, I refrain from subsuming them under the term 'temporal regime of shrinkage'. However, in their entirety they still constituted something like a morphology of the future in this particular space and time – a set of cross-references, which compose a framework for local temporal practices and agency.

Throughout the book, I have explored this morphology of the local future. In Chapter 1, I introduced the ways in which my informants produced and deployed ideas of contexts, with which they attempted to embed their hometown's and their own personal dramatic changes. I read these attempts in their variety against our own anthropological constructions of contextual knowledge, engaging critically with the concept of postsocialism and its inherent historical and determinist bias. In Chapter 2, I narrowed down this contextual knowledge to forms of temporal reasoning. The intergenerational and political clashes I depicted emerged around different forms of temporal reasoning and included references to the past and the future. Chapter 3 took this perspective further and focused more specifically on aspects of the future. With material from urban planning discourses, contrasted with other public interventions in debates about the city's future, I tried to show how the presumed and at first sight apparent evacuation of the near future was challenged by a multiplicity of other references to – and appropriations of – the near future. Having developed the idea of an unexpected abundance of future references in a shrinking city, in the remaining chapters I expanded my toolkit and perspectives with further elements of relevance for studying the future, addressing the pressing issues of outmigration, urban governance and citizens' participation, which shaped Hoyerswerda's understanding of itself and its futures during the time of my fieldwork. Chapter 4 tried to think through incidents when affect is imposed on other people. Chapter 5 deployed theories of practice and ethics to think through the efficacy of future knowledge regarding practices of maintenance, endurance and permanence and their inherent teleologies. They all helped to map the local economy of knowledge about the future.

The many references to the future that I encountered during my fieldwork not only guided me through the complexity of my ethnographic material – they also helped me probe a more complex analytical approach to the future. In this conclusion, I summarize this presentist approach and point at its theoretical limits, benefits and implications. Moreover, I suggest a few future directions in which studies of the future could potentially be taken. As I laid out in this book's introduction: the main point of my take on the future is that I approach the future methodologically as a matter of only ever present knowledge practices, regardless of whether their predictions turn out to be right. For its analysis, I draw on the rich tradition of the anthropology of knowledge. To put it briefly, I consider the future as a matter of time; time, in turn, as a matter of knowledge; and knowledge as a matter of concrete and situated practice (see Rabinow 1986). Approaching the future in this way embeds it in analytical terms thoroughly in particular situational (epistemic, practical, relational etc.) contexts. It thereby renders the social, ethical and political contexts of its practices ethnographically accessible. I claim that this conceptualization of the role the future plays in human life and experience is radical in at least three different ways.

First, my approach to the yet-to-come is radically presentist – especially since it is based on a similarly presentist methodology of anthropological fieldwork. That means that in contrast to Bloch, for instance, I do not deploy a deterministic understanding of time and the future. In my understanding of presentism, the future always remains open – hence my emphasis on notions of surprise and the unexpected. As the philosopher Craig Bourne (2006) pointed out, even the fact that only one out of all possible futures turns out to become the present in the future does not mean that this future was predetermined to become a future present, that is, that it somewhat pre-existed and then inevitably emerged in the present. To take such an ex post facto construction as true, as I argued in the Introduction, constitutes what Bourne calls a 'deterministic fallacy' (ibid.: 61f). It is only in the present that references to the future dimension are made; consequently, it is not the future-to-be that leans into – and has effects on – this present. Rather, it is only the present that reaches out into the future, as much as it reaches (back?) into the past.[1] Approaches to time based on phenomenology and practice theory follow a similar logic. Husserl's famous 'retention' and 'protention', Koselleck's 'space of experience' (*Erfahrungsraum*) and 'horizon of expectation' (*Erwartungshorizont*), and Gell's 'temporal maps' are examples of such approaches.

Second, this presentist claim involves the observation that even the after all non-existing actual future (as well as all others) does depend for its existence in the present on its epistemic representation. The term 'temporal reasoning' captures the framework in which these representational practices occur, but it is only one of the many sets of practices that create a relationship to the future. Other practices involve straightforward extensions of the present into the future (planning, construction and realization rather than reasoning or representations per se) or affects as non-representational expressions of knowledge about the future in the present (especially hope and fear). Importantly, temporal aspects are not an inherent characteristic of particular objects, situations or ideas – as the term 'temporality' suggests (Ringel 2016b). There is nothing like a futurity in the form of some inherent drive to the future in whatever analytical object we look at. Such a determined position in time can only be constructed retrospectively, especially regarding the future. Elements of a given present then come to be seen as having a history and as having (always?) been directed towards the future. However, this construction 'after the fact' does not account for the present under consideration and its openness to the future. It does also not explain the sudden loss of this characteristic, since it does not make its reproduction through time dependent on practice and further investments. If a temporal aspect of a thing, an idea or a situation has to be created and maintained via continuous (knowledge and other) practices, then time overall can be seen as an issue of knowledge. The many different temporal references, particular temporal epistemic logics and affects, and distinct forms of temporal reasoning that I presented in this book are prime examples of temporal knowledge. Like any other knowledge, they are heavily embedded in the ethical, social and political contexts in which they are produced, disseminated and deployed. I have discerned these contexts in my account in order to understand the complexity of the epistemic and affective repercussions of Hoyerswerda's factual shrinkage and to show how my informants – against common expectations for people severely affected by postindustrial and other decline – deploy an astonishing temporal, that is, epistemic flexibility in continuous practices and difficult processes of social negotiation and the communal production of meaning.

Third, this also implies a radical deployment of the theoretical concerns of contingency and indeterminacy. Once we strip off the term 'temporality' from its future dimension – since the future is a matter of representation in the present – then all that remains from its presumed analytic worth is the aspect of historicity. Historicity involves an idea of the past as predetermining the present, even in its infamous enabling and restricting effects (see Hirsch and Stewart 2005). Seen from a presentist approach, it presumes that what and how we know in any present is determined or conditioned by the past – by a history that has not only made our knowledge into what it is, but also imbues its existence in time with a particular force and directionality. My approach – without fully disputing the

conditioned character of the present – questions the presumed directionality that is springing from any idea of historical determination.
The retrospective analytical detection of historical trends and patterns does make sense when deploying long-term historical perspectives as Foucault did in his histories of systems of thought. In such
cases, we can abstractly determine the longstanding temporal characteristics of particular analytical objects such as problematizations,
assemblages and apparatuses (Rabinow 2003: 55ff). But for a presentist, this does not constitute an ontological aspect of the present analysed. Although Foucault's analysis of knowledge includes a variety
of concrete practices, I would also observe that he links knowledge
unambiguously to power as a transhistorical force, or rather as a thoroughly historically embedded force that transcends human lifespans.
From a presentist point of view, Foucault's observations of long-term
change have less relevance for an understanding of the present. They
remain if at all – and as initially intended – only a doubtlessly important and necessary *history* of the present, not an intricate *analysis* of
the contemporary (cf. Rabinow et al. 2008). However, as Gell (1992)
claimed, the past's impact on the present is similarly contingent as
that of the future. Processes of change, but even more so actual representations of past, present and future, are the contingent outcome
of human practice. A presentist approach therefore makes it possible
to finally put the past and the future on an equal footing in whatever
present we are concerned about.

Beyond Shrinkage?

One major repercussion of this presentist approach affects the last
decade's general trend in the anthropology of postsocialism and
broader academic considerations of topics such as memory, culture
and change. First, this book has shown that it is analytically unhelp-
ful and theoretically flawed to dismiss the temporal dimension
of the future in analyses of social life. In response, there has been
an upsurge in academic concerns with the future over the last two
decades – paralleling Hoyerswerda's sudden and intense problematization of the future in the same post-Cold War period. People's manifold attempts to reach out in time make future matters count in their
epistemic and mundane practices, and assist them in understanding
their own position in time. Analysing these attempts profits from a
fuller consideration of the future and its role in – and subsequent
impact on – the present. In the anthropology of postsocialism, this

is even more relevant due to its inherent reference to the socialist past (compare Knudsen and Frederiksen 2015). Similar to James
Ferguson's critique of development discourses, postsocialist scholars
have deconstructed narratives of transition. However, these analyses remained subject to analytical 'enforced presentism' by focusing
on issues of survival and mundane pragmatism – which emptied out
their informants' ability to creatively reach out in time and especially
into the future (see for instance Oushakine 2000).

But the anthropology of postsocialism is obviously much more
heterogeneous than a retrospective tendency of culturalizing one's
informants' existence in time suggests. Despite the fact that many of
these informants exactly proved the point that no subjugation to –
or determination by – any dominant regime is ever total, they were
quickly transformed from the celebrated heroes of the late-socialist
revolutions to the postsocialist other, who is somehow 'stuck' in the
past and unwilling or unable to overcome it. The anthropology of
East Germany is eager to point out that practices of Ostalgie were
not expressions of a presumed fixation to the past or an ontological
matter of being postsocialist. As the works of Borneman, Berdahl,
Glaeser and Boyer underline, the abundance of references to the
socialist past was rather an outcome of particular temporal politics. Postsocialist studies as a whole increasingly reflect upon their
analytical tools', terms' and logics' implications in such temporal
politics – as should the whole discipline of anthropology. However,
as Gilbert et al. (2008; see also Gilbert 2006) have pointed out, the
anthropology of postsocialism more generally faces severe challenges
with periodization. But what can the perspective from a shrinking
postsocialist city, the extreme case of the more general processes of
postsocialist transformation, deindustrialization and growing global
inequality, propose as a better relationship to the future?

First, as a postsocialist shrinking city, Hoyerswerda provides
an example of a locale where the temporal regime of transition or
postsocialism is accompanied, if not overcome, by a new temporal
framework: that of shrinkage. Second, it shows that Jane Guyer's
inspiring ideas of enforced presentism and fantasy futurism are challenged through a variety of local practices. Initially, I intended to
present these challenges as resistant or rebellious reappropriations of
the near future until I realized that they could be as well embedded
in what I came to call 'enforced futurism'. However, to substitute
their forms of relating to the future with other ones would neither
solve the actual problems with the future nor transcend the opposite
of enforced presentism, namely 'enforced futurism'. It would also

contradict my presentist inclinations to account for people's temporal agency. Also, ethnographically, a reappropriation of the future did not provide a convincing answer to the present's epistemic crisis with regard to the local future. From Boyer's perspective, this is just an expression of a 'nostalgia for the future' (Boyer 2010). But does this urge for the future entail a coming to terms with the future, a mastering of the future, a step of epistemic survival, which would be setting an end to shrinkage and decline (or at least its repercussions on local temporal knowledge practices)?

This brings me back to the strategic representational problems presented at the beginning of this book – that is, to avoid presenting the city either through the perspective of decline or through that of survival. Shrinkage itself has a similar deterministic relationship to the future like decline and survival. Although I have criticized the notion of shrinkage and have shown its limits and deficiencies, I still use it as an analytical tool and descriptive device. Reflecting upon my own development, the sixteen months of fieldwork now appear as consisting of two phases: one of an intellectual appropriation of the term *Schrumpfung* and the other of a critical distancing from it. It seems that the biggest achievement in this process was to be able to finally ask the question 'What does come after shrinkage?' – that is, to open up the present yet again for a different relationship to the future. This ability to imaginatively transcend the determinate process of shrinkage (and other dominant temporal logics and regimes) made it possible to put an imaginary end to this framework and be able to reflect upon and accordingly shape the present from a new vantage point in the future. This left the temporal regime of shrinkage behind by radically redirecting knowledge, which created a previously lost form of hope for the future – not, as Miyazaki (2004) suggests, the other way round. However, as this shows, before coming to this conclusion, I had still been bound up in some form of enforced futurism in order to overcome the enforced presentism prevalent in official planning discourses.

In the last ethnographic discussion of this book, I will scrutinize my own hopes. I search for a relationship to the future that I can pose against those that I found in the temporal regimes and dominant forms of temporal reasoning, which I criticized in this book. I also try to answer the introduction's question by Gundermann about how we are to catch the future and accordingly how am I to write a *hopeful* ethnography about a shrinking fieldsite's future. This requires an introduction of one last aspect of the temporal and analytical logics of the future. This step presents the reconsideration of one's relationship to the future as the regaining of critical faculty. Investments in the future not only result in the creation of something new and further emergence (the major hope expressed in the academic literature on utopia) or the production of permanence, maintenance and endurance – they also create a new relationship to the present.

Crapanzano is interested in the latter relation between the future and the present. As he claims: 'Our images, dreams, projections, calculations, and prophecies may give form and substance to the beyond, but as they do, they destroy it, they assure its displacement' (2004: 14). He thereby draws our attention to the 'paradoxical ways in which the irreality of the imaginary impresses the real on reality and the real of reality compels the irreality of the imaginary' (ibid.: 15). In his eyes, our ability for utopian thought is a distancing faculty from the present. Crapanzano quotes literary critic Jean Starobiski's work from the 1970s: imagination is also a 'distancing power ... thanks to which we ... distance ourselves from the present realities' 'because it anticipates and previews, serves action, draws before us the configuration of the realizable before it can be realized' (ibid.: 19). I see this act of previewing the yet-to-come as a form of anticipatory presentism, and it is precisely this present concern to which Hoyerswerda's inhabitants aspired. However, 'nothing can ... guarantee the success of the anticipatory imagination. It may end up producing only "an empty image of hope"' (ibid.). What then do my informants (as much as I) hope for when reclaiming the future, or respectively the present?

'Hoyerswerda is Alive!'

Later on the first day of my return, I was dragged to a training session for the sequel of a community dance project whose first part had taken place in the first summer after my leaving. There it was again, in this little run-down gym from the 1960s, adjacent to the former Yuri Gagarin School: the Hoyerswerda that had inspired me with its commitment and joy of life, with its openness to new forms and ideas, and with the actual stamina and courage to put them into reality. Approximately sixty people of all age groups swarmed the small space. Dirk, one of my host uncles, who has time and again appeared in this book, was warming up the heterogeneous crowd. All different kinds and shapes of bodies were twisting around, stretching as far as possible, moving in bizarre gestures. Dirk was showing the participants new dancing steps and group choreographies. The breaks between were very welcome. They were filled with chitchat and laughter, but there was also a sense of professionalism, which made the pain and little embarrassments all the more endurable. When I – for the very last time – visited Hoyerswerda again in order to attend their performance, I could attest that all the suffering had been worth it. As the project's title 'Hoyerswerda is Alive – A City is Dancing!' (*Hoyerswerda lebt – Eine Stadt tanzt!*) indicated, for the participants, the city's survival and its quality of life were actually a real concern – and their excellent show was an impressive expression of their very will to answer to this concern.

Only one of my hopes was not fulfilled whilst watching the second part of the show. I had expected this sequel to provide the audience with the answer to the very distinct question that Dirk and the dancers so ingeniously raised at the end of part one: how does life look *after shrinking*? The very intense first part had given the audience a space to work through the loss of the future. People showed very strong emotional reactions: tears, bitterness, but also a lot of hope. However, the sole and potentially affective proposition for overcoming the crisis of shrinkage that was given then was the one of 'pure joy of life' (*echte Lebensfreude*). This proclamation was powerful because it stayed in the discursive paradigm of that time; it was responding defensively to all the internal and external accusations of Hoyerswerda's unworthiness and its lack of quality of life. It was the first step in a more self-confident stance from which to produce new and different knowledge about the city, its future and one's life in it. As a first step, it did not produce much content. There were no representations of what 'a good life' in a future after shrinking would actually look like.

The self-proclaimed aim of Dirk and his advisers was to provide exactly such an idea in the sequel. He was inspired by East German philosopher Wolfgang Engler's book *Citizen, without a Job*, a provocative call for the radical reorganization of society. Instead of being based on wage labour, the postindustrial society should account for the fact that there are no longer enough jobs, which the author celebrates as a 'civilizing achievement' (Engler 2005). What Engler, like many others, proposes is the introduction of a general basic income. Every citizen *qua* being citizen is entitled to this general income, which covers all basic existential, social and cultural needs. Understanding Hoyerswerda as an extreme case of postindustrial decline – indeed, a new vanguard city of a process that will affect most parts of the former industrialized world – Dirk initially intended to deploy Engler's idea to Hoyerswerda as a case study. He wanted to explore with his team and dancers and for the audience what such a fundamental restructuring of society would actually entail. The very concrete concerns on his agenda were questions such as: how will people in the future live, define work and value family life, social relations, culture or art? What will be the definitions of happiness and fulfilment – indeed, of the quality of life – in such a future?

In the course of the second project, participants were asked to produce knowledge about their hometown's potential postindustrial futures. In a weekend workshop, they were given the task to imagine that a miracle had happened in Hoyerswerda. The amateur dancers were then supposed to assemble answers to questions such as 'How would that miracle look like?' or 'How would one notice that it had actually happened?' Such questions pushed the participants' stance to the future to its limits – how does one imagine a miracle and its detailed repercussions? Interestingly, the distilled answers came down to five words – no more – and were thus only in a very abstract way presented on stage. The five words were future, togetherness, happiness, courage and strength – or rather agency, as I would like the last term to be understood in translation (*Zukunft, Miteinander, Glück, Mut* and *Kraft*). The reduction of a detailed future imaginary to five terms makes their analysis difficult. However, these terms still say a lot about the ways in which their authors, a group of passionate amateur dancers from Germany's fastest-shrinking city, want to relate to the future; indeed, the ways in which they imagine this future to be like (compare Zipes 1988). Even more so, they indicate what the amateur dancers longed for and held dearly in the present – and whose lack they would regret in the future. They did so by deploying yet another register for relating to the future: the affective language of art. This form of expression and representation of the future does not allow me to find the concrete and detailed answers to the question that I started with. However, they still aimed to answer the same question. Perhaps the continuous training sessions and the many social relations cultivated in them already practically created the city that they had wished for?

The urges to the future, to a togetherness in this future, and to happiness, courage and agency, which the dancers expressed in front of their fellow citizens, could be seen in Miyazaki's sense as a radical reorientation of knowledge. But hope, in this case, did not redirect knowledge. There was not much knowledge being produced about the future. Rather, hope here redirected practice, especially communal practice – or let us say gave it a direction in the first place. Miyazaki's 'method of hope' played a role in the continuation of concrete attempts at producing maintenance and endurance as described in the last chapter. In other arenas, hope also directed affect and ethics. And in professional planning practices, the evacuation of the near future suggested that a hopeful method actually did not have any considerable effects either way. Despite their vagueness, the five terms of the dance project, first, reclaimed the future and, second, circumscribed a new register to relate to the future. The project's future knowledge, although imprecise, redirected relations to the future – in the present. It reproblematized and then deproblematized the local future, and created an arena in which the radical redirection of knowledge can continuously be reconsidered. Most importantly, it answered the question posed by Gundermann at the very outset of this book. As the outcome of hard work, endless negotiations and continuous reconceptualizations, some Hoyerswerdians have chosen a different way of catching the future bullet that carries their name on it: with one's fellow (dancing) citizens, with bravery, strength and happiness. The liveliness of this dance underlined that this was a *performative* performance of ideas about the future in the present; it made these ideas real.

At the end of my fieldwork, I suggested something similarly abstract and 'ethical', following not just coincidentally the same local problematization as much as finding similar answers to it. At my own goodbye party, I was asked to give some anthropological advice on Hoyerswerda's future. I recommended three things: *Mensch, Miteinander, Moderne* – anthropos, togetherness, modernity. My own idea for a better future – Hoyerswerda's miracle – which I had contemplated for several months by then was also abstract and less concerned with the detail of actual urban life and its organization. Under the category of human or *anthropos* (*Mensch*), I first suggested that the city should concentrate on the sole location factor (*Standortfaktor*) that remained in it: the people. Detached from the broader economic and political networks, the hope for salvation granted by external investors or enormous amounts of state funding seemed unrealistic. Rather, human beings living here should redefine their own role and responsibilities (and all that without the potential neoliberal overtones). This indeed involves a problematization and scrutinization of *anthropos* – the human presented as an object of thought. I claimed that such an approach should lead to a strategy of togetherness (*Strategie des Miteinander*). Together, the Hoyerswerdians should solve the problems that face them. In order to do so, they had to overcome some of the weaknesses of humanity, which is captured by the German term *menscheln*, which translates

Figure 6.2 *Remains, 'ArtBlock' building (during its demolition), November 2008*

as 'being too human'. This term refers to all ludicrous and piti-able weaknesses exhibited by human beings. By some of my infor-mants, these weaknesses are seen to prevent concrete solutions for Hoyerswerda's future: egoism, nepotism, betrayal, prejudices, fear, cowardice and incompetence, to name but a view. Instead of small-mindedness, provincialism and mediocrity, Hoyerswerda should return to its vanguard modern tradition – indeed, to the temporal dimension of the present with an eye on the future. I thus encour-aged my informants to deploy a recaptured ethos of modernity, being newly drawn towards the future in concise, optimistic and self-determined ways.

Retrospectively, these suggestions seem naïve, to say the least. But in that very situation they made absolute sense, and they were felicitous as speech acts. Shall I now dismiss them as romantic invo-cations of a harmonic, social and vanguard future – following Sara Ahmed's (2008) trenchant critique? What are the epistemic opera-tions involved in my or the dancers' utterances and their form of tem-poral reasoning? Such idealistic proclamations did have considerable effects. First, they deproblematized the present. My take on a more relaxed form of relating to the future and of being in the present – a form of cultivated presentism (*Gegenwärtigkeit*) – was later even quoted in the city's own new promotional magazine. Second, at the same time, these proclamations opened up the future for political and social negotiation, sparking further public debates about the future. Third, they created an image of the future that ethically and practically guided and directed practice in the present. The actual effects of such linguistic representations of the future remained indeterminate. Fourth, another part of their efficacy worked in affective terms – that is, the dancers definitely wanted to disseminate a sense of optimism and confidence. Lastly, these operations also entailed the crucial aspect pointed out by Crapanzano *pace* Starobiski: that all that which pertains to the future is actually a remark on and in the present. Let me recapture how this last ethnographic observation fits into the book's overall argument.

Belonging to the Present

Reflecting upon the future also means regaining a critical stance to the present, since this perspective might in contrast allow us to widen, mark and invest in the present more thoroughly. In this light, Boyer's observation that the East Germans were excluded from defining their own and the national future is crucially a remark on the politics of the present. Their general exclusion from a future other than the Western one, which – as they were continuously reminded – they failed to achieve in the present, mounted up to an exclusion from both temporal dimensions more generally, not to mention the past. East Germans were to work through the latter and then prove their worthiness to actually belong to the post-reunification present and future. People in Hoyerswerda faced quite different problems. The past played a role in local discourses only when relating to contemporary concerns with the future. Working on one's present relations to the future entailed the potential to newly position oneself in time, thereby producing new solutions for the present *and* changing dominant temporal politics.

I have tried to map relations to the future by presenting the actual ethnographic objects that made up the future in Hoyerswerda. I see my contribution as a diversification of our theoretical and analytical understanding of – and methodological approaches to – the future. Although I continuously underlined that this diversification was directed at a better understanding of the future, I can now conclude that the concern with the future in my study was in fact only yet another, very important perspective on the present – opened up from the vantage point of future knowledge. Hence, this overall presentist account is not about the future. Rather, this book is an extensive observation of the role the future plays in the present. It examines the epistemic operations the future requires as much as allows with regard to the present in which it is represented. This is also the reason why the title of this book might be somewhat misleading. Beyond enforced presentism, this book wanted to show a way back to the postindustrial future (whatever follows this condition will hopefully be a good surprise and better than expected), but it wanted to do this by opening up the postindustrial present, whose inequalities and injustices, I believe, demand rigorous attention.

My future-orientated approach to the present emerges out of a longstanding engagement with the anthropology of postsocialism. I see this body of literature as prone to contributing to theoretical understandings of time and change, implying potential contributions to theories of knowledge, practice and agency. With my presentist perspective, I aim to push postsocialist studies to introduce theories of the future more thoroughly into their analyses of change and transformation. Against an understanding of the postsocialist present being determined by the past, I posed temporal complexity and temporal flexibility as two concepts with which to explore that present differently. They are supposed to ensure a more general awareness of the diverse and heterogeneous vocabularies, registers and practices at play in a context where the future is rendered problematic. However, these multiple elements of relations or references to the future remain grounded in the present and its particular social, political and ethical dynamics. My analysis depicts them as evidence of how the inhabitants of Hoyerswerda, and East Germans more generally, attempted to determine their own futures rather than remaining occupied with their past. The self-determination of the future stems from a very peculiar position in the present: a development that is seen to be unprecedented in peacetime and hence incites the production of not yet stabilized, partially unframed knowledge, especially of knowledge about the future.

Akin to the studies of East German nostalgia (*Ostalgie*), I came to understand that knowledge about any other temporal dimension than the present is *still* about the present. The present is the point from where these temporal references are made and in which they gain meaning and relevance, rendered anew in every novel present. This is also how I understand the Gundermann quote: a future is to come either way, so our (limited) choice is to try to determine our position vis-à-vis this future in the present. Some options can be excluded from the social imaginary, for instance, due to ideological and political conflicts or the dominance of particular forms of temporal reasoning. Since representations of – and claims to – the future remain indeterminate, the communal process of negotiating them also remains contingent. Art practices, ethical consideration and sociocultural, pedagogical projects can be as effective in working on the future as professional public discourses and official negotiations. In their entirety they constitute Hoyerswerda's process of coming to terms with the problem of the future, and thereby of finding a way of belonging to the present. This process of 'Zukunftsbewältigung' mirrors the German idea of mastering the past (*Vergangenheitbewältigung*), presuming that there is a need to talk about and deal with the loss of the future. Against horrifying demographic predictions, the inhabitants of this city sought to open up the present to the future without determining in detail what that future should look like. The way in which the Hoyerswerdians were forced to do this in a period that could rightly be referred to as *post*postsocialist was impressive and I applaud them for it. The Hoyerswerdians were hoping for a kiss rather than a torpedo. This did not solve the economic and demographic problems at hand, but it helped to rid them of some of the emerging epistemic problems they faced.

My explorations of the role the future played in Germany's fastest-shrinking city is just another step in the studies of the post-industrial era. The restructuring of formerly industrialized societies might seem less of a troubling change than the unexpected postsocialist revolution. Nonetheless, it also yields temporal and epistemic repercussions. In Hoyerswerda, two strategic economic pursuits gained increasing influence during my fieldwork: tourism and renewable energy. Whereas the former follows the neoliberal shift towards the service and entertainment economy, the latter strategy entails another fascinating image of the future: that of sustainability. Sustainability creates the idea of a moment in the future, which is somewhat out of time: a stabilized present in the future. The process of shrinkage would at that moment stop and the future present would be self-perpetuating, finally overcoming ideologies of growth and progress as much as its opposite narratives of vanishing and decline. For such an analysis, there is yet neither a coherent theory of knowledge nor of the future. To create new insights into postindustrial changes, the study of temporal knowledge looks promising and could be taken further. In particular, the more subtle changes of temporal knowledge, the creation or emergence of new temporal outlooks and logics, their embeddedness in particular contexts, in short, the flexibility, adaptability and malleability of knowledge more generally, still deserves further investigation. The issue of form might be a good starting point for that, as Ong and Collier's book *Global Assemblages* (2005) indicates. In it, the contributing authors redefined their approach to the all-encompassing notion of globalization by paying attention to a variety of deterritorializable and reterritorializable (global) forms. This insight into spatial issues could also be of use when thinking through the temporal dimension of human life, investigating how particular aspects and objects of a temporal dimension different from the present are *de-actualized and re-actualized* in it. Generally, the formal aspects of knowledge add immensely to a consideration of how knowledge exists and operates in time. Such future explorations could illuminate the contemporarily dominant configurations of future relations, mapping the epistemic regimes of not just postsocialism and shrinkage, but also of the post-Cold War, postindustrial era, which I have here approached through an exemplary small city, its publics, concerns and specific socialities, its politics and temporal affects, and its multiplicity of temporal relations to the future.

This brings me one more time back to my informants. Throughout my work, it has been their commitment to their hometown that has inspired me most. Their quest for a better quality of life in Hoyerswerda wanted to interpellate its future not as a, in local terms, *Wohnstadt*, a City for Dwelling, which it long was as the settlement for the nearby industrial complex, but as a *Lebensstadt*, a City for Living, a 'creative city', as one of my host mothers envisioned. By doing so in continuous social practices, many Hoyerswerdians have already performed and realized this vision in the present. On a normal day during my fieldwork, I encountered a variety of communal events that do not fit into conceptions of life in a city of decline. On a typical day, I would have a chat with retiree Rosemarie and the elderly women and men at the Spätlese club for their weekly meetings over coffee and cakes, then rush to a seminar in the Senior's Academy about contemporary China and its influence on global politics, and leave quickly just to make it in time for a discussion of some Kirghiz author at a Kunstverein event in Hoyerswerda's castle. From there I would find my way to the *KuFa* to attend a late-night planning meeting for the next big youth project or the grand annual prohibition party. I could also have gone to one of the many sports clubs, meetings of friends or family festivities that all made up local life. I do not say that life in Hoyerswerda was perfect and the loss of the future had after all only been an epistemic problem. Rather, this kind of knowledge, local and temporal, was so complex and intricately efficacious that it warranted careful consideration, especially when it is knowledge about the future that takes away the quality of life in the present.

Gundermann wrote defiantly in the song 'I was Born Here' and in response to Hoyerswerda's post-reunification decline: 'Here, it is today not better than yesterday, and here, there is no tomorrow after all' (*hier isses heute nicht besser als gestern, und ein Morgen gibt es hier nicht*). However, this description was ironic in tone; indeed, it was full of care and commitment to Hoyerswerda. He concluded 'here, my journeys don't take me far, but they take me deep' (*hier führt mich meine Reise bringt nicht weit, aber tief*), expressing an appreciation of his hometown despite its many problems. As he put it rather casually in another song, 'stay alive, at least until tomorrow, because then everything will have turned around again' (*Überlebe wenigstens bis morgen, denn dann kommt es wieder andersrum*). As Hoyerswerda's turbulent recent history shows, there is, indeed, always a time for surprise or the unexpected.

This account questioned the role and efficacy of knowledge, especially temporal knowledge, in times of accelerated change. It did so in order to carve out a space in the present that is 'presentist' not in the sense of enforced presentism and 'futurist' not in the sense of enforced futurism. This presentism's epistemic relations to the future are serene – and critical and committed at the same time. Gundermann was only one of the many voices I have assembled here that advanced other knowledges about the past, present and the future in order to capture these current changes differently and stabilize one's existence in them – for producing a feeling of belonging in the present in terms at least partially self-determined, a relief from the restrictions that particular temporal regimes, or rather concrete temporal politics, impose on them.

Let me then finish this book by returning one very last time to WK 10. Not far away from where the 'ArtBlock' building stood, another, this time community-based art residency took place. The 'PaintBlock' building (*Malplatte*; see Ringel 2013b) used three entrances, comprising thirty-six flats altogether. It took place in June 2009 and was opened to Hoyerswerda's wider public for two weeks. The idea was simple. Before these apartments were demolished, everybody was invited to fill them in a grand communal effort 'with art, life and laughter', as a friend put it. Participants could choose any

Figure 6.3 *Artwork in 'PaintBlock' building, 'That much construction for deconstruction', summer 2009*

of the abandoned rooms, stairways or balconies. The façade overlooking one of the main federal roads crossing Hoyerswerda also became a popular canvas. The organizers provided paints, brushes, ladders, buckets and everything else needed for transforming this empty block before its inevitable deconstruction. More than 300 Hoyerswerdians, mostly teenagers, but also several pensioners, worked in these empty rooms and created very different works of art, which in turn were seen by more than 2,000 visitors. Before its final deconstruction, this former apartment block was painted all over, inside and outside. Instead of a passive endurance of the process of shrinkage, this block's dispensable space was temporarily *re*appropriated (literally – a few of the young artists had previously lived in these flats) and finally bid farewell with a grand gesture. Maybe at last this made amends for all the goodbye parties never celebrated?

One participant summarized the enormous collective effort in his ironic, but spot-on remark: 'That much construction for deconstruction!' (*So'n Aufriß für'n Abriß!*). Even the goodbye party at the end of the project with its joyful, relaxed atmosphere differed enormously from the expectable melancholy in sight of the 'PaintBlock' building's upcoming demolition. After the farewell party, the entrances were closed, but the house still stood in its new dress for a few months, proudly exhibiting many colourful details as well as the famous Goethe quote from Faust, 'Verweile Doch!' (the abbreviation of 'Stay, thou are so beautiful'), as a last hopeful, if somewhat ironic and even devilish reminder. And the project did have some endurance or aftermath.

The fact that it took place in Hoyerswerda alone proved to many that: 'Hoyerswerda is by far not a ghost town!' The 'I ♥ HY' slogan, often depicted in the block's staircases and rooms, after all, had shown some efficacy. As the Lord Mayor said in his introduction to the catalogue, a collection of postcards depicting many of the pieces of art produced during the 'PaintBlock' project: 'In Hoyerswerda, there was and is an especially creative spirit of art. And this spirit will survive the hard times of the demographic ruptures – of that I am certain.' By 'the spirit of art', he also meant the city's spirit, the hopes, lust for life, creativity and, I hasten to add, temporal agency of its inhabitants, which were so colourfully expressed in this project. The times of shrinkage normally produced less optimistic statements, and even the Lord Mayor in his daring prediction seemed to have reached out to the times after shrinkage. It might come as no surprise then that in yet another project in WK 10, the Time-Out (*Auszeit*) project of 2012 (which in 2016 gave the name for the new café in the finally rebuilt and reopened Braugasse 1 building), the organizers from the Cultural Factory passionately underlined that this project, finally, was not about shrinkage. In its seven laboratories, participants were instead allowed to take a rest out of time – and to think about the ways in which they could realize new vanguard projects already in this very present.

Note

1. In comparison to the future, the past is widely presumed to have another ontological status, since it has once existed, which is seen to give it another efficacy in the present. In my understanding of a presentist approach, this looks questionable and in any case does not explain present references to the past.

Bibliography

Abram, S., and G. Weszkalnys (eds). 2013. *Elusive Promises: Planning in the Contemporary World*. New York and Oxford: Berghahn Books.

Adam, B. 1990. *Time and Social Theory*. Cambridge: Polity Press.

Ahmed, S. 2004. 'Affective Economies', *Social Text 79* 22(2): 117–39.

———. 2008. 'Multiculturalism and the Promise of Happiness', *New Formations* 63: 121–37.

Alexander, C. 2007. 'Soviet and Post-Soviet Planning in Almaty, Kazakhstan', *Critique of Anthropology* 27(2): 165–81.

Allison, A. 2013. *Precarious Japan*. Durham, NC: Duke University Press.

Anderson, B. 2002. 'Principle of Hope: Recorded Music, Listening Practices, and the Immanence of Utopia', *Geografiska Annaler B* 84: 211–27.

———. 2006a. 'Becoming and Being Hopeful: Towards a Theory of Affect', *Environment and Planning D: Society and Space* 24: 733–52.

———. 2006b. 'Transcending without Transcendence: Utopianism and an Ethos of Hope', *Antipode* (38): 691–710.

———. 2007. 'Hope for Nanotechnology: Anticipatory Knowledge and the Governance of Affect', *Area* 39(2): 156–65.

Antze, P., and M. Lambek. 1996. *Tense Past: Cultural Essays in Trauma and Memory*. London: Routledge.

Appadurai, A. 1981. 'The Past as a Scarce Resource', *MAN New Series* 16(2): 201–19.

———. 1995. 'The Production of Locality', in R. Fardon (ed.), *Counterworks: Managing the Diversity of Knowledge*. London: Routledge, pp. 205–25.

———. 2002. 'The Right to Participate in the Work of the Imagination: Interview by Arjun Molder', *Transurbanism* 32–47.

———. 2013. *The Future as Cultural Fact: Essays on the Global Condition*. New York: Verso.

Bach, J. 2002. 'The Taste Remains: Consumption, (N)ostalgia, and the Production of East Germany', *Public Culture* 14(3): 545–56.

Barth, F. 2002. 'An Anthropology of Knowledge', *Current Anthropology* 43(1): 1–18.

Baxstrom, R. 2012. 'Living on the Horizon of the Everlasting Present: Power, Planning and the Emergence of Baroque Forms of Life', in L. Chua, J. Cook, N. Long and L. Wilson (eds), *Southeast AsianPerspectives on Power*. London: Routledge, pp. 135–50.

Bear, L. 2014. *Doubt, Conflict, Mediation: The Anthropology of Modern Time*. Special Issue, *Journal of the Royal Anthropological Institute (N.S.)* 20(S1).

———. 2015. *Navigating Austerity: Currents of Debt along a South Asian River*. Stanford, CA: Stanford University Press.

Beck, U. 1992. *Risk Society: Towards a New Modernity*. London: Sage Publications.

Berdahl, D. 1999. *Where the World Ended: Re-unification and Identities in the German Borderland*. Berkeley, CA: University of California Press.

———. 2009. *The Social Life of Postsocialism: Memory, Consumption, Germany*. Bloomington, IN: University of Indiana Press.

Berdahl, D., M. Lampland and M. Bunzl (eds). 2000. *Altering States: Ethnography of Transition in Eastern Europe and the Former Soviet Union*. Ann Arbor, MI: University of Michigan Press.

Berlant, L. 2011. *Cruel Optimism*. Durham, NC: Duke University Press.

Biehl, J., and P. Locke. 2010. 'Deleuze and the Anthropology of Becoming', *Current Anthropology* 51 (3): 317–51.

Bloch, E. 1986 [1959]. *The Principle of Hope*, vols. 1–3. Oxford: Blackwell.

Borneman, J. 1992. *Belonging in the Two Berlins: Kin, State, Nation*. Cambridge: Cambridge University Press.

———. 1997. *Settling Accounts, Violence, Justice, and Accountability in Postsocialist Europe*. Princeton, NJ: Princeton University Press.

Bourne, C. 2006. *The Future of Presentism*. Oxford: Oxford University Press.

Boyer, D. 2001a. 'On the Sedimentation and Accreditation of Social Knowledges of Difference: Mass Media, Journalism, and the Reproduction of East/West Alterities in Unified Germany', *Cultural Anthropology* 15(4): 459–91.

———. 2001b. 'Media Markets, Mediating Labors, and the Branding of East German Culture at Super Illu', *Social Texts* 68(19): 9–33.

———. 2005. 'Visiting Knowledge in Anthropology: An Introduction', *Ethnos* 70(2): 141–48.

———. 2006. '*Ostalgie* and the Politics of the Future in Eastern Germany', *Public Culture* 18(2): 361–81.

———. 2010. 'From Algos to Autonomos: Nostalgic Eastern Europe as Postimperial Mania', in M. Todorova and Z. Gille (eds), *Postcommunist Nostalgia*. New York and Oxford: Berghahn Books.

Boyer, D., and C. Howe. 2010. 'Portable Analytics and Travelling Theory', EASA Biannual Conference, Maynooth, Ireland, August 2010.

Brennan, T. 2004. *The Transmission of Affect*. Ithaca, NY: Cornell University Press.

Bridger, S., and F. Pine (eds). 1998. *Surviving Post-socialism: Local Strategies and Regional Responses in Eastern Europe and the Former Soviet Union.* London: Routledge.

Bude, H., T. Medicus and A. Willisch (eds). 2011. *ÜberLeben im Umbruch. Am Beispiel Wittenberge: Ansichten einer fragmentierten Stadt.* Hamburg: Verlag Hamburger Edition.

Burawoy, M., and K. Verdery (eds). 1999. *Uncertain Transition: Ethnographies of Change in the Postsocialist World.* Oxford: Rowman & Littlefield.

Buyandelgeriyn, M. 2008. 'Post-post-transition Theories: Walking on Multiple Paths', *Annual Review of Anthropology* 37: 235–50.

Cañás Bottos, L. 2008. *Old Colony Mennonites in Argentina and Bolivia: Nation Making, Religious Conflict and Imagination of the Future.* Leiden: Brill Academic Publishers.

Carrithers, M. 2007. 'Story Seeds and the Inchoate', *Durham Anthropology Journal* 14(1): 1–20.

Clifford, J., and G. Marcus. (eds). 1986. *Writing Culture: The Poetics and Politics of Ethnography.* Berkeley, CA: University of California Press.

Cliver, G., and C. Smith-Prei (eds). 2014. *Boom and Bust: Urban Landscapes in the East since Reunification.* New York and Oxford: Berghahn Books.

Cole, J. 2004. 'Fresh Contact in Tamatave, Madagascar: Sex, Money, and Intergenerational Transformation', *American Ethnologist* 31(4): 573–88.

———. 2005. 'The Jaombilo of Tamatave (Madagascar), 1992–2004: Reflections on Youth and Globalization', *Journal of Social History* 38(4): 891–914.

Cole, J., and D. Durham (eds). 2007. *Generations and Globalization: Youth, Age and Family in the New World Economy.* Bloomington, IN: Indiana University Press.

———. 2008. *Figuring the Future: Globalization and the Temporalities of Children and Youth.* Santa Fe, NM: School for Advanced Research Press.

Collier, S., and A. Lakoff. 2005. 'Regimes of Living', in A. Ong and S. Collier (eds), *Global Assemblages:Technology, Politics, and Ethics as Anthropological Problems.* Oxford: Blackwell Publishing, pp. 22–39.

Collier, S, and A. Ong. 2005. 'Global Assemblages, Anthropological Problems', in A. Ong and S. Collier (eds), *Global Assemblages: Technology, Politics, and Ethics as Anthropological Problems.* Oxford: Blackwell Publishing, pp. 3–21.

Crapanzano, V. 2003. 'Reflections on Hope as a Category of Social and Psychological Analysis', *Cultural Anthropology* 18(1): 3–32.

———. 2004. *Imaginative Horizons: An Essay in Literary-Philosophical Anthropology.* Chicago, IL: University of Chicago Press.

———. 2007. 'Co-futures' (Commentary), *American Ethnologist* 34(39): 422–25.

De Certeau, M. 1984. *The Practice of Everyday Life*. Berkeley, CA: University of California Press.

De Pina-Cabral, J. 2000. 'The Ethnographic Present Revisited', *Social Anthropology* 8(3): 341–48.

De Soto, H., and N. Dudwick. 2000. *Fieldwork Dilemmas: Anthropologists in Postsocialist States*. Madison, WI: University of Wisconsin Press.

Decker, M., M. Kolodziej, K. Schäfer and D. Lienig. 2010. *Geschichten eines Umbruchs: Hoyerswerda 1989/1990*. Hoyerswerda: Scholz Publishing House.

Dunn, E. 2004. *Privatizing Poland: Baby Food, Big Business, and the Remaking of Labor*. Ithaca, NY: Cornell University Press.

Durham, D. 2004. 'Disappearing Youth: Youth as a Social Shifter in Botswana', *American Ethnologist* 31(4): 589–605.

———. 2008. 'New Horizons: Youth at the Millennium', *Anthropology Quarterly* 81(4): 945–58.

Esbenshade, R. 1995. 'Remembering to Forget: Memory, History, National Identity in Central Eastern Europe', *Representations* 49: 72–96.

Engler, W. 1999. *Die Ostdeutschen: Kunde von einem verlorenen Land*. Berlin: Aufbau Verlag.

———. 2002. *Die Ostdeutschen als Avantgarde*. Berlin: Aufbau Verlag.

———. 2005. *Bürger, ohne Arbeit: Für eine Neugestaltung der Gesellschaft*. Berlin:Aufbau Verlag.

Escobar, A. 1995. *Encountering Development: The Making and Unmaking of the Third World*. Princeton, NJ: Princeton University Press.

Fabian, J. 1983. *Time and the Other: How Anthropology Makes its Object*. New York: Columbia University Press.

Fardon, R. 1995. 'Introduction: Counterworks', in R. Fardon (ed.), *Counterworks: Managing the Diversity of Knowledge*. London: Routledge, pp. 1–22.

Faubion, J. 2001. 'Toward an Anthropology of Ethics: Foucault and the Pedagogies of Autopoesis', *Representations* 74: 83–104.

Ferguson, J. 1999. *Expectations of Modernity: Myths and Meanings of Urban Life in the Zambian Copperbelt*. Berkeley, CA: University of California Press.

Foucault, M. 1991 [1984]. 'On the Genealogy of Ethics: An Overview of Work in Progress', in P. Rabinow (ed.), *The Foucault Reader*. London: Penguin, pp. 340–72.

Foucault, M. 2004 [1961]. *Madness and Civilization: A History of Insanity in the Age of Reason*. London: Routledge.

Foucault, M. 2005 [1966]. *The Order of Things: An Archaeology of the Human Sciences*. London: Routledge.

Gaibazzi, P. 2015. *Bush Bound: Young Men and Rural Permanence in Migrant West Africa*. New York and Oxford: Berghahn Books.

Gell, A. 1992. *The Anthropology of Time: Cultural Constructions and Temporal Maps and Images*. Oxford: Berg.

Gilbert, A. 2006. 'The Past in Parenthesis: (Non)Post-socialism in Post-war Bosnia-Herzegovina', *Anthropology Today* 22(4): 14–18.

Gilbert, A., J. Greenberg, E. Helms, and S. Jansen. 2008. 'Reconsidering Postsocialism from the Margins of Europe: Hope, Time and Normalcy in Post-Yugoslav Societies', *Anthropology News* November: 10–11.

Glaeser, A. 2000. *Divided in Unity: Identity, Germany, and the Berlin Police.* Chicago, IL: University of Chicago Press.

———. 2001. 'Conclusion: Why Germany Remains Divided', in T. Herzog and S.L. Gilman (eds), *A New Germany in a New Europe.* London: Routledge, pp. 173–95.

———. 2011. *Political Epistemics: The Secret Police, the Opposition, and the End of East German Socialism.* Chicago, IL: University of Chicago Press.

Graeber, D. 2004. *Fragments of an Anarchist Anthropology.* Chicago, IL: Prickly Paradigm Press.

———. 2008. 'Hope in Common'. Retrieved 15 February 2011 from http://news.infoshop.org/article.php?story=20081122005935877.

———. 2009. *Direct Action.* Edinburgh: AK Press.

Greenberg, J. 2011. 'On the Road to Normal: Negotiating Agency and State Sovereignty in Postsocialist Serbia', *American Anthropologist* 113(1): 88–100.

Greenhouse, C.J. 1996. *A Moment's Notice: Time Politics across Cultures.* Ithaca, NY: Cornell University Press.

Greenhouse, C.J., E. Mertz and K.B.B. Warren (eds). 2002. *Ethnography in Unstable Places: Everyday Lives in Contexts of Dramatic Political Changes.* Durham, NC: Duke University Press.

Gupta, A., and J. Ferguson (eds). 1997. *Culture, Power, Place: Explorations in Critical Anthropology.* Durham, NC: Duke University Press.

Guyer, J. 2007. 'Prophecy and the Near Future: Thoughts on Macroeconomic, Evangelical, and Punctuated Time', *American Ethnologist* 34(3): 409–21.

Guyer, J., et al. 2007. 'Temporal Heterogeneity in the Study of African Land Use: Interdisciplinary Collaboration between Anthropology, Human Geography and Remote Sensing', *Human Ecology* 35(1): 3–17.

Hage, G. 2003. *Against Paranoid Nationalism: Searching for Hope in a Shrinking Society.* Annandale, Australia: Pluto Press Australia.

Hann, C.M. (ed.). 2002. *Postsocialism: Ideals, Ideologies and Practices in Eurasia.* London: Routledge.

Hann, C.M., C. Humphrey and K. Verdery. 2002. 'Introduction: Postsocialism as a Topic of Anthropological Investigation', in C.M. Hann (ed.), *Postsocialism: Ideals, Ideologies and Practices in Eurasia.* London: Routledge, pp. 1–21.

Hannemann, C. 1996. *Die Platte: Industrialisierter Wohnungsbau in der DDR.* Braunschweig and Wiesbaden: Vieweg.

———. 2003. 'Schrumpfende Städte in Ostdeutschland – Ursachen und Folgen einer Stadtentwicklung ohne Wirtschaftswachstum', *Aus Politik und Zeitgeschichte* B28: 16–24.

Haraway, D. 1988. 'Situated Knowledge: The Science Question in Feminism and Privilege of Partial Perspective', *Feminist Studies* 14(3): 575–99.

Harvey, D. 2000. *Spaces of Hope*. Edinburgh: Edinburgh University Press.

Harris, O. 1996. 'The Temporalities of Tradition: Reflection on a Changing Anthropology', in V. Hubinger (ed.), *Grasping the Changing World: Anthropological Concepts in the Postmodern Era*. London: Routledge, pp. 1–16.

———. 2004. 'Braudel: Historical Time and the Horror of Discontinuity', *History Workshop Journal* 57: 161–74.

Hastrup, K. 1990. 'The Ethnographic Present: A Reinvention', *Current Anthropology* 5(1): 45–61.

Hemmings, C. 2005. 'Invoking Affect: Cultural Theory and the Ontological Turn', *Cultural Studies* 19(5): 548–67.

Hirsch, E., and C. Stewart. 2005. 'Introduction: Ethnographies of Historicity', *History and Anthropology* 16(3): 261–74.

Hirschkind, C. 2001. 'The Ethics of Listening: Cassette-Sermon Audition in Contemporary Cairo', *American Ethnologist* 28: 623–49.

Hobsbawm, E., and T. Ranger (eds). 1983. *The Invention of Tradition*. Cambridge: Cambridge University Press.

Hodges, M. 2008. 'Rethinking Time's Arrow: Bergson, Deleuze and the Anthropology of Time', *Anthropological Theory* 8: 399–429.

Holbraad, M., and A.M. Pedersen (eds). 2013. *Times of Security: Ethnographies of Fear, Protest and the Future*. New York: Routledge.

Humphrey, C. 2002a. *The Unmaking of Soviet Life: Everyday Economies in Russia and Mongolia*. Ithaca, NY: Cornell University Press.

———. 2002b. 'Does the Category of "Postsocialist" Still Make Sense?', in C.M. Hann (ed.), *Postsocialism: Ideals, Ideologies and Practices in Eurasia*. London: Routledge, pp. 12–15.

James, J. 2012. *Preservation and National Belonging in Eastern Germany: Heritage Fetishism and Redeeming Germanness*. New York: Palgrave Macmillan.

Jameson, F. 1971. *Marxism and Form: Twentieth-Century Dialectical Theories of Literature*. Princeton, NJ: Princeton University Press.

———. 2005. *Archaeologies of the Future: The Desire Called Utopia and Other Science Fictions* New York: Verso.

Jansen, S. 2014. 'Hope for/against the State: Gridding in a Besieged Sarajevo Suburb', *Ethnos* 79(2): 238–60.

Kalb, J. 2002. 'Afterword: Globalism and Postsocialist Prospects', in C.M. Hann (ed.), *Postsocialism: Ideals, Ideologies and Practices in Eurasia*. London: Routledge, pp. 317–34.

Kaneff, D. 2003. *Who Owns the Past?: The Politics of Time in a 'Model' Bulgarian Village*. New York and Oxford: Berghahn Books.

Kemper, S. 2001. *Buying and Believing: Sri Lankan Advertising and Consumers in a Transnational World.* Chicago, IL: University of Chicago Press.

Kertzner, D. 1983. 'Generation as a Sociological Problem'. *Annual Review of Sociology* 9: 125–49.

Kil, W. 2004. *Luxus der Leere: Vom schwierigen Rückzug aus der Wachstumswelt.* Wuppertal: Verlag Müller & Busmann KG.

———. 2007. *Das Wunder von Leinefelde: Eine Stadt erfindet sich neu.* Dresden: Sandstein Verlag.

Kleist, N., and S. Jansen. 2016. 'Introduction: Hope of Time-Crisis, Immobility and Future-Making', *History and Anthropology* 27(4): 373–92.

Knudsen, I.H., and M.D. Frederiksen (eds). 2015. *Ethnographies of Grey Zones in Eastern Europe: Relations, Borders and Invisibilities.* London: Anthem Press.

Koselleck, R. 1989. *Vergangene Zukunft: Zur Semantik geschichtlicher Zeiten, Begriffsgeschichte und Sozialgeschichte.* Frankfurt am Main: Suhrkamp.

Kraftl, P. 2007. 'Utopia, Performativity, and the Unhomely', *Environment and Planning D: Society and Space* 25: 120–43.

Krøijer, S. 2015. *Figurations of the Future: Forms and Temporalities of Left Radical Politics in Northern Europe.* New York and Oxford: Berghahn Books.

Kumar, K. 2010. 'The Ends of Utopia', *New Literary History* 41(3): 549–69.

Laidlaw, J. 2002. 'For an Anthropology of Ethics and Freedom', *Journal of the Royal Anthropological Institute* 8: 311–32.

Laidlaw, J. 2014. *The Subject of Virtue: An Anthropology of Ethics and Freedom.* Cambridge, Cambridge University Press.

Lakoff, A., and S. Collier. 2004. 'Ethics and the Anthropology of Modern Reason', *Anthropological Theory* 4(4): 419–34.

Levitas, R. 2000. 'For Utopia: The (Limits of) the Utopian Function in Late Capitalist Society', *Critical Review of International Social and Political Philosophy* 3(2–3): 25–43.

Malkki, L. 2000. 'Figures of the Future', in D. Holland and J. Lave (eds), *History in Person: Enduring Struggles, Contentious Practices, Intimate Identities.* Santa Fe: School of American Research Press, pp. 325–48.

Mahmood, S. 2001. 'Feminist Theory, Embodiment, and the Docile Agent: Some Reflections on the Egyptian Islamic Revival', *Cultural Anthropology* 16: 202–35.

———. 2005. *Politics of Piety: The Islamic Revival and the Feminist Subject.* Princeton, NJ: Princeton University Press.

Marcus, G. 1998. *Ethnography through Thick and Thin.* Princeton, NJ: Princeton University Press.

Masco, J. 2008. '"Survival is Your Business": Engineering Ruins and Affect in Nuclear America', *Cultural Anthropology* 23(2): 361–98.

Maurer, B. 2005. 'Chronotypes of the Alternative: Hope for the New

Economy', Hope in the New Economy Conference, Cornell University (quoted with the author's kind permission).

Mertz, E. 2002. 'The Perfidy of Gaze and the Pain of Uncertainty: Anthropological Theory and Search for Closure', in C.J. Greenhouse, E. Mertz and K.B.B. Warren (eds), *Ethnography in Unstable Places: Everyday Lives in Contexts of Dramatic Political Changes.* Durham, NC: Duke University Press, pp. 355–78.

Miyazaki, H. 2004. *The Method of Hope: Anthropology, Philosophy, and Fijian Knowledge.* Stanford, CA: Stanford University Press.

———. 2006. 'Economy of Dreams: Hopes in Global Capitalism and its Critiques', *Cultural Anthropology* 21(2): 147–72.

———. 2010. 'The Temporality of No Hope', in C.J. Greenhouse (ed.), *Ethnographies of Neoliberalism.* Berkeley, CA: University of California Press, pp. 238–50.

Miyazaki, H., and A. Riles. 2005. 'Failure as an Endpoint', in A. Ong and S. Collier (eds), *Global Assemblages: Technology, Politics, and Ethics as Anthropological Problems.* Oxford: Blackwell, pp. 320–31.

Moroşanu, R., and F. Ringel. 2016. 'Time-Tricking: A General Introduction', *Cambridge Journal of Anthropology* 34(1): 17–21.

Morris, B. 2005. *Anthropology and Anarchy: Their Elective Affinity.* London: Goldsmiths University.

Munn, N. 1992. 'The Cultural Anthropology of Time: A Critical Essay', *Annual Review of Anthropology* 21: 93–123.

Nafus, D. 2006. 'Post-socialism and Notions of Context in St Petersburg', *Journal of the Royal Anthropological Institute* 12: 607–24.

Navaro-Yashin, Y. 2009. 'Affective Spaces, Melancholic Objects: Ruination and the Production of Anthropological Knowledge', Malinowski Memorial Lecture, *Journal of the Royal Anthropological Institute* 15: 1–18.

Nielsen, M. 2011. 'Futures Within: Reversible Time and House-Building in Maputo, Mozambique', *Anthropological Theory* 11(4): 397–423.

———. 2014. 'A Wedge of Time: Futures in the Present and Presents without Futures in Maputo, Mozambique', *Journal of the Royal Anthropological Institute* 20(S1): 166–82.

Ong, A., and S. Collier (eds). 2005. *Global Assemblages: Technology, Politics, and Ethics as Anthropological Problems.* Oxford: Blackwell.

Oswalt, P. (ed.) 2005. *Shrinking Cities. Vol. 1: International Research.* Ostfildern-Ruit: Hatje Cantz Publishers.

———. (ed.) 2006. *Shrinking Cities. Vol. 2: Interventions.* Ostfildern-Ruit: Hatje Cantz Publishers.

Oswalt, P., and T. Tieniets (eds). 2006. *Atlas der schrumpfenden Städte/ Atlas of Shrinking Cities.* Ostfildern-Ruit: Hatje Cantz Publishers.

Oushakine, S. 2000. 'In the State of Post-Soviet Aphasia: Symbolic Development in Contemporary Russia', *Europe-Asia Studies* 52(6): 991–1016.

Pedersen, M.A. 2012. 'A Day in a Cadillac: The Work of Hope in Urban Mongolia', *Social Analysis* 56(2): 1–16.

Pelkmans, M. 2003. 'The Social Life of Empty Buildings: Imaging the Transition in Post-Soviet Ajaria', *Focaal* 41: 121–35.

Pels, P. 2015. 'Modern Times: Seven Steps towards the Future', *Current Anthropology* 56(6): 779–95.

Persoon, G., and D. van Est. 2000. 'The Study of the Future in Anthropology in Relation to the Sustainability Debate', *Focaal* 35: 7–28.

Pfeiffer, J. 2004. 'Condom Social Marketing, Pentecostalism, and Structural Adjustment in Mozambique: A Clash of AIDS Prevention Messages', *Medical Anthropology Quarterly* 18(1): 77–103.

Povinelli, E. 2011. *Economies of Abandonment: Social Belonging and Endurance in Late Liberalism.* Durham, NC: Duke University Press.

Rabinow, P. 1986. 'Representations are Social Facts: Modernity and Post-modernity in Anthropology', in J. Clifford and G. Marcus (eds), *Writing Culture: The Poetics and Politics of Ethnography.* Berkeley, CA: University of California Press, pp. 234–61.

———. 2003. *Anthropos Today.* Princeton, NJ: Princeton University Press.

———. 2005. 'Midst Anthropological Problems', in A. Ong and S. Collier (eds), *Global Assemblages: Technology, Politics, and Ethics as Anthropological Problems.* Oxford: Blackwell, pp. 40–53.

———. 2007. *Marking Time: On the Anthropology of the Contemporary.* Princeton, NJ: Princeton University Press.

———. 2009. 'Prosperity, Amelioration, Flourishing: From a Logic of Practical Judgement to Reconstruction', *Law and Literature* 21(3): 301–20.

Rabinow P., G. Marcus, J. Faubion and T. Rees. 2008. *Designs for an Anthropology of the Contemporary.* Durham, NC: Duke University Press.

Rabinow, P., and A. Stavrianakis. 2013. *Demands of the Day: On the Logic of Anthropological Inquiry.* Chicago, IL: University of Chicago Press.

Reimann, B. 1998. *Alles schmeckt nach Abschied. Tagebücher 1964–1970*, ed. by Angela Drescher. Berlin: Aufbau Verlag.

Riles, A. 2000. *The Network Inside out.* Ann Arbour: University of Michigan Press.

Ringel, F. 2012. 'Anarchisms in the Making: Creative Presentism, Vanguard Practices and Anthropological Hopes', *Critique of Anthropology* 32(2): 173–88.

———. 2013a. 'Differences in Temporal Reasoning: Local Temporal Complexity and Generational Clashes in an East German Town', *Focaal* 66: 25–35.

———. 2013b 'Epistemic Collaborations in Contexts of Change: On Conceptual Fieldwork and the Timing of Anthropological Knowledge' *Laboratorium* 5: 36–55.

———. 2014. 'Post-industrial Times and the Unexpected: Endurance and Sustainability in Germany's Fastest-Shrinking City', *Journal of the Royal Anthropological Institute* 20(S1): 52–70.

———. 2016a. 'Can Time Be Tricked? On the Future of Temporal Agency', *Cambridge Journal of Anthropology* 34(1): 22–31.

———. 2016b. 'Beyond Temporality: Notes on Time from a Shrinking Fieldsite', *Anthropological Theory* 16(4): 390–412.

Ringel, F., and R. Moroșanu (eds). 2016. *Time-Tricking: Reconsidering Temporal Agency in Troubled Times*. Special Issue in *Cambridge Journal of Anthropology* 34(1): 17–129.

Robbins, J. 2009. 'Value, Structure, and the Range of Possibilities: A Response to Zigon', *Ethnos* (74): 277–85.

Rose, N. 1996. 'The Death of the Social? Refiguring the Territory of Government', *Economy and Society* 25(3): 327–56.

———. 1999. *Powers of Freedom: Reframing Political Thought*. Cambridge: Cambridge University Press.

Rosenberg, D., and S. Harding. 2005. *Histories of the Future*. Durham, NC: Duke University Press.

Schieffelin, B. 2002. 'Marking Time: The Dichotomizing Discourse of Multiple Temporalities', *Current Anthropology* 43: S5–S17.

Schielke, S. 2009a. 'Being Good in Ramadan: Ambivalence, Fragmentation, and the Moral Self in the Lives of Young Egyptians', *Journal of the Royal Anthropological Institute*: S24–S40.

———. 2009b. 'Ambivalent Commitments: Troubles of Morality, Religiosity and Aspiration among Young Egyptians', *Journal of Religion in Africa* 39: 158–85.

Shoshan, N. 2016. *The Management of Hate: Nation, Affect and the Governance of Right-Wing Extremism in Germany*. Princeton, NJ: Princeton University Press.

Simon, G.M. 2009. 'The Soul Freed of Cares? Islamic Prayer, Subjectivity, and the Contradictions of Moral Selfhood in Minangkabau, Indonesia', *American Ethnologist* 36: 258–75.

Strathern, M. 1988. *The Gender of the Gift: Problems with Women and Problems with Society*. Berkeley, CA: University of California Press.

———. 1991. *Partial Connections*. Lanham, MD: Rowman and Littlefield.

———. (ed.) 1995a. *Shifting Contexts: Transformations in Anthropological Knowledge*. London: Routledge.

———. 1995b. 'The Nice Things about Culture is that Everyone Has it', in M. Strathern (ed.), *Shifting Contexts: Transformations in Anthropological Knowledge*. London: Routledge, pp. 153–76.

———. (ed.). 2000. *Audit Cultures: Anthropological Studies in Accountability, Ethics and the Academy*. London: Routledge.

———. 2005. 'Robust Knowledge and Fragile Futures', in A. Ong and S. Collier (eds), *Global Assemblages: Technology, Politics, and Ethics as Anthropological Problems*. Oxford: Blackwell, pp. 464–81.

———. 2006. 'A Community of Critics? Thoughts on New Knowledge', *Journal of the Royal Anthropological Institute* 12: 191–209.

Ssorin-Chaikov, N. 2006. 'On Heterochrony: Birthday Gifts to Stalin: 1949', *Journal of the Royal Anthropological Institute* 12: 355–75.

Stewart, K. 2007. *Ordinary Affects*. Durham, NC: Duke University Press.
Ten Dyke, E.A. 2001. *Dresden: Paradoxes of Memory in History*. London: Routledge.
Thelen, T. 2011. 'Shortage, Fuzzy Property and Other Dead Ends in the Anthropological Analysis of (Post)Socialism', *Critique of Anthropology* 31(1): 43–61.
Thrift, N., 2004. 'Intensities of Feeling: Towards a Spatial Politics of Affect', *Geografiska Annaler* 86 B(1): 57–78.
———. 2008. *Non-representational Theory: Space/Politics/Affect*. London: Routledge.
Tsing, A. 2005. *Friction: An Ethnography of Global Connection*. Princeton, NJ: Princeton University Press.
Turner, V. 1987. *The Anthropology of Performance*. New York: PAJ Books.
Vacarro, I., K. Harper and S. Murray. (eds). 2016. *The Anthropology of Postindustrialism: Ethnographies of Disconnection*. London: Routledge.
Verdery, K. 1996. *What was Socialism, and What Comes Next?* Princeton, NJ: Princeton University Press.
———. 2002. 'Whither Postsocialism?', in C.M. Hann (ed.), *Postsocialism: Ideals, Ideologies and Practices in Eurasia*. London: Routledge, pp. 16–21.
Walley, C.J. 2013. *Exit Zero: Family and Class in Postindustrial Chicago*. Chicago, IL: University of Chicago Press.
Weszkalnys, G. 2010. *Berlin Alexanderplatz: Transforming Place in a Unified Germany*. New York and Oxford: Berghahn Books.
Wilk, R. 2007. 'It's about Time: A Commentary on Guyer', *American Ethnologist* 34(3): 440–43.
Willisch, A. (ed.) 2012. *Wittenberge ist überall: Überleben in schrumpfenden Regionen*. Berlin: Ch. Links Verlag.
Wolf, E. 1982. *Europe and the People without History*. Berkeley, CA: University of California Press.
Young, G. 2013. *Teardown: Memoir of a Vanishing City*. Berkeley, CA: University of California Press.
Yurchak, Alexei. 2006. *Everything was Forever until it was No More: The Last Soviet Generation*. Princeton, NJ: Princeton University Press.
Zigon, J. 2006. 'An Ethics of Hope: Working on the Self in Contemporary Moscow', *Anthropology of East Europe Review* 24(2): 71–80.
———. 2007. 'Moral Breakdown and Ethical Demand: A Theoretical Framework for an Anthropology of Moralities', *Anthropological Theory* 7: 131–50.
———. 2009. 'Within a Range of Possibilities: Morality and Ethics in Social Life', *Ethnos* 74: 251–76.
Zipes, J. 1988. 'Introduction', in J. Zipes and F. Mecklenberg (eds), *Ernst Bloch: The Utopian Function of Art and Literature: Selected Essays*. Cambridge, MA: MIT Press, pp. xi–xlv.

Index

EASA Series

Published in Association with the European Association of Social Anthropologists (EASA)

Series Editor: Aleksandar Bošković, University of Belgrade

Social anthropology in Europe is growing, and the variety of work being done is expanding. This series is intended to present the best of the work produced by members of the EASA, both in monographs and in edited collections. The studies in this series describe societies, processes, and institutions around the world and are intended for both scholarly and student readership.

www.ingramcontent.com/pod-product-compliance
Lightning Source LLC
Chambersburg PA
CBHW070922030426
42336CB00014BA/2495